Ernest George Hardy

Christianity and the Roman Government

Ernest George Hardy

Christianity and the Roman Government

ISBN/EAN: 9783337008680

Printed in Europe, USA, Canada, Australia, Japan

Cover: Foto ©ninafisch / pixelio.de

More available books at **www.hansebooks.com**

CHRISTIANITY

AND THE

ROMAN GOVERNMENT

A STUDY IN IMPERIAL ADMINISTRATION

BY

E. G. HARDY, M.A.

FORMERLY FELLOW OF JESUS COLLEGE, OXFORD

LONDON
LONGMANS, GREEN, AND CO.
AND NEW YORK: 15 EAST 16th STREET
1894

All rights reserved

PREFACE

THE origin of this little book, which is written from the point of view of Roman rather than of Christian history, may be explained in a few words. It was suggested by, and owes its existence to, an article by Professor Mommsen in the 'Historische Zeitschrift' of 1890, entitled, *Der Religionsfrevel nach römischem Recht*. The criticism of Professor Mayor and others on the insufficient and too hastily written essay on Pliny and the Christians in my edition of 'Pliny's Correspondence with Trajan' had led me to go into the subject with more thoroughness than I had hitherto given to it; and I was already convinced that on two points at least—viz. the importance of the Neronian persecution, and the connexion of Pliny's action in Bithynia with the government attitude towards *collegia*—I had followed quite erroneous views. It was Mommsen's article, however, which first seemed to give a clear and consistent account of the principles which underlay the action of the imperial government, not only towards the Christians, but towards foreign religions of all kinds, and I determined by means of the clue furnished by it to attempt an historical *résumé* of the relations between Christianity and the Roman government during the first two centuries.

I had been working at the literature of the subject and collecting materials for nearly a year and a half when Professor Ramsay's lectures on the Christian communities of Asia Minor were announced and delivered. As it was understood that these lectures were to be published, I put aside my own work, feeling that the ground was covered by his book, and intending, if possible, to make use of my materials in reviewing his lectures when they appeared. Subsequently, however, wishing to make somewhat more use than this would have allowed of my own work, such as it was, I altered my mind and reverted to my former intention, in the hope that there would be found sufficient difference in scope, method and arrangement to justify the existence of my little book side by side with, though at a respectful distance from, Professor Ramsay's.

To say that I have produced it quite independently of 'The Church in the Roman Empire' is impossible, and would be ungracious, because no one could read the book, as I have done with care, without being indebted to it in innumerable ways. Still it is to Mommsen's article that I am bound to acknowledge my chief indebtedness, and I am not conscious that my treatment of the subject is in any essential respect different from what it would have been if I had written it before Professor Ramsay's book appeared.

In addition to Mommsen's article, already alluded to, I have found most assistance from the following books: K. J. Neumann, 'Der römische Staat und die allgemeine Kirche;' C. Franklin Arnold, 'Die Neronische Christenverfolgung' and 'Studien zur Geschichte der Plinianischen Christenverfolgung;' Overbeck, 'Studien zur Geschichte der alten Kirche;' Keim, 'Rom und das Christenthum;' Lightfoot, 'The Apostolic Fathers;' Friedländer, 'Sittengeschichte Roms,' vol. iii., 'Die religiösen Zustände;' Marquardt, 'Staatsverwaltung,' vol. iii., 'Das Sacralwesen;' W. Liebenam, 'Zur Geschichte und Organisation des römischen Vereinswesens;' Schürer, 'Die Gemeindeverfassung der Juden in Rom in der Kaiserzeit.'

E. G. H.

OXFORD: *January* 25, 1894.

CONTENTS

SECTION I

THE ATTITUDE OF THE REPUBLIC TOWARDS FOREIGN CULTS, 1-17

	PAGE
Statement of the problem and its difficulty	1
The nature of the Roman toleration only to be discovered by looking at its treatment of religions generally	3
The Roman religion national and political	4
Foreign gods brought to Rome	5
Foreign cults gradually adopted, such as those of Cybele and Bellona	6
Other cults not authorised	7
Instances of interference by government with foreign cults limited to Roman citizens	8
Increasing laxity in this respect, instanced in cult of Magna Mater	9
State action exemplified in Bacchanalian conspiracy	10
Insufficiency of national religion and need for something more emotional	13
Treatment of Isis cult	14
Practical policy of the government	15

SECTION II

THE TREATMENT OF JUDAISM, 18–37

	PAGE
Attitude towards religion in the provinces	18
Problems presented by monotheism	19
Wide extension of the Jewish race	20
Its political position	21
Semi-political unity of the Jews and their readiness to sacrifice this for religious toleration	22
Privileges and immunities granted to the Jews	23
Motives of the government	25
Different treatment of Jews at Rome and in the provinces	26
Action of Augustus and Tiberius	26
Of Claudius	28
Possible danger of the Roman policy towards the Jews	29
Consequences of the destruction of Jerusalem	31
Arrangement of Vespasian: the *religio licita*	32
Hatred and dislike of the Jews	33
Summary of the limitations to Roman toleration	35

SECTION III

FIRST APPEARANCE OF CHRISTIANITY IN THE EASTERN PROVINCES, 38–53

A new problem presented by the non-nationality and universality of Christianity	38
Christianity at first regarded as a Jewish sect	39
The gospel first preached to Jews	39
Persecution on the part of the Jews	40
Roman government at first looked on Christians as Jews and protected them	41
Origin and growth of the name 'Christiani'	42
Political charges made by Jews against Christians	42
Gradual distinction between Jews and Christians	44
Growing unpopularity of the Christians	44

	PAGE
Christianity a social revolution	45
Persecution by Gentiles in the Acts	49
Disintegrating tendency of Christianity	50
Opposition between Church and world	51
Rumours of *flagitia* at Christian meetings	52
Summary of the evidence up to Nero	53

SECTION IV

CHRISTIANITY IN ROME UNDER NERO, 54–77

First collision of government with Christianity in Rome	54
The community in Rome probably Gentile-Christian	55
First traces of Christianity in Rome	56
Paul in Rome	58
Nero's action as reported by Tacitus	59
Difficulties in the account: view of Schiller	60
Objections to his view	61
Merivale's view: objections to it	62
Reasons for thinking the account of Tacitus correct	63
Course which the trial took	65
The punishment of the Christians	70
Evidence of Clemens Romanus	71
Of Melito and Suetonius	72
'Odium generis humani:' what it implied	73
The whole matter one of police administration	74
The Neronian victims punished as Christians	77

SECTION V

CHRISTIANITY UNDER THE FLAVIAN EMPERORS, 78–101

Influence of the Neronian trials on the provinces	78
Jews and Christians distinguished from one another	79
Was the Flavian policy different? Professor Ramsay's view	80
Objections to it	81

xii   CONTENTS

	PAGE
The Christians potentially outlaws and brigands since Nero	82
Policy of Titus as evidenced by Sulpicius Severus	83
The persecution of Christians a standing one, but spasmodic	84
Access of severity under Domitian	85
Evidence of Dio Cassius, of Suetonius, of Eusebius	86
Christianity of Flavius Clemens, Domitilla, and Acilius Glabrio	87
Course probably taken by the trials	88
The accused usually punished *qua* 'Christiani'	89
Influence of the popular hatred	91
Grounds on which Christians could be executed	91
Religious fanaticism greater in the provinces	92
Test probably established under Domitian to identify the Christians	93
The imperial cult	94
More generally enforced under Domitian	95
Evidence of persecution in the Apocalypse	96
The imperial cult used only as a test	98
No imperial policy as yet towards Christians	99
The matter left to discretion of provincial governors	100
Christianity a criminal offence in virtue of its *obstinatio*	101

SECTION VI

TRAJAN AND THE CHRISTIANS, 102–124

Fortunate preservation of Pliny's letter	102
Christianity in Bithynia	103
Mission of Pliny: his correspondence with Trajan	104
Course first taken by Pliny	107
Probably based on precedents in accordance with the Neronian principle	108
Fresh cases of a more complicated kind	109
Suspicions of *flagitia*: further investigations made by Pliny	110
Reason why Trajan is consulted	111
Pliny's questions involve a reconsideration of the whole matter	112
Trajan's rescript	114

	PAGE
Its meaning	115
Opposite interpretations of it	116
Tertullian's criticism	117
Outward respect to the state worship expected of all	118
The Christians alone refused it	119
Not considered a practical danger, and toleration the rule	120
Except when popular hatred was too strong	121
Origen's statement as to small number of victims	122
Trajan's rescript primarily local and not an edict either of proscription or toleration	122
Probable source of the accusations in Bithynia	123

SECTION VII

PERSECUTION FOR THE NAME, 125–140

Date at which the 'nomen' alone was punished	125
Professor Ramsay's view discussed	126
Were those condemned for the name *rei maiestatis*?	127
Grounds on which the Christians might be punished	128
The policy of Trajan's rescript continued through the second century	130
Evidence of the Apologists	131
The Christians still punished for the name	133
Recantation followed by pardon	134
The Christians not sought out	137
Persecution due to popular hatred	138
The emperors themselves generally inclined to indulgence	139

SECTION VIII

ATTITUDE OF HADRIAN, PIUS, AND MARCUS AURELIUS, 141–167

Rescript of Hadrian	141
Letters of Antoninus Pius to cities in Greece	145
Persecution under Marcus Aurelius	146
Neumann's view: objections to it	146

	PAGE
Consideration of the evidence	148
Probably no change of policy under Marcus Aurelius	152
Contrast drawn by Professor Ramsay between emperors of first and second centuries	154
The government as yet had no steady policy	155
No systematic persecutions	156
Professor Ramsay antedates the Christian organisation	157
Number of Christians probably small	158
Beginnings of intercommunication between Churches	160
Interchange of letters	161
Christian unity still ideal and not dangerous to the government	162
Beginnings of closer organisation	163
The Catholic Church	164
Meeting of synods	164
Changing character of government action under Severus and Maximin	165
Systematic persecution first under Decius	166
General results	167

SECTION IX

CHRISTIANITY IN ITS RELATION TO *COLLEGIA*, 168–195

How did Christianity avoid the laws against *collegia*?	168
The Lex Iulia	169
Licences required for *collegia*	169
Trajan's suspicion of *collegia*	170
Resemblances between Christian communities and *collegia*	171
Inscriptions show that many *collegia* must have been unlicensed	172
Reasons for hostility to *collegia* not equally strong in all cases	174
Political danger of *collegia* in republican times	174
Opportunist policy of the empire	176
Practical impossibility of enforcing the Lex Iulia	177
Policy of emperors and governors varied	178
Collegia put down if political danger was suspected	179
Collegia opificum and *collegia sodalicia*	180

CONTENTS xv

	PAGE
Collegia funeraticia or *tenuiorum*	182
Possibility, in spite of the law, for Christian communities to exist uninterfered with	183
Certain features about Christianity which might call down interference	185
The Agapae	185
Action of Bithynian Christians in giving up the Agapae	187
Possibly the same was done elsewhere	188
Evidence that Christians were sometimes regarded as members of a *collegium illicitum*	189
Tertullian represents the Christians as a *collegium tenuiorum*	190
Probably recognised as such by the state	191
But this did not affect their general position in the empire	194

APPENDIX ON TWO 'ACTA MARTYRUM' 196–208

CHRISTIANITY

AND THE

ROMAN GOVERNMENT

I

THE ATTITUDE OF THE REPUBLIC TOWARDS FOREIGN CULTS

The policy of the Roman government towards the Christians is involved in not a few difficulties, and though many attempts have been made to give a consistent explanation of the facts which from various sources are supplied to us, none of them can be said to have met with universal acceptance. This is, perhaps, to a certain extent inevitable. Our information, such as it is, comes to us from one of two sources—from Roman writers or from Christian—and while it is almost impossible not to presuppose a certain amount of bias on both sides, there is this further and special obstacle to our arrival at the truth: that while the heathen writers in the too few and too brief notices which have come down to us treat the matter as one of only a passing and superficial interest, our Christian authorities, on the other hand, are men of one idea, to whom Christianity is the one important feature in the history of the time. Add to this that neither on the one side nor the other is there any consecutive account of the spread and fate of Christianity, either in Rome or other parts of the empire, but rather isolated notices which seem to assume on the part of the reader knowledge which we at least, separated from the facts by so many centuries, do not possess. Finally, even assuming that by the synthesis of scattered notices, by inference from indirect evidence, and by the weighing of probabilities with the aid of whatever critical apparatus is at our disposal, we can make to a certain extent continuous what we find disjointed, there still remains the fact that the evidence on which we have ultimately relied is on the one side tainted with the hatred, contempt, and mistrust which the unintelligible and therefore unpardonable 'obstinacy' of the Christians produced in the heathen mind, and on the other with the passionate sense of injustice which rankled in and undoubtedly warped the minds of the Christian writers.[1]

How is the treatment to which the Christians were subjected during the first two centuries (for to that period we shall confine ourselves) consistent with the toleration with which the Roman government in religious matters has generally been credited?

[1] The tone adopted by the writer of the Apocalypse is a case in point. Professor Ramsay argues from the extreme bitterness of the Apocalypse that the persecutions of the first century must have been severer than those of the second. His argument is noticed below on 96, note 2.

Was this toleration less complete than we have been used to suppose? or has the extent, severity, and meaning of the persecutions been, as Gibbon was the first to suggest, exaggerated or misrepresented?[1] It is the great merit of Mommsen's article in the 'Historische Zeitschrift'[2]—an article which has laid the foundation for a more systematic treatment of the subject—to have pointed out that neither the one question nor the other can be fairly considered as long as we confine ourselves to the case of the Christians alone. Their treatment was only a part— no doubt as time went on always tending to be the most important part—of the general policy of the Roman government in those matters where religious, social, and political interests touched and overlapped. Christianity was not the only foreign cult with which the government had to deal; it was not the only foreign cult with which it had to interfere; and while it may be possible, perhaps, at the outset to define generally the Roman policy in religious matters, such a definition will carry us a very little way—partly because of the growing indifference to the national religion which was insensibly reflected in the action of the government, but mainly because a 'religious policy' tended more and more to become an abstraction, the concrete embodiments of which were modified by diverse political and social considerations, which were never the same in any two cases. In order, therefore, to form a well-grounded judgment on the

[1] See Gibbon's two famous chapters xv. and xvi.
[2] Vol. lxiv. 1890, *Der Religionsfrevel nach römischem Recht.*

treatment of Christianity, we have not only to discover from the often conflicting and uncertain evidence what that treatment was, but to connect it generally, if possible, with any underlying principles of Roman policy, and to show how these were or may have been modified by political and social circumstances, really or apparently involved in the nature of Christianity as it developed through the empire, or in the conditions amid which the Roman empire itself had coalesced, and on which its stability seemed to depend.

The Roman religion was essentially and before all things a national religion ; its object was primarily, not the honour of the gods, but the safety of the state, of which the goodwill of the gods was supposed to be the necessary condition.[1] Its observance was therefore the duty of every citizen, and was an even more necessary part of patriotism than service in the army, because the sin of a single recusant might call down the anger of the neglected gods on the whole state. It was, therefore, in early times the duty of the executive to enforce on citizens the observance of the national religion, and, if necessary, to punish its neglect. But the simple state of things which the principle so stated implies was of no long duration. The mission of the Roman state was a mission of conquest, and each fresh conquest, whether within Italy or without, opened out new mercantile communications with foreign nations. Foreigners from all quarters came to Rome, and with them necessarily

[1] See Boissier, *La Religion Romaine*, vol. i. p. 10 seq.

came their gods; and henceforward Roman policy was the outcome of two principles; different, indeed, but not essentially opposed, the exclusiveness of a national religion, modified, though by no means destroyed, by the comprehensiveness which is inherent in all polytheism. It is, as we should expect, the latter principle which is the most patent and easy to trace. Gradually the number of deities included in the national religion increased as the Roman citizenship was extended over Italy and as communication with the Greek nation became closer and more continuous. What were originally foreign cults could always be incorporated by the executive—who, however, would never take action without the support of a senatorial decree [1]—in the national worship, and so come under the general superintendence of the pontifices as 'sacra populi Romani;' the only distinction between these 'dii novensiles,' [2] as they were called, and the 'dii indigetes' being that the former, unless they were identified under another name with one of the old deities, were not allowed within the pomerium.

In this way were gradually adopted into the Roman state worship not only such Italian deities

[1] Tert. *Apol.* 5: 'Vetus erat decretum ne quis deus ab imperatore consecraretur, nisi a senatu probatus;' and 13, 'Status dei cuiusque in senatus aestimatione pendebat.'

[2] Arnobius, iii. 38: 'Cincius numina peregrina novitate ex ipsa appellata pronuntiat; nam solere Romanos religiones urbium superatarum partim privatim per familias spargere, partim publice consecrare, ac ne aliquid deorum multitudine aut ignorantia praeteriretur, brevitatis et compendii causa uno pariter nomine cunctos novensiles invocari.' Cf. Liv. viii. 9.

as Juno Regina from Veii,[1] or Diana from Aricia, but Apollo,[2] Aesculapius,[3] Ceres,[4] Dis, and—to a great extent through the influence of the Sibylline books[5] —almost all the Hellenic gods; so that long before the unification of Italy it was true 'cunctas caerimonias Italicis in oppidis et numinum effigies iuris atque imperii Romani esse.'[6] Nor were Greek and Italian cults alone thus received and recognised by the state. The same procedure was adopted as early as 204 B.C. in reference to the Oriental cult of Cybele, whose image, symbolised in a sacred stone, was, in accordance with the directions of the Sibylline books, brought to Rome from Pessinus in Galatia; and, in consequence apparently of her identification with the Italian Magna Mater, was ultimately placed in a temple within the pomerium on the Palatine itself.[7] Similarly, in the course of the Mithridatic wars, the worship of the Cappadocian goddess, centring round Comana, was introduced into Rome and identified with the Italian deity Bellona.[8] Manifestly this

[1] Liv. v. 21: 'Te simul, Juno regina, quae nunc Veios colis, precor, ut nos victores in nostram, tuamque mox futuram, urbem sequare.'

[2] Liv. iv. 25 and 29; cf. xxv. 12.

[3] Val. Max. i. 8, 2: 'Cura sacerdotum inspectis Sibyllinis libris animadvertit non aliter pristinam recuperari salubritatem posse, quam si ab Epidauro Aesculapius esset accersitus.' Liv. x. 47.

[4] Val. Max. i. 1, 1; Dionys. 6, 17; Tac. *Ann.* 2, 49; Cic. *pro Balb.* 24, 55.

[5] Marquardt, *Staatsverw.* iii. pp. 42, 52, and 358.

[6] Tac. *Ann.* iii. 71.

[7] Liv. xxix. 10 and 14: xxxvi. 36.

[8] Plut. *Sull.* 9: Λέγεται δὲ μετὰ τοὺς ὕπνους αὐτῷ Σύλλᾳ φανῆναι θεὸν ἣν τιμῶσι 'Ρωμαῖοι παρὰ Καππαδόκων μαθόντες, εἴτε δὴ Σελήνην οὖσαν εἴτε Ἀθηνᾶν εἴτε Ἐνυώ.

enlargement of the state worship was due to political considerations; the narrower circle of 'dii indigetes' no longer satisfied a population so varied and heterogeneous as that of Rome was fast becoming. And in the case of an Oriental cult, like that of Cybele, it naturally seemed more advisable, by recognising it as part of the state cult, to place it under the control of the government, represented by the pontifices, and so to sanction its restricted observance by the whole citizen body, rather than, by allowing free scope within a limited number of the population to a worship characterised in its native form by a certain sensuousness and extravagance, to run the risk of a general corruption of religion or morality.

But in a population so large and so mixed as that of Rome in the last century of the republic other strange and unfamiliar cults could not but creep in, not recognised by the government, and so beyond the control of the pontifices. With regard to these, the state policy seems to have been in the main one of watchful toleration. So far as the public morality was not endangered,[1] and so far as Roman citizens were not led to neglect or to violate the national worship, these cults were not interfered with. Nor was this a mere *laisser-faire* procedure, at any rate at first. The government knew its own strength; the executive magistrates were armed with a very wide police authority, which enabled them to step in at once, with or without the support of the senate, whenever

---

[1] Serv. ad *Aen.* iv. 303: 'Sacra Nyctelia quae populus Romanus exclusit causa turpitudinis.'

public order or public morality or public religion seemed in any way endangered. As might be expected the occasions for this interference were not wanting.

As early as 425 B.C. the aediles, in consequence of the invasion of new sacrificial rites, are ordered to take care 'ne qui nisi Romani dii neu quo alio more quam patrio colerentur.'[1] In 213 B.C. the anxieties of the Hannibalic war had made both men and women more inclined to have recourse to strange and foreign rites, and Roman citizens in the publicity of the Forum and the Capitol had not shrunk from celebrating non-national modes of worship. So open a scandal imperatively called for the interference of the government; the executive were censured by the senate, and the praetor at the command of the same body issued an edict, 'ne quis in publico sacrove loco novo aut externo ritu sacrificaret.'[2] That many other instances of the same sort occurred we may be quite certain, though few of them are recorded. 'How often,' asks Postumius in 188 B.C., 'in the time of our fathers and grandfathers were instructions given to the magistrates *ut sacra externa fieri vetarent*?'[3] In all these cases it is probably safe with Mommsen to assume that

---

[1] Liv. iv. 30: 'Nec corpora modo adfecta tabo sed animos quoque multiplex religio et pleraque externa invasit: novos ritus sacrificandi vaticinando inferentibus in domos quibus quaestui sunt capti superstitione animi: donec publicus iam pudor ad primores civitatis pervenit, cernentes in omnibus vicis sacellisque peregrina atque insolita piacula pacis deum exposcendae.'

[2] *Id.* xxv. 1: 'Tanta religio, et ea magna ex parte externa, civitatem incessit, ut aut homines aut dii repente alii viderentur facti,' &c.

[3] *Id.* xxxix. 16: 'Quoties hoc patrum avorumque aetate negotium est magistratibus datum, ut sacra externa fieri vetarent, sacri-

the particular point which called for interference on the part of the government was not the celebration of the foreign cult in itself, but the participation in it of Roman citizens or its intrusion within the limits of the pomerium. But even on this point the vigilance of the magistrates tended to become relaxed. Even in the use of an adopted cult like that of the Magna Mater this tendency towards greater laxity in course of time declared itself. The cult was at first placed under strict regulations: the priests who conducted the worship were Phrygians, and though a procession with some of the national rites, such as the blowing of trumpets and the clashing of cymbals, was allowed to pass through the city, the worship was stripped of its most extravagant features, and above all Roman citizens were forbidden by decree of the senate personally to participate in the ministrations of the cult.[1] Dionysius writes, indeed, as if these restrictions were still observed in the time of

ficulos vatesque foro, circo, urbe prohiberent, vaticinos libros conquirerent comburerentque, omnem disciplinam sacrificandi, praeterquam more Romano abolerent? Indicabant enim prudentissimi viri omnis divini humanique iuris nihil aeque dissolvendae religionis esse quam ubi non patrio sed externo ritu sacrificaretur.'

[1] Dionys. ii. 19: καὶ ὃ πάντων μάλιστα ἔγωγε τεθαύμακα καίπερ μυρίων ὅσων εἰς τὴν πόλιν ἐληλυθότων ἐθνῶν οἷς πολλὴ ἀνάγκη σέβειν τοὺς πατρίους θεοὺς τοῖς οἴκοθεν νομίμοις, οὐδενὸς εἰς ζῆλον ἐλήλυθε τῶν ξενικῶν ἐπιτηδευμάτων ἡ πόλις δημοσίᾳ, ὃ πολλαῖς ἤδη συνέβη παθεῖν· ἀλλὰ καὶ εἴ τινα κατὰ χρησμοὺς ἐπεισηγάγετο ἱερά, τοῖς ἑαυτῆς αὐτὰ τιμᾷ νομίμοις, ἅπασαν ἐκβάλλουσα τερθρείαν μυθικὴν, ὥσπερ τὰ τῆς Ἰδαίας ἱερά. θυσίας μὲν γὰρ αὐτῇ καὶ ἀγῶνας ἄγουσιν ἀνὰ πᾶν ἔτος οἱ στρατηγοὶ κατὰ τοὺς Ῥωμαίων νόμους· ἱέραται δὲ αὐτῆς ἀνὴρ Φρὺξ καὶ γυνὴ Φρυγία· καὶ περιάγουσιν ἀνὰ τὴν πόλιν οὗτοι μητραγυρτοῦντες, ὥσπερ αὐτοῖς ἔθος, τύπους τε περικείμενοι τοῖς στήθεσι, καὶ καταυλούμενοι πρὸς τῶν

Augustus. If so, it was perhaps in consequence of the Augustan religious reformation; but more probably he is describing a state of things which had long since passed away. At any rate it did ultimately pass away. We know from inscriptions that the *archigallus* or chief priest of Cybele was usually a Roman,[1] and certainly the cult was celebrated under the empire with much, if not all, of its Oriental enthusiasm.[2]

Livy's account of the Bacchanalian conspiracy[3] puts into the clearest light both the action of the government in cases where public morality or public security seemed to be endangered by foreign cults, and also the extent to which such cults might spread even among Roman citizens without attracting the attention of the government. These Bacchic rites, of undoubtedly Oriental origin, and for centuries common enough in Greece and Asia Minor, were apparently introduced into Etruria by a Greek adventurer, and from there spread with extreme rapidity both in Italy

ἑπομένων τὰ μητρῷα μέλη καὶ τύμπανα κροτοῦντες. Ῥωμαίων δὲ τῶν αὐθιγενῶν οὔτε μητραγυρτῶν τις οὔτε καταυλούμενος πορεύεται διὰ τῆς πόλεως ποικίλην ἐνδεδυκὼς στολὴν οὔτε ὀργιάζων τὴν θεὸν τοῖς Φρυγίοις ὀργιασμοῖς κατὰ νόμον καὶ ψήφισμα βουλῆς. οὕτως εὐλαβῶς ἡ πόλις ἔχει πρὸς τὰ οὐκ ἐπιχώρια ἔθη περὶ θεῶν.

[1] See *C. I. L.* vi. 2183, and other inscriptions collected by Marquardt, p. 369.

[2] See especially the description in Apuleius, *Met.* viii. 27; also Mart. ii. 84, 3-4; Stat. *Theb.* x. 170 foll.; Seneca, *Agam.* 687 foll.:

'Non, nisi molles imitata viros
Tristis laceret brachia tecum
Quae turritae turba parenti
Pectora rauco concita buxo
Furit, ut Phrygium lugeat Attin.'

[3] Liv. xxxix. 8 foll.

and Rome. At first women only were admitted into the θίασοι, or secret associations, which formed the basis of the cult: the initiation took place by day, and the meetings were only held three times a year. But all this was now changed: men were initiated as well as women; the initiated were to be under twenty years of age. Meetings were held five times in every month, and took place under the secrecy of night. The inevitable enormities did not fail to follow, and the Bacchic associations became hotbeds not only of moral corruption, but of civil crimes, such as forgery and murder, and even of political conspiracy. Accident brought this state of things to the notice of the government. The consul whose duty it was to take action laid the whole matter before the senate; an extraordinary investigation was held, and the cult was put down throughout Italy with energy and promptitude. More than 7,000 men and women were found to be implicated, and of these more than half were executed, while Bacchic associations were forbidden for the future. That political and moral rather than purely religious considerations guided the government action in this matter is clear from the whole account of Livy, and is proved by a saving clause in the senatorial decree abolishing the cult, to the effect that if individuals deemed it incumbent on them to celebrate any Bacchic rites, they might do so on obtaining a licence from the *praetor urbanus*, so long as no more than five persons, two men and three women, met together for the purpose.[1]

[1] See S. C. de Bacchanalibus, in Brun's *Fontes Iuris Rom. Ant.*

This event took place in 188 B.C. A hundred years later the government would have found it perhaps a less easy matter to put down so effectually an intrusive Oriental cult. At least the history of the Isis cult and the attitude of the government towards it tend to favour this supposition. By the last century of the republic popular belief in the national religion was very greatly undermined. The very toleration which characterised it might easily lead to indifferentism; its frequent resort to new modes of worship, especially in times of public danger and anxiety, was in itself a confession of insufficiency and weakness.[1] The upper classes, permeated with the sceptical philosophy of Greece, hardly took the trouble to keep up a decent appearance of belief:[2] popular poets scoffed openly at the established religion. More important still was the avowedly political character of the religion; it was a state religion, but the state was an oligarchy, and therefore the religion established and supported by the government tended to become a party religion—a religion of the minority—which, if indifferent to its own

p. 146: 'Sacra in oquoltod (occulto) ne quisquam fecise velet; neve in poplicod neve in preivatod neve extrad urbem sacra quisquam fecise velet, nisei pr. urbanum adieset, isque de senatuos sententiad .... jousiset.' Cf. Liv. xxxix. 18 *ad fin.*

[1] So, on the occasion of a plague in 395 B.C., Dionysius says (x. 53): καὶ πολλὰ ἐνεωτερίσθη ‘Ρωμαίοις οὐκ ὄντα ἐν ἔθει περὶ τίμας τῶν θεῶν ἐπιτηδεύματα οὐκ εὐπρεπῆ. Dio Cass. *Frag.* 24, 1 (Bekk): οἱ ‘Ρωμαῖοι πολλὰς μάχας μαχεσάμενοι καὶ πολλὰ καὶ παθόντες καὶ δράσαντες τῶν μὲν πατρίων ἱερῶν ὠλιγώρησαν, πρὸς δὲ τὰ ξενικὰ ὡς καὶ ἐπαρκέσοντά σφισιν ὥρμησαν: also the passages in Livy already cited, iv. 30 and xxv. 1.

[2] Cic. *De Nat. Deor.* ii. 3, 9.

supporters, was worse than indifferent to the masses and the subject classes. Reasons of a more subjective kind, and therefore more difficult to trace, came, there is no doubt, in time to be among the attractions towards Oriental cults. The national religion made little appeal to individuals; it was a state cult, and individuals were no longer bound up in the state, as they had been in 'the brave days of old.' There was more scope for personal interests and personal aspirations; greater subjectivity of feeling; and in proportion as this developed the less satisfying the old religion was felt to be, with its rigid ceremony and its unemotional character. But it was precisely here that the Oriental religions exercised their paramount influence. Mysterious rites of initiation, sensuous music, a worship crowded with symbolism no less awe-inspiring that it was imperfectly or not at all understood; and above all a system of expiatory and purificatory rites, in which there was enough of asceticism to satisfy the craving for something personal in religion and enough of licence to attract the crowd in its non-religious moods, all these things made the population of Rome peculiarly susceptible to the influence of cults like the Egyptian.[1]

At what date the worship of Isis was first introduced into Rome is uncertain, probably early in the last century of the republic. At any rate we know that a *collegium* of *pastophori*—the priests who presided at

[1] See on this, Keim, *Rom und das Christenthum*, p 9 foll., and for the bibliography of the subject see Marquardt, *Staatsverw.* iii. pp. 80–1.

her worship—was established in the time of Sulla.¹ The cult, however, was not a licensed one; it was peculiarly un-Roman in its character; it attracted a large number of citizens; it intruded itself on the very Capitol,² and above all it was believed to sanction grave immoralities. On account of all these reasons we find repeated action taken by the government. In 58 B.C. the cult was excluded from the Capitol by the consuls of the year;³ five years later the private shrines were ordered by the senate to be destroyed;⁴ in 50 B.C. the temples of Isis and Serapis were destroyed, not without some manifestation of popular feeling;⁵ two years later we find the same thing happening again, this time in consequence of action taken by the augurs.⁶ So far there had been a consistent attempt, clearly not very successful, on the part of the government to put down this cult. But in

---

¹ Apul. *Met.* xi. 17 : ' Coetu pastophorum quod sacrosancti collegii nomen est. . . . Collegium vetustissimum et sub illis Sullae temporibus conditum.'   Cf. Diodor. Sic. i. 29.

² *C. I. L.* i. 1034.   Suet. *Dom.* 1.   Tac. *Hist.* iii. 74.

³ Tert. *Apol.* 6 : ' Serapidem et Isidem . . . Capitolio prohibitos, id est curia Deorum pulsos, Piso et Gabinius consules . . . abdicaverant.'

⁴ Dio Cass. xl. 47 : τοὺς γὰρ ναοὺς αὐτοῦ οὓς ἰδίᾳ τινὲς ἐπεποίηντο καθελεῖν τῇ βουλῇ ἔδοξεν· οὐ γὰρ δὴ τοὺς θεοὺς τούτους ἐπὶ πολὺ ἐνόμισαν, καὶ ὅτι γε καὶ ἐξενίκησεν, ὥστε καὶ δημοσίᾳ αὐτοὺς σέβεσθαι ἔξω τοῦ πωμηρίου σφᾶς ἱδρύσαντο.

⁵ Val. Max. i. 3, 3 : ' L. Aemilius Paulus, consul cum senatus Isidis et Serapis fana diruenda censuisset, eaque nemo opificum attingere auderet, posita praetexta securim arripuit templique eius foribus infixit.'

⁶ Dio Cass. xlii. 26 : ἔδοξε γνώμῃ τῶν μάντεων πάντα αὖθις τά τε ἐκείνης [Isis] καὶ τὰ τοῦ Σεράπιδος τεμενίσματα κατασκάψαι.

43 B.C., amidst the anarchy of the civil wars, a temple of Isis was built by the triumvirs.[1] From this time the cult, though not formally adopted by the state, was nevertheless practically tolerated in Rome.[2] Augustus, indeed, excluded it from the pomerium,[3] Agrippa even from the suburbs,[4] though we know that there must have been a shrine of Isis on the Capitol at the end of Nero's reign;[5] and noble Romans like Otho participated openly in the cult.[6] But it was not without its vicissitudes. The attention of Tiberius was drawn to a particularly revolting instance of immorality perpetrated under cloak of its rites, and for the time the cult was put down with a strong hand—the temples destroyed, the priests crucified, and the devotees of the goddess banished from Italy.[7] This action, however, no more than the repeated

[1] Dio Cass. xlvii. 15: τὸν μὲν οὖν ἐνιαυτὸν ἐκεῖνον ταῦτά τε οὕτως ἐποίησαν, καὶ νεὼν τῷ τε Σεράπιδι καὶ τῇ Ἴσιδι ἐψηφίσαντο.
Cf. Lucan, viii. 831:
'Nos in templa tuam Romana accepimus Isin.'

[2] Arnob. ii. 73: 'Quid vos, Aegyptiaca numina, quibus Serapis atque Isis est nomen, non post Pisonem et Gabinium consules in numerum vestrorum rettulistis deorum?'

[3] Dio Cass. liii. 2: καὶ τὰ μὲν ἱερὰ τὰ Αἰγύπτια οὐκ ἐσεδέξατο εἴσω τοῦ πωμηρ'ου.

[4] *Id.* liv. 6: τά τε ἱερὰ τὰ Αἰγύπτια ἐπεισιόντα αὖθις ἐς τὸ ἄστυ ἀνέστειλεν· ἀπειπὼν μηδένα μηδὲ ἐν τῷ προαστείῳ αὐτὰ ἐντὸς ὀγδόου ἡμισταδίου ποιεῖν.

[5] Tac. *Hist.* iii. 74, and Suet. *Dom.* 1: 'Ardente templo [i.e. of Jupiter Capitolinus] apud aedituum clam pernoctavit, ac mane Isiaci celatus habitu interque sacrificulos vanae superstitionis,' &c.

[6] Suet. *Oth.* 12: 'Sacra etiam Isidis saepe in lintea religiosaque veste propalam celebrasse.'

[7] See the account in Joseph. *Ant. Iud.* 18, 3, 4, and cf. Tac. *Ann.* 2, 85.

expulsion of Jews from Rome implied any change of policy towards the religion as such. Not only, indeed, in Rome, but throughout Italy and the provinces numerous inscriptions testify to the wide extent of the cult.[1] Under the Flavian dynasty it was especially favoured. In the reign of Titus the temple was accidentally burnt down, but a new Iseum was built by Domitian,[2] and the remains at Pompeii testify to the extent to which the cult was celebrated in the Italian municipalities. Minucius Felix, writing towards the end of the second century, can say : ' Haec tamen Aegyptia quondam sacra nunc et Romana sunt.'[3] The history of the Isis cult reveals clearly enough the fact that in the last century of the republic and throughout the period of the empire the attempt to control Roman citizens in religious matters was to a very large extent given up. The extension of the franchise first throughout Italy, and then to large classes of individuals in the provinces, could hardly fail to impair and undermine the national feeling, on which the continued existence of the national religion as a living force depended.[4] Cults which were allowed to non-citizens in Rome and in the provinces could only be forbidden to citizens by a policy which would have seemed reactionary, and would have proved impracticable. As a matter of

[1] They are collected by Marquardt, *Staatsverw*. iii. p. 78.
[2] Eutrop. 7, 23.
[3] Min. Felix, *Octav*. 22, 1.
[4] Tert. *Apol*. 6 : ' Ubi religio, ubi veneratio maioribus debita a vobis ? Habitu, victu, instructu, sensu, ipso denique sermone proavis renuntiastis. Laudatis semper antiquitatem et nove de die vivitis.'

fact, therefore, government interference became limited to two kinds of cases—(1) to those in which a strange religion was dangerous to public morality or social order or political security; (2) to those in which the foreign religions did not reciprocate the state toleration with an equal toleration of their own, but were as rigidly exclusive of all worships but their own as the national religion had been in theory in times that were almost prehistoric. With the last of these conditions the Egyptian cults sufficiently complied : the first, as we have seen, led more than once to state action, though not to permanent proscription.

II

THE TREATMENT OF JUDAISM

So far the cases which we have considered have had relation almost exclusively to Rome itself, or at most to Rome and Italy. In the provinces Roman citizens were for a long time comparatively few in number, and therefore cases in which the government could have had any sufficient motive for interference with the native religions were altogether exceptional, and, as a matter of fact, these religions met with the most complete toleration both under the republic and under the empire. No doubt this toleration was not unconditional, but it was subject to fewer conditions than in Italy. The supervision of public morality, incomplete or nominal as of necessity it became even in Rome, was hardly attempted in the provinces, and only where such enormities as human sacrifices were involved in a cult, as in that of Saturn in Africa,[1] or as was believed to be the case with Druidism in

---

[1] Tert. *Apol.* 9 : 'Infantes penes Africam Saturno immolabantur palam usque ad proconsulatum Tiberii, qui ipsos sacerdotes in eisdem arboribus templi sui obumbratricibus scelerum votivis crucibus exposuit.'

Gaul,[1] do we hear of any cases of interference with the polytheistic religions of the native races. In the latter case, indeed, Augustus had contented himself with interdicting the worship to Roman citizens, and when Claudius resolved to put down Druidism entirely, it was probably because it seemed to contain within itself in a concentrated form the surviving national feeling of the Gallic tribes, which, in view of the annexation of Britain, might appear a real danger to the peace of the Western provinces.

But a somewhat new problem had to be faced when the empire came into contact with the monotheistic religions of the East—first Judaism, then Christianity—and in treating of the Roman policy towards the Christians it is of 'the greatest importance to remember that this problem of how to deal with an exclusive, intolerant, monotheistic religion had been before the government for considerably more than fifty years before the existence of Christianity as something distinct, and needing distinct treatment, could by any possibility have been realised.

That there were Jews in Rome under the republic is certain; they were even expelled from the city and from Italy 139 B.C.,[2] apparently on the charge of

---

[1] Plin. *H. N.* xxx. 1, 13: 'S. C. factum est ne homo immolaretur. .... Gallias utique possedit, et quidem ad nostram memoriam. Namque Tiberii Caesaris principatus sustulit Druidas eorum et hoc genus vatum medicorumque.' Suet. *Claud.* 25: 'Druidarum religionem apud Gallos dirae immanitatis et tantum civibus ab Augusto interdictam penitus abolevit [Claudius].' Cf. Strab. iv. 5, p. 198.

[2] Val. Max. i. 3, 2: 'C. Cornelius Hispalus praetor peregrinus . Popillio Laenate M. Calpurnio coss. . . . Iudaeos qui Sabazi

tainting Roman manners with their cult; and since the time of Pompeius there were large numbers of Jewish freedmen, originally brought over from the East as slaves. But it was in the Oriental provinces rather than in Rome that the government was confronted with the Jewish problem. And for the most part it was a political problem, especially at first.[1] The Jews differed from the other nationalities with which the Romans came into contact in this, that, bound together as they were by the closest national ties, they were neither united by a common political government nor were they all collected within the local boundaries of a single country. On the contrary, Judaea, though the centre, was only the nucleus of the race. The Jewish race was scattered throughout the Oriental provinces; in almost every one of the great Hellenistic cities which had sprung up since the time of Alexander there was a considerable Jewish population. Usually, perhaps, as in Alexandria, where two out of the five regions of the city were inhabited by Jews, they lived together more or less distinct from the rest of the population; but, whether in this way or mingled with the other inhabitants, they were to be found in the cities of Syria and Asia, of Cilicia, Pamphylia, Bithynia, and Pontus, in the purely Greek provinces of Macedonia and Achaia, and even

Iovis cultu Romanos inficere mores conati erant repetere domus suas coegit.'

[1] See on the subject of the Jews in the Roman empire Mommsen's important chapter 'Judäa und die Juden,' *Röm. Gesch.* v. p. 487 foll.

in the larger islands of the Aegean.[1] But they were naturally not citizens of the towns in which they resided. To become such they would by the constitutional laws of the empire have ceased to be Jews, and they would have had to submit in all respects to the municipal government of the various cities. This was in their case impossible; their legal position, therefore, was that of *incolae* or μέτοικοι. But while ordinary *incolae*, though no doubt, like the 'Berytenses cultores Iovis Heliopolitani qui Puteolis consistunt,'[2] forming associations within the alien cities for purposes of their national worship, were content to merge their other interests, as far as they were allowed by law, in the civic conditions around them, the case was always different with the Jews. Their associations—συναγωγαί—no doubt took their place among the other religious associations in the East for foreign or other cults, but they were different, nevertheless, in several important and essential points. That they were exclusive, and even aggressive towards other religions, might attract less attention in Oriental cities, where factions were numerous, and the party feeling and jealousy which sprang from them a standing danger to the public peace; but there was a close and intimate connexion between the local συναγωγαί, or, as they were from this point of view,

[1] Philo, *Leg. ad Caium*, p. 1032; Mang. 587. Strab. in Joseph. *Ant. Iud.* xiv. 7, 2; Joseph. *Bell. Iud.* ii. 16, 4; Acts ii. 5-11. Cf. Seneca, fragm. in August. *Civ. Dei*, vi. 11: 'Cum interim usque eo sceleratissimae gentis consuetudo convaluit, ut per omnes iam terras accepta sit, victi victoribus leges dederunt.'
[2] Orell. 1246 = Wilm. 2002.

πολιτεύματα,[1] and the centre at once of the religion and the race at Jerusalem, which made this exclusiveness more marked, and might seem to make it more dangerous. Moreover, included under this exceptional religious unity there was a certain political or semi-political unity, involved though hardly expressed, which made the Jewish problem both difficult, ambiguous, and complex to the Roman government.

To the Jews themselves, indeed, this political unity was of altogether secondary importance. They had, indeed, played their part, as a national and political unity, but always with a tendency to recur in some form or other to the theocracy which, according to national traditions, was proper to the race. Hence they had with comparatively little difficulty adapted themselves to the Seleucid *régime*, under which the loss of political independence was compensated by religious freedom,[2] and hence in later times they were content to accept the position merely of a 'religio licita' after all national unity had been proscribed. But at the time when the Jews first came within the sphere of Roman politics the national unity still existed, and it was reflected in the claim made by the συναγωγαί of the Diaspora to certain semi-political rights, such as jurisdiction over their own members, freedom from tribute, and exemption from service in the army.[3] Such claims joined to their religious fanaticism and their peculiar and exclusive customs,

---

[1] Cf. the πολίτευμα τῶν ἐν Βερενίκῃ Ἰουδαίων, *C. I. Gr.* 5261.
[2] Momms. *Röm. Gesch.* v. p. 487.
[3] Joseph. *Ant. Iud.* xiv. 10.

made them often an object of dislike and jealousy in the cities where they settled, and of scorn not unmixed with suspicion to the Roman government.

To Cicero their religion was a 'barbara superstitio,' and Flaccus was, in his opinion, justified in refusing to allow the annual Temple tax to be sent by the Jews of Asia to Jerusalem.[1] Julius Caesar, however, in regulating the Oriental provinces, partly from general considerations of policy or equity, partly with the view of rewarding the past services and securing the future good faith of Herod, who was in the position of a client-king of Judaea, inaugurated a more favourable policy towards the Jews, and granted them a number of exceptional privileges, some of which were semi-political in their effect, but all had more or less direct reference to the existence of Judaism as a religion. These privileges were defined and embodied in a series of edicts sent at the order of Caesar, or, after his death, of Antonius, by the provincial governors to the various cities in which Jewish συναγωγαί existed. The principal concession was the free exercise of their national religion, and the exemption from any duties or services which were irreconcilable with this. They were allowed unimpeded to send the annual Temple tax to Jerusalem; they were excused from appearing in court on the Sabbath; they were exempted from military service; they were formally allowed a cer-

---

[1] Cic. *pro Flacc.* xxviii. 67 : 'Quum aurum Iudaeorum nomine quotannis ex Italia et ex omnibus provinciis Hierosolyma exportari soleret, Flaccus sanxit edicto ne ex Asia exportari liceret. Quis est, iudices, qui hoc non vere laudare possit?'

tain jurisdiction over their own members,[1] and their συναγωγαί were expressly excepted from the edict by which almost all the *collegia* and θίασοι were put down, while later on, when the imperial cult was established in the Eastern provinces, the Jews were excused from a compliance which would have contradicted the first principles of their religion.[2] By these privileges the Jews were placed in an exceptionally favourable position, and this notwithstanding the fact that their religion was distinctly aggressive, and was even a proselytising religion, and that by reason of this aggressiveness they were generally the objects of dislike, suspicion, and even hatred. But

---

[1] Cf. Acts ix. 2, xxii. 19, xviii. 12-17, xxvi. 11 ; 2 Cor. xi. 24.

[2] Joseph. *Ant. Iud.* xiv. 10, 6, to the magistrates of Paros : καὶ γὰρ Γάϊος Καῖσαρ ὁ ἡμέτερος στρατηγὸς καὶ ὕπατος ἐν τῷ διατάγματι κωλύων θιάσους συνάγεσθαι κατὰ πόλιν μόνους τούτους οὐκ ἐκώλυεν, οὔτε χρήματα συνεισφέρειν οὔτε σύνδειπνα ποιεῖν· ὁμοίως δὲ κἀγὼ τοὺς ἄλλους θιάσους κωλύων τούτους μόνους ἐπιτρέπω κατὰ τὰ πάτρια ἔθη καὶ νόμιμα συνάγεσθαί τε καὶ ἵστασθαι.

Ibid. xiv. 10, 12, an edict of Dolabella to the Ephesians : Ἀλέξανδρος πρεσβευτὴς Ὑρκανοῦ ἀρχιέρεως καὶ ἐθνάρχου τῶν Ἰουδαίων ἐνεφάνισέ μοι περὶ τοῦ μὴ δύνασθαι στρατεύεσθαι τοὺς πολίτας αὐτοῦ διὰ τὸ μήτε ὅπλα βαστάζειν δύνασθαι μήτε ὁδοιπορεῖν αὐτοὺς ἐν ταῖς ἡμέραις τῶν σαββάτων, μήτε τρόφων τῶν πατρίων καὶ συνήθων κατ' αὐτοὺς εὐπορεῖν. Ἐγώ τε οὖν αὐτοῖς, καθὼς καὶ οἱ πρὸ ἐμοῦ ἡγεμόνες, δίδωμι τὴν ἀστρατείαν καὶ συγχωρῶ χρῆσθαι τοῖς πατρίοις ἐθισμοῖς ἱερῶν ἕνεκα καὶ ἁγίων συναγομένοις, καθὼς αὐτοῖς νόμιμον.

Ibid. xiv. 10, 17, to the magistrates of Sardis : Ἰουδαῖοι πολῖται ἡμέτεροι προσελθόντες μοι ἐπέδειξαν ἑαυτοὺς σύνοδον ἔχειν ἰδίαν κατὰ τοὺς πατρίους νόμους ἀπ' ἀρχῆς, καὶ τόπον ἴδιον ἐν ᾧ τά τε πράγματα καὶ τὰς πρὸς ἀλλήλους ἀντιλογίας κρίνουσι· τοῦτό τε αἰτησαμένοις ἵν' ἔξῃ αὐτοῖς ποιεῖν, τηρῆσαι καὶ ἐπιτρέψαι ἔκρινα.

See also the decrees of the citizens of Pergamus, Halicarnassus, Sardis, and Ephesus. Joseph. xiv. 10, 22-25. Cf. Suet. *Caes.* 84, where the Jews especially mourn his death.

on the one hand their existence was a fact with which the empire, in dealing with the Eastern provinces, had to take account, and there were really only two alternatives—to protect them or to put them down— because a neutral policy would have meant perpetual friction and disturbances which no well-ordered government could allow. And there was no sufficient reason for departing from the usual toleration of provincial cults, and putting down a religion which, though not complying with all the normal conditions of toleration, was nevertheless not suspected of being immoral, and which, in spite of proselytising tendencies, seemed to be narrowed down by its strictly national basis so far as to make any dangerous extension of it a remote improbability. Besides, as Mommsen has pointed out with much likelihood, these privileges, though bearing more or less directly on their religious position, were granted primarily to Jews in a political sense, and could not be claimed by, though they might often be allowed to, the proselytes of non-Jewish birth, while conversely national Jews by becoming Roman citizens would lose the right to these special exemptions. The latter case would seldom arise in the provinces, for which these regulations were primarily intended, but it might and did often occur in Rome, where a large proportion of the Jews were apparently of the freedman class, and therefore Roman citizens. Partly owing to this cause, and partly to the different conditions in Rome, where the Jewish communities were brought face to face with the central government, they were treated with less favour, or at least there were more exceptions to their entire freedom from interference in Rome than in the provinces. This, however, was not the case under Augustus, who, in spite of his attempts to infuse fresh life into the national or state religion, not only expressly confirmed and renewed all the privileges granted by the dictator to the Jews in the East,[1] but, as Philo expressly says, left the manumitted Jews in Rome in the undisturbed practice of their religion, neither expelling them from the city nor depriving them of their citizenship.[2] He even went so far as to order that when the distribution of corn took place on the Sabbath any Jews entitled to

---

[1] Joseph. *Ant. Iud.* xvi. 6, 2 : ἔδοξέ μοι καὶ τῷ ἐμῷ συμβουλίῳ μετὰ ὁρκωμοσίας γνώμῃ δήμου Ῥωμαίων τοὺς Ἰουδαίους χρῆσθαι τοῖς ἰδίοις θεσμοῖς κατὰ τὸν πάτριον αὐτῶν νόμον, καθὼς ἐχρῶντο ἐπὶ Ὑρκανοῦ ἀρχιέρεως θεοῦ ὑψίστου, τά τε ἱερὰ εἶναι ἐν ἀσυλίᾳ, καὶ ἀναπέμπεσθαι εἰς Ἱεροσόλυμα καὶ ἀποδίδοσθαι αὐτὰ τοῖς ἀποδοχεῦσιν Ἱεροσολύμων, ἐγγυᾶς τε μὴ ὁμολογεῖν αὐτοὺς ἐν σάββασιν.

Philo, *Leg. ad Caium*, p. 1035 ; Mang. 591 : Τὸ μὲν γὰρ πρῶτον ἀπέστειλε τοῖς ἐπιτρόποις τῶν κατὰ τὴν Ἀσίαν ἐπικρατειῶν, πυθόμενος ὀλιγωρεῖσθαι τὰς ἱερὰς ἀπαρχάς, ἵνα ἐπιτρέπωσι τοῖς Ἰουδαίοις μόνοις εἰς τὰ συναγώγια συνέρχεσθαι· μὴ γὰρ εἶναι ταῦτα συνόδους ἐκ μέθης καὶ παροινίας ἐπὶ συστάσει ὡς λυμαίνεσθαι τὰ τῆς εἰρήνης .... εἶτα κελεύει μηδένα ἐμποδὼν ἵστασθαι τοῖς Ἰουδαίοις μήτε συνιοῦσι μήτε συνεισφέρουσι.

[2] *Ibid.* p. 1014 ; Mang. 568 : Τὴν πέραν τοῦ Τιβέρεως ποταμοῦ μεγάλην τῆς Ῥώμης ἀποτομὴν ἣν οὐκ ἠγνόει κατεχομένην καὶ οἰκουμένην πρὸς Ἰουδαίων. Ῥωμαῖοι δὲ ἦσαν οἱ πλείους ἀπελευθερωθέντες· αἰχμάλωτοι γὰρ ἀχθέντες εἰς Ἰταλίαν ὑπὸ τῶν κτησαμένων ἠλευθερώθησαν, οὐδὲν τῶν πατρίων παραχαράξαι βιασθέντες. Ἠπίστατο οὖν καὶ προσευχὰς ἔχοντας καὶ συνιόντας εἰς αὐτὰς καὶ μάλιστα ταῖς ἱεραῖς ἑβδόμαις, ὅτε δημοσίᾳ τὴν πάτριον ἐπαιδεύοντο φιλοσοφίαν. Ἠπίστατο καὶ χρήματα συναγαγόντας ἀπὸ τῶν ἀπαρχῶν ἱερὰ, καὶ πέμποντας εἰς Ἱεροσόλυμα διὰ τῶν τὰς θυσίας ἀναξόντων. Ἀλλ᾽ ὁ μὲν οὔτε ἐξῴκισε τῆς Ῥώμης ἐκείνους, οὔτε τὴν Ῥωμαϊκὴν αὐτῶν ἀφείλετο πολιτείαν ὅτι καὶ τῆς Ἰουδαϊκῆς ἐφροντίζοντο.

the dole should have their portion reserved till the next day.[1] Tiberius[2] and Claudius,[3] while confirming all the Jewish privileges in the provinces, though the latter in his edict to the provincial governors found it necessary to recommend some reciprocal toleration to the Jews, came into a certain amount of collision with the Jews of the capital. In Rome every form of religious innovation tended to take root, and unattractive as the Jewish ritual might seem to be, it was not without its adventitious adherents, especially among women, while it grew to be a fashionable form of dilettanteism to observe certain parts of the Jewish ritual without formally becoming Jews.[4] Possibly this tendency may have considerably increased between the accession of Augustus and the time of Tiberius, while we know that the growth of foreign superstitions was a subject of some anxiety under Claudius.[5] At any rate Tiberius, using as an occasion the fact that a noble Roman lady, a convert to Judaism, had been induced to part with money for the adornment

[1] Philo, *Leg. ad Caium*, p. 1015; Mang. 569.

[2] *Ibid.* p. 1033; Mang. 591: Τί δὲ ὁ ἕτερός σου πάππος Τιβέρ.ος Καῖσαρ; Ἐν γὰρ τρίσιν καὶ εἴκοσιν ἔτεσιν οἷς αὐτοκράτωρ ἐγένετο, τὴν κατὰ τὸ ἱερὸν ἐκ μηκίστων χρόνων παραδεδομένην θρησκείαν ἐτήρησεν, οὐδὲν αὐτῆς παραλύσας ἢ παρακινήσας μέρος. Cf. also p. 1015; Mang. 569.

[3] Joseph. *Ant. Iud.* xix. 5, 3: Καλῶς οὖν ἔχειν τοῖς Ἰουδαίοις τοῖς ἐν παντὶ τῷ ὑφ' ἡμᾶς κόσμῳ τὰ πάτρια ἔθη ἀνεπικωλύτως φυλάσσειν, ἐν οἷς καὶ αὐτοῖς ἤδη νῦν παραγγέλλω μου ταύτῃ τῇ φιλανθρωπίᾳ ἐπιεικέστερον χρῆσθαι καὶ μὴ τὰς τῶν ἄλλων ἐθνῶν δεισιδαιμονίας ἐξουθενίζειν, τοὺς ἰδίους δὲ νόμους φυλάσσειν.

[4] Hor. *Sat.* i. 9, 69; Ovid, *Ars Am.* i. 415; Pers. v. 179; Juv. xiv. 97, &c.

[5] Tac. *Ann.* xi. 15.

of the Temple in Jerusalem, which was appropriated
by certain Jewish adventurers, took decisive measures
against the communities in Rome.[1] That the religion
itself was for the time put down, those who refused
to give up their profane rites being banished from
Italy, seems clear from the accounts of Suetonius and
Tacitus. But it is no less clear that the main brunt
of the repression fell upon those who were Roman
citizens. Of these no less than 4,000 were compul-
sorily enlisted in the army—since as Roman citizens,
and so no longer politically Jews, they lost their right
of exemption—and sent to Sardinia to put down the
brigandage there. The repression was only temporary: according to Philo, indeed, it was due to the
personal influence of Sejanus;[2] and under Claudius
the Jews in Rome were again very numerous. Under
that emperor we hear again of their expulsion from
the city, perhaps in consequence of disputes with the
Christians,[3] though Dio Cassius says that, as they
were too numerous to be expelled, Claudius simply
put in force against them the regulations forbidding

---

[1] Tac. *Ann.* ii. 85: 'Actum et de sacris Aegyptiis Iudaicisque pellendis: factumque Patrum consultum, ut quatuor milia libertini generis, ea superstitione infecta, quis idonea aetas, in insulam Sardiniam veherentur, coercendis illic latronibus, et, si ob gravitatem caeli interissent, vile damnum: ceteri cederent Italia, nisi certam ante diem profanos ritus exuissent.' Cf. Suet. *Tib.* 36.

Josephus, *Ant. Iud.* xviii. 3, 4, describes the whole affair: Τιβέριος κελεύει πᾶν τὸ Ἰουδαϊκὸν τῆς Ῥώμης ἀπελαθῆναι, κ.τ.λ.

[2] Philo, *Adv. Flacc.* ad init., and *Leg. ad Caium,* p. 1015; Mang. 569.

[3] Suet. *Claud.* 25: 'Iudaeos impulsore Chresto assidue tumultuantes Roma expulit.' Cf. Acts xviii. 2.

unlicensed *collegia*.¹ But whatever form the repression took it was clearly due to some temporary cause. It was getting to be against the spirit of the age to expect that a Jew, from the mere fact of being manumitted, should put off his national religion and conform to the established cult. Tiberius and Claudius may have deemed it advisable for the moment to assert the state's right to such compliance, but in the absence of some distinctly political or social danger the national religion had no longer sufficient hold on the public mind, and was no longer sufficiently the care of the government, to justify any permanent reversal of the Augustan policy; or to place the Jews in a position less favourable than that of the worshippers of Isis.

There was, however, as Mommsen points out,² always a distinction between the Roman policy towards the Jews in the East and in the West. In the former they were a political factor of which account had to be taken; in the latter they were immigrants to be tolerated at the most, but not encouraged. Nor is it possible to deny that in his policy towards the Jews of the Diaspora Augustus had admitted principles which might, in conceivable circumstances, prove a danger to the empire. The indulgence shown to their rigid monotheism in

---

¹ Dio Cass. lx. 6: τούς τε Ἰουδαίους πλεονάσαντας αὖθις, ὥστε χαλεπῶς ἂν ἄνευ ταραχῆς ὑπὸ τοῦ ὄχλου σφῶν τῆς πόλεως εἰρχθῆναι, οὐκ ἐξήλασε μέν, τῷ δὲ δὴ πατρίῳ νόμῳ βίῳ χρωμένους ἐκέλευσε μὴ συναθροίζεσθαι.

² *Röm. Gesch.* v. p. 499.

exempting them from the imperial cult, intended as it was to be a bond of unity in and allegiance to the empire, was in itself, perhaps, from the imperial point of view, a doubtful step; but the national and political unity, such as it was, granted to this dispersed race, really on the ground of this religious recusancy, was still more in contradiction both to the imperial and municipal policy which the government in other cases adopted. It was the recognition, on however small a scale, of a State within the State. The ill-considered attempt of Caligula to force the imperial cult, contrary to all these expressly granted privileges, first on the synagogues of Alexandria, and finally to place his statue in the central Temple of Jerusalem,[1] proved, to a certain extent, the wisdom of the Augustan policy, to which, as we have seen, Claudius at once reverted; but the political difficulties were greater, and it is doubtful whether the catastrophe of the Jewish war at the end of Nero's reign could by any possibility have been permanently avoided. Ever since Judaea was made into a province, and the Jews were brought into direct contact with the Roman officials, procurators, military officers, and tax-gatherers, in spite of every wish on the part of the Roman government to avoid causes of collision, these proved less and less able to be avoided. Individual cases of misgovernment on the one hand were met by an increasing tendency on the part of the Jewish authorities to play into the hands of the extreme party, and when the war broke out it was

[1] Philo, *Leg. ad Caium*, p. 1019; Mang. 573, &c.

merely the natural consummation of relations which were mutually incompatible.

The war had important consequences in several directions. Politically, after the destruction of Jerusalem, the deposition of the high priest, and the dissolution of the Sanhedrim, the Jews ceased to exist. In the eyes of the Roman law they were henceforth 'cives nullius certae civitatis—peregrini dediticii'—and an inscription of Hadrian's time rightly describes them as οἵ ποτε 'Ιουδαῖοι.[1] But though their political privileges were abolished their religion was still not only tolerated but protected. In fact, as Mommsen says, into the place of the privileged nation there now stepped the privileged confession—the 'religio licita.'[2] The Jews of the Diaspora remained in their position of μέτοικοι in the Eastern cities, but there was now no sort of political union with any centre of the race. Technically a Jewish community could no longer be described, as before the war, by the term πολίτευμα, but simply as a συναγωγή, or rather as a collection of συναγωγαί. The Jews in Rome and those in the provinces now stood on exactly the same footing. Their worship was protected by the state from all interference; their συναγωγαί were still exempted from the regulations against *collegia*; their members were no more than before compelled to conform to the imperial cult; their scruples as to the Sabbath were respected; and they were excused from military service. But

[1] Momms. *Histor. Zeitschr.* lxiv. p. 424. C. I. Gr. 3148.
[2] Ibid. p. 425.

these privileges were no longer free to all who called themselves Jews, whether by birth or by conversion. Only those were recognised as Jews by the State who were members of one of the συναγωγαί, and who formally entered their names (*profiteri*) as such, and received a licence from the proper official. And for this licence a tax had to be paid. The two drachmae which all Jews had hitherto paid to the Temple at Jerusalem were now to be paid to the temple of Jupiter Capitolinus.[1] So that though the Jews retained their freedom of worship, it was a 'vectigalis libertas.' Several ends were gained by this institution. The supremacy and dignity of the national religion were to a certain extent vindicated against the exclusive and haughty monotheism by the tax paid to the centre of Roman worship; a supervision by the licensing of individual members was secured over the συναγωγαί, which made their concession less of a real exception to the imperial policy in this matter than at first sight it seemed to be; while the possibility of checking any dangerous spread of the religion through an access of proselytising zeal was placed always within the power of the government, which also had

[1] Joseph. *B. I.* vii. 6, 6: φόρον δὲ τοῖς ὁπουδήποτε οὖσιν Ἰουδαίοις ἐπέβαλε, δύο δραχμὰς ἕκαστον κελεύσας ἀνὰ πᾶν ἔτυς εἰς τὸ Καπετώλιον φέρειν, ὥσπερ πρότερον εἰς τὸν ἐν Ἱεροσολύμοις νεών.
Dio Cass. lxvi. 7 : καὶ ἐπ' ἐκείνου δίδραχμον ἐτάχθη τοὺς τὰ πάτρια ἀπῶν ἔθη περιστέλλοντας τῷ Καπιτωλίῳ Διΐ κατ' ἔτος ἀποφέρειν. Suet. *Dom.* 12 : 'Praeter ceteros Iudaicus fiscus acerbissime actus est, ad quem deferebantur qui vel improfessi Iudaicam viverent vitam, vel dis inulata origine imposita genti tributa non pependissent.' Tert. *Apol.* 18 : 'Sed et Iudaei palam lectitant ; vectigalis libertas vulgo aditur sabbatis omnibus.' Juv. iii. 15.

an easy means of preventing, if it wished, Roman citizens from becoming proselytes. Under this arrangement Jews by birth were not as such bound to pay the tax, but only if they attended the synagogues and were therefore Jews by religion. On the other hand, proselytes, whether Roman citizens or others who had obtained the licence, were entitled to all the religious privileges of the Jews, though apparently both classes might in private, and as long as they were not members of a synagogue, practise Jewish manners ('vita Iudaica') without, by registration, making themselves liable to the tax.[1]

But though the war had not caused any repression of the Jewish religion, which, as Tertullian says, was 'certe licita,'[2] it had very strongly increased the feeling of antipathy to the Jews entertained in a less degree even before by the educated classes at Rome. Tacitus is the best representative of this feeling, to which, however, expression is given clearly enough by Juvenal,[3] Quintilian,[4] and Pliny.[5] According to Tacitus[6] it is a 'gens taeterrima'—'proiectissima ad

---

[1] So I interpret the passage of Suetonius, *Dom.* 12, cited above.
[2] Tert. *Apol.* 21.
[3] Juv. xiv. 100:
  'Romanas autem soliti contemnere leges,
  Iudaicum ediscunt et servant ac metuunt ius,
  Tradidit arcano quodcunque volumine Moyses.'
[4] Quint. *Instit. Or.* iii. 7, 21 : 'Est et conditoribus urbium infame contraxisse aliquam perniciosam ceteris gentem, qualis est primus Iudaicae superstitionis auctor.'
[5] Plin. *H. N.* xiii. 4 : 'Gens contumelia numinum insignis.'
[6] Tac. *Hist.* v. 2-5: 'Profana illic omnia quae apud nos sacra: rursum concessa apud illos quae nobis incesta.... Cetera instituta

libidinem '—characterised by an 'hostile odium' towards all outside its own circle, teaching its converts 'contemnere deos, exuere patriam, parentes liberos fratres vilia habere.' That in spite of this very strong feeling—a feeling which must inevitably have been heightened by the internecine war under Trajan, and by the frightful atrocities perpetrated by the Jews in Cyprus and other places [1]—the toleration extended to the Jews should still have been maintained, so that even so late as the beginning of the third century we find Callistus banished to Sardinia for disturbing a Jewish congregation at Rome,[2] while it is expressly affirmed in the Theodosian Code, 'Iudaeorum sectam nulla lege prohibitam satis constat,'[3] is a sufficiently remarkable circumstance, and would seem, at any rate, to justify the general assertion that in religious matters the Roman government was both forbearing and tolerant.

But before we pass on to consider its dealings with the second monotheistic religion with which it came into contact—Christianity—it will, perhaps, be well just to sum up the limitations to this toleration which we have seen to constitute its practical or working

---

sinistra foeda pravitate valuere. Nam pessimus quisque spretis religionibus patriis tributa et stipes illuc gerebant: unde auctae Iudaeorum res, et quia apud ipsos fides obstinata, misericordia in promptu, sed adversus alios omnes hostile odium.... Transgressi in morem eorum idem usurpant, nec quidquam prius imbuuntur quam contemnere deos, exuere patriam, parentes liberos fratres vili habere.'

[1] Euseb *H. E.* iv. 2; Dio Cass. lxviii. 32; Oros. vii. 12.
[2] Hippolstus, *Philosoph.* ix. 12.
[3] *Cod. Theod.* xvi. 8, 9.

policy towards foreign cults. In the first place, then, putting on one side the received cults which thus became parts of the national worship, foreign religions were tolerated in so far as they did not injure the national and established worship. Strictly, and at first, this would mean that aliens but not Roman citizens might participate in them. But a rigid enforcement of this principle was practically impossible and it became so far modified as to permit Roman citizens to participate in these cults in so far as they were not thereby prevented from showing due honour to the national gods—in other words, in so far as the toleration was reciprocal. In the course of time, and under the empire—or, as Mommsen puts it, 'unter dem die alten Ordnungen verflachenden und zerrüttenden Regiment der Cäsaren und ihrer Beamten'—even this condition was in certain cases overlooked, and no doubt many Roman citizens were Jews or even Christians without drawing down upon themselves, in fact, any State interference. If the question had been a purely religious one the government policy would have been summed up in what has been said. But it was not. It was a characteristic of many of the immigrant religions, especially of those of an Oriental origin, to foster and encourage gross immoralities. No doubt in this connexion any line drawn between what might be permitted and what not was an arbitrary one, but still the existence of such a line was always tacitly recognised, not only in the policy of the government, but even, if we may use such a term of such times, in the moral sense of the community; and, as we have seen, the government occasionally, sometimes with, sometimes without the support of popular feeling, took decisive action and put down a cult on the score of its immorality. More important still was the potential interference of the government with foreign religions from political considerations. Long after religious belief had practically disappeared, the national religion was upheld as the emblem or symbol of the political supremacy of Rome. It is of little importance for the present question whether we look to Rome or Italy with their sphere of state-recognised deities whose cults were under the ultimate superintendence of the pontifex maximus—who himself, under the empire, was always the executive head of the state—or to the provinces, where, by the institution of Augustus, the imperial cult—the worship of 'Rome and Augustus'—was to provide some kind of religious unity for the empire, as the representation and symbol of its political cohesion.[1] In the one case as in the other, viewed in its severest light, religious recusancy was tantamount potentially to political disaffection. Not by any means that in all cases it was actually so regarded. That would depend on a number of circumstances, collective and individual, local and imperial. Sometimes opposite considerations might have to be balanced against one another, as, *e.g.*, when it seemed a smaller political danger to condone and even to sanction the religious recusancy of the Jews—which,

[1] See an article in the *English Historical Review*, No. 18, on the Provincial Concilia,' p. 226 foll.

based as it was on the narrow limits of an obscure nationality, seemed incapable of any appreciable development—rather than to risk a general conflagration of religion and national hatred in all the great cities of the East by interfering with the religious freedom and its semi-political consequences among the scattered but important Jewish communities. But because an aggressive and morose monotheism, resting on a narrow national basis, was tolerated by the government, all the circumstances of the case being taken into account, it by no means necessarily followed that an aggressive monotheism, equally exclusive and equally indifferent to the political obedience which was implied in religious conformity, and at the same time claiming to overstep all limits of nationality, and without disguise aiming at a universality which the Roman empire was prevented by the history of all its institutions from conceiving apart from political consequences—it by no means followed that such a religion would receive the same treatment from the state.

III

FIRST APPEARANCE OF CHRISTIANITY IN THE EASTERN PROVINCES

HISTORICALLY Christianity originated as an offshoot from Judaism, and it is probably an undisputed fact that to all outside the Jewish communities, perhaps at first even to the Jews themselves outside Judaea, Christianity was regarded merely as a Jewish sect. It is no less certain that the first spread of Christianity was aided and conditioned by the extent and number of the Jewish communities scattered over the provinces of Syria and Asia Minor. That the earliest converts in Jerusalem, rising with extreme rapidity from 120[1] to 3,000,[2] and then to 5,000[3]—the large number being accounted for by the fact that multitudes of Jews from all parts of the empire happened to be at Jerusalem for the feast of Pentecost[4]—still continued to worship in the Temple is expressly attested.[5] The fact that Stephen was brought before the Sanhedrim[6] proves that in the eyes of that body he was a recusant Jew, over whom, therefore, they had

---

[1] Acts i. 15. [2] Acts ii. 41. [3] Acts iv. 4.
[4] Acts ii. 5-11. [5] Acts. ii. 46. [6] Acts vii. 12.

the right of jurisdiction, while the certainly illegal action of putting him to death could only have been overlooked by the Roman government because they regarded it as one of those regretable incidents which the internal animosities among the Jews sometimes occasioned, and at which it was better to connive than to interfere with. The persecution, a purely Jewish one, which followed was the first means of spreading the new sect through the cities of Judaea and Samaria,[1] and then to such places as Damascus,[2] Cyprus, and Antioch[3]—all places where there were large Jewish communities, and in which it is expressly stated that the refugees 'spake the word to none save to the Jews only.'[4] So, too, a few years later, when, through the missionary activity of Paul, the new religion—for such it was gradually becoming —spread north and west of the Taurus range, it was to the Jews first that Paul invariably announced the message that he had to bring. This was the case at Salamis in Cyprus,[5] at Antioch in Pisidia,[6] at Iconium,[7] at Philippi,[8] at Thessalonica,[9] at Beroea,[10] at Ephesus,[11] and no doubt at all the other cities where he preached. But though many Jews became converts to the 'new way' it had been from the first discountenanced and even proscribed by the central authorities at Jerusalem.[12] Just as Saul was sent by

---

[1] Acts viii. 1.   [2] Acts ix. 1.   [3] Acts xi. 19.
[4] μηδενὶ λαλοῦντες τὸν λόγον εἰ μὴ μόνον Ἰουδαίοις. xi. 19.
[5] Acts xiii. 5.   [6] Acts xiii. 14.   [7] Acts xiv. 1.
[8] Acts xvi. 13.   [9] Acts xvii. 1.   [10] Acts xvii. 10.
[11] Acts xviii. 19 and xix. 8.   [12] Acts iv. 18 and v. 28.

the high priest with letters to the synagogues of Damascus against the Christians,[1] so no doubt there were emissaries to the various cities of the Diaspora. At Antioch in Pisidia the Jews were so hostile that Paul at this early stage of his missionary journey declared his intention of turning to the Gentiles.[2] They were driven out of Iconium by the Jewish faction,[3] who, together with the Jews of Antioch, followed the missionaries to Lystra, causing them to be stoned there and left for dead,[4] while in subsequent journeys similar treatment was experienced from the Jews of Thessalonica[5] and Corinth.[6] That the Christians were subject to persecution during the early growth of the religion is indisputable, but the persecution would seem to have been neither systematic nor continuous, and to have fallen mainly not on the ordinary members of the new brotherhood, whether Jews or Gentiles, but on the apostles and leaders, who went about from place to place, unsettling existing conditions[7] and undermining the binding force of the Jewish law.[8] Above all the persecution came at this period exclusively from the Jews.[9] Indeed, the Roman government, in so far as it was brought into contact with the Christians at all, acted rather as a protecting and moderating influence,

---

[1] Acts ix. 2.   [2] Acts xiii. 47.   [3] Acts xiv. 5.
[4] Acts xiv. 19.   [5] Acts xvii. 5.   [6] Acts xviii. 12.
[7] Acts xvii. 6 : τὴν οἰκουμένην ἀναστατώσαντες.
[8] Acts xviii. 13 : παρὰ τὸν νόμον ἀναπείθει οὗτος τοὺς ἀνθρώπους σέβεσθαι τὸν θεόν. Cf. xxiv. 5.
[9] Cf. for instances of Jewish hostility Acts vii. 58, viii. 3, xi 14, xvii. 7 and 13, xviii. 13, xxi. 28, xxiv. 5, xxv. 8, xxvi. 10.

either by preventing violence and outrage,[1] or, when accusations were brought by the Jews before the imperial tribunals, by altogether refusing to abet or assist the religious bigotry of the Jews, or to interfere in their sectarian differences. This was the course taken at once and brusquely by Junius Gallio, the proconsul of Achaia,[2] and it was practically also adopted, though with greater patience and a greater semblance of interest and judicial investigation, by Antonius Felix,[3] and afterwards by Porcius Festus,[4] procurators of Judaea, to whom the whole question seemed to turn on ζητήματά τινα περὶ τῆς ἰδίας δεισιδαιμονίας,[5] and who would have dismissed the Jewish charges altogether had not Paul claimed as a Roman citizen to be tried before the emperor.[6] Bu though the government officials, so far as all our evidence goes, were agreed in taking this view of the case, and regarded the Christians as an extreme sect of the Jews—so much so that Claudius Lysias suspected that Paul was a leader of the Sicarii,[7] and Tertullus, the Jews' own advocate, designated him as πρωτοστάτης τῆς τῶν Ναζαραίων αἱρέσεως[8]—i seems to be pretty clear that the term 'Christians,' the derisive *sobriquet* first attached to the new sect by the flippant wit of the Greek populace of Antioch

---

[1] Acts xxi. 31, 32.
[2] Acts xviii. 14-15: εἰ μὲν ἦν ἀδίκημά τι ἢ ῥᾳδιούργημα πονηρόν, ὦ Ἰουδαῖοι, κατὰ λόγον ἂν κατεσχόμην ὑμῶν· εἰ δὲ ζητήματά ἐστι περὶ λόγου καὶ ὀνομάτων καὶ νόμου τοῦ καθ' ὑμᾶς, ὄψεσθε αὐτοί.
[3] Acts xxiv. 1-27.   [4] Acts xxv. 14 foll.   [5] Acts xxv. 19.
[6] Acts xxvi. 32.   [7] Acts xxi. 38.   [8] Acts xxiv. 5.

about 48 A.D.,[1] disowned and ignored at first by the Christians themselves,[2] and not adopted by the Jews,[3] was nevertheless becoming familiar to the population of the Eastern provinces, and probably to the Roman officials there.[4] Connected, too, with this, and in the end far more important, was the fact that the Jews continued the policy which they had begun in the case of Jesus himself before Pontius Pilate, of mingling with their own complaints more or less outspoken accusations of disloyalty on the part of the Christians to the Roman government. This in the case of Paul comes out only indirectly. Thus Paul says, clearly in answer to charges made, Οὔτε εἰς τὸν νόμον τῶν Ἰουδαίων οὔτε εἰς τὸ ἱερὸν οὔτε εἰς Καίσαρά τι ἥμαρτον,[5] while the very fact of his being sent to Rome precludes us from supposing that petty violations of Jewish ritual were the only charges made, though the procurator was clear-sighted enough to see that this was the real point, and to attach no value to the others.

At Thessalonica, however, we have definite evidence that political charges were made, not, indeed, in this case before the government officials, but before the municipal magistrates. Οὗτοι πάντες ἀπέναντι τῶν δογμάτων Καίσαρος πράσσουσιν, βασιλέα ἕτερον λέγοντες εἶναι Ἰησοῦν.[6] Nor can there be any reasonable doubt

---

[1] Acts xi. 26: ἐγένετο . . . χρηματίσαι πρώτως ἐν Ἀντιοχείᾳ τοὺς μαθητὰς Χριστιανούς.

[2] Notice how Paul ignores it, Acts xxvi. 29.

[3] To the Jews the Christians were Ναζαραῖοι, Acts xxiv. 5.

[4] It was used in the presence of Festus, Acts xxvi. 28.

[5] Acts xxv. 8.   [6] Acts xvii. 7.

that the same thing took place in other cities, where the Jews were at once indignant at the rise of the new αἵρεσις and jealous of the extension of its membership to the heathen? If this was so, we can well understand that, though the Christians were still, and would be for years to come, taken by the Roman officials for a Jewish sect, and as such protected from riotous behaviour on the part of their co-religionists and privileged in their own religious worship, yet the way was being prepared more and more for the thorough discrimination between them, which, whenever it began, was, as all agree, an accomplished fact at the beginning of the second century. What of course naturally aided this discrimination was the really wider line of separation which, apart from any views on the subject, either by Jews or Romans, gradually came to mark off the Christians from the Jewish bodies. If the earliest members of the Christian communities were probably in almost all cases Jewish, it is no less true that at a very early date the tendency of Christianity to sever itself from all national limitation was begun. At Antioch in Pisidia Paul announced his intention of turning to the Gentiles [1]— a declaration made still more emphatically in Macedonia,[2] and before long the Gentile Christians became, there is no doubt, the preponderating element in all the Christian Churches both in the East and in the West. At first, indeed, the heathen, and especially

[1] Acts xiii. 47.
[2] Acts xviii. 6: τὸ αἷμα ὑμῶν ἐπὶ τὴν κεφαλὴν ὑμῶν· καθαρὸς ἐγώ· ἀπὸ τοῦ νῦν εἰς τὰ ἔθνη πορεύσομαι.

the Greek population, were far from hostile to the new religion. If the Jewish monotheism, morose, and in certain aspects repellent, as it seemed, nevertheless attracted numerous proselytes from the Hellenistic cities,[1] Christianity, with its wider appeals to humanity, was even more likely to do this. Professor Ramsay with perfect justification emphasises the point that Paul, almost from the first, clearly conceived of Christianity as the universal religion, the limits of which were to be co-extensive with the Roman empire, and that it was with this idea in his mind that he chose out, especially in his missionary journeys, the centres not only of Greek civilisation, but of the Roman organisation and government.[2] That he did do this, from whatever motive, is indisputable, and amid the general decay of the old religions the missionaries of the new found the masses not altogether indisposed to give them a favourable hearing, whilst even the more educated classes, though seldom converts, regarded them at any rate at first with no stronger feeling than a somewhat sceptical curiosity.

But this favourable or neutral attitude was not destined to be permanent; by the beginning of the second century it had generally given way to an intense and often violent hatred, and the change, whenever it came about—and it probably came about gradually—was due to several causes, the beginnings of some of which we are able to trace at this earlier

---

[1] Tacitus, *Hist.* v. 5 : ' Nam pessimus quisque spretis religionibus patriis tributa et stipes illuc gerebant.'

[2] *The Church in the Roman Empire*, pp. 56, 57. Cf. also p. 147.

period and in our chief authority for it—the Acts of the Apostles.

That the unpopularity of the Christians was caused by purely religious animosities is of all suppositions the least likely. As Professor Ramsay says, 'the ordinary pagan did not care two straws whether his neighbour worshipped twenty gods or twenty-one.'[1] But Christianity constituted a social revolution even more than a religious one, or rather its social (to received ideas they seemed anti-social) effects were far more patent and striking than the religious ideas which produced them. And it was this divergence from the social life in its widest sense around them, often amounting to an aggressive interference with the established conditions of society, with trade interests, with family life, with popular amusements, with everyday religious observances, with the lax but conventional morality of the time, which gave to Christianity an appearance of misanthropy, of an *odium generis humani*, which in time was more than repaid by the general execration of paganism. It is important to look, if we can, at the early Christians from the heathen point of view, and above all to avoid any idealisation of the primitive communities. We may grant at once that in matters of morality, and especially in the relations of the sexes, the Christians were far superior to the populations in whose midst they lived. But it would be a mistake to suppose that it was the loftier elements of Christianity which most strongly attracted converts, or that conversion introduced them neces-

[1] *Op. cit.* p. 130.

sarily into a higher plane of life or enlightenment. To a great extent it was the tendency to level distinctions of property or differences of social life, the hopes it held out of a shortly coming Saviour, and the idea of a future beyond the grave, in which compensation would be made for the inequalities of the present—which drew the lower classes to Christianity. We cannot judge of the ordinary Christian of Corinth or Antioch, or Ephesus, or Rome, from the leaders and teachers of the sect. The Christians of the Eastern provinces shared the characteristics of the Oriental population; they were not less fanatical or less ignorant, or less excitable, or less credulous. In the eyes of their fellow-citizens there was nothing about them to justify what seemed the extravagant claims they made on behalf of their religion. They were fanatical, exclusive, and intolerant, and for a religion which, so to speak, to Gentile eyes had nothing to show for itself, no stately temples, no famous shrines, no imposing priesthood, no impressive ceremonial.

But it was not so much as religious enthusiasts that the Christians attracted popular attention. Their fanaticism took certain apparently anti-social forms, which, there can be little doubt, made them the Nihilists of the day. In the first place the very belief—and in the first century it was a vivid one—of the approaching end of the world and the second coming of Christ involved a restless expectation and in some respects a recklessness of action which were quite inconsistent with the ordinary duties, domestic, social, or political, of an orderly subject of the empire.

Then, again, the communistic ideas of the sect must have interfered, often in a very exasperating way, with social and family relations. The mere fact that members of a family were induced to leave their relations, to desert the religion of their fathers and to join these enthusiasts, was in itself enough to cause heart-burning and rancour; but to see part of the family property appropriated to the common Christain funds must greatly have embittered these feelings, and inspired the moneyed classes of society at any rate with hatred and apprehension. Again, there was a manifest disinclination on the part of the Christians to marriage and the duties and obligations of married life. This in connexion with the comparatively large number of female converts must often have led to episodes like that in the history of Paul and Thekla, where a maiden of good social standing is induced to refuse the marriage arranged by her parents. Nor did cases of this kind appear accidental and occasional: they rather followed from the maxims of the Founder of the sect—maxims which, imperfectly understood, and obeyed in the letter rather than the spirit, were no doubt constantly in the mouths of his followers. 'It is easier for a camel to pass through the eye of a needle than for a rich man to enter into the kingdom of heaven.' 'Think not that I am come to give peace on the earth. I tell you nay, but rather division.' 'If any man cometh unto me and hateth not his father and mother, and wife and children and brother . . . he cannot be my disciple.' 'The sons of this world marry and are given in marriage, but they that are accounted worthy to attain unto that world and the resurrection from the dead neither marry nor are given in marriage.' These and other 'hard sayings' put into practice without discrimination or qualification were tantamount, so far as they extended, to an upheaval of existing social relations, and might well seem to lay the Christians open to the charge of turning the world upside down.

Only less intolerable than this disregard of the primary rights and obligations of social and family life was the absolute refusal of the Christians to join in any religious festival, to appear in the courts where an oath had to be taken, to illuminate their doors at festivals, to join in the amusements of the amphitheatre; their unwillingness, if not refusal, to serve in the army, and their aversion to all civic duties and offices. It was this apparently 'hostile odium' towards all outsiders which had made the Jews so generally unpopular as they were, and in explaining the hatred felt for the Christians we must remember that, as Mommsen says, 'der Hass der Massen von den Juden auf die Christen sich übertrug.'[1] The Christians to a certain extent, apart from any characteristics of their own, inherited, as a Jewish sect or αἵρεσις, the aversion with which the Jews were regarded. As has, however, already been said, the intense animosity of the second century was only of gradual growth, and it no doubt grew with the growth of Christianity. Things quite unimportant, when the communities were small and insignificant, would be looked at with very different eyes as the number of

[1] *Histor. Zeitschr.* p. 412. Cf. *Expositor*, July 1893, p. 2.

converts increased. In the Acts there are only two instances recorded in which there was any manifestation of popular feeling against the Christians on the part of the heathen, and in both cases the reason was the same—interference with trade relations, pecuniary loss or the fear of it from the existence of Christianity. At Philippi the occasion of the tumult was a trivial one: the sympathy of the crowd with a few individuals whose hope of gain from the prophecies of a mad soothsayer was disappointed by Paul's action in healing her. Naturally the accusation before the *duoviri* of the *colonia* took a somewhat different form, viz. that the apostles were setting forth customs which it was not lawful for Roman citizens to receive;[1] but that the magistrates did not treat this accusation seriously and only took action at all to appease the mob is clear from their order to release the prisoners without further formality next morning. The affair at Ephesus is a better instance still. Here the workmen who made the silver shrines presented by her worshippers to Artemis, instigated by Demetrius, the head of their guild, took fright at the increasing number of the Christians, not only in Ephesus but throughout the province of Asia, which threatened, by interfering with the worship of the goddess, to injure their trade.[2] The matter was not on this occasion brought before either the municipal or the state

---

[1] Acts xvi. 20 : καὶ προσαγαγόντες αὐτοὺς τοῖς στρατηγοῖς εἶπον. Οὗτοι οἱ ἄνθρωποι ἐκταράσσουσιν ἡμῶν τὴν πόλιν Ἰουδαῖοι ὑπάρχοντες, καὶ καταγγέλλουσιν ἔθη ἃ οὐκ ἔξεστιν ἡμῖν παραδέχεσθαι οὐδὲ ποιεῖν Ῥωμαίοις οὖσιν.

[2] Acts xix. 23 foll.

authorities, but the whole incident is very significant of what might soon be expected to occur on a larger scale, the attitude of the craftsmen at Ephesus being an anticipation of what, as we shall see, Pliny probably found in Bithynia sixty years later. It is noticeable, too, that the charge of atheism, though not insisted on, is implied in the words of Demetrius— ὁ Παῦλος οὗτος λέγει ὅτι οὐκ εἰσὶν θεοὶ οἱ διὰ χειρῶν γιγνόμενοι—though it is clear from verse 37 that the Christians were not as yet generally regarded as *sacrilegi* or blasphemers of the national cults.[1] At the same time the social hatred, as it grew, was almost certain in time either to support itself by, or actually to develop into, a religious hatred.

But the apparent interference of the Christians with social relations was not confined to matters of trade or commercial gain. Family life was affected by it: it is almost certain that a large proportion of the earliest converts were slaves, and as these endeavoured to convert other members of the household, dissensions and divisions would arise in numerous families, and Christianity would seem a dividing and disintegrating element,[2] dangerous to social stability. Added to these particular causes of unpopularity there was the general tendency of Christianity to separate itself from the ordinary concerns of life.[3] To a certain extent the communistic tenden-

---

[1] Acts xix. 37: ἠγάγετε γὰρ τοὺς ἄνδρας τούτους οὔτε ἱεροσύλους οὔτε βλασφημοῦντας τὴν θεὸν ἡμῶν.

[2] Luke xxi. 16.

[3] Tertullian enumerates many things which were impossible for

cies of Christianity would naturally lead to this result; still more, perhaps, the confident expectation of the earliest converts that the end of the world was approaching. At any rate the opposition between the Church and the world was perhaps at no time more marked than during the first century; it existed long before the opposition of Church and State had formulated itself. The Christians were strangers and pilgrims in the world around them;[1] their citizenship was in heaven;[2] the kingdom to which they looked was not of this world.[3] The consequent want of interest in public affairs came thus from the outset to be a noticeable feature in Christianity. The Christians were, in the words of Tertullian, 'infructuosi in negotiis,'[4] and on this ground alone, in cities, where individuals were so closely bound up in the state, they became natural objects of suspicion to their fellow-citizens. The avoidance of the numerous religious

---

a conscientious Christian, as involving idolatry: *e. g.* the oath usual at contracts; the illumination of doors at festivals, &c.; all Pagan religious ceremonies; the games and the circus; the profession of teaching secular literature; military service; public offices. *De Idol.* 17: *De cor. mil.* i. 15.

[1] Tert. *Apol.* 1: 'Scit se peregrinam in terris agere, inter extraneos facile inimicos invenire, ceterum genus, sedem, spem, gratiam, dignitatem in caelis habere.' 41: 'Nihil nostra refert in hoc aevo nisi de eo quam celeriter excedere.' *Epist. ad Diognet.* 5, § 5: πᾶσα ξένη πατρίς ἐστιν αὐτῶν καὶ πᾶσα πατρὶς ξένη. § 9: ἐπὶ γῆς διατρίβουσιν, ἀλλ' ἐν οὐρανῷ πολιτεύονται. Cf. Hebrews xi. 13, 1 Pet. ii. 11.

[2] Philipp. iii. 20.

[3] Cf. Justin. *Apol.* i. 11: καὶ ὑμεῖς ἀκούσαντες βασιλείαν προσδοκῶντας ἡμᾶς ἀκρίτως ἀνθρώπινον λέγειν ὑπειλήφατε, ἡμῶν τὴν μετὰ θεοῦ λεγόντων.

[4] Tert. *Apol.* 42 ad init.

festivals, the refusal to take part in the amusements of the circus or the amphitheatre, indifference to civic honours, probably in many cases reluctance to serve in the army—all these things seemed to mark the Christians out as haters of their kind. And if they refused to participate in ordinary religious observances, they had what seemed a secret worship of their own : their meetings, not in synagogues, like those of the Jews, but in private houses, had probably a certain air of mystery, and this mystery was certain to lead to rumours as to what went on; and in a state of society like that in the Oriental cities it was almost certain that anything like a secret worship would be credited with immoralities of a more or less grave description. At exactly what date the suspicions arose that children were sacrificed and eaten at the Christian rites, and that incestuous orgies were permitted, is uncertain. If, however, as seems not unlikely, they arose through the malevolent stories of the Jews, the date was probably an early one, and, as we shall see later on, these stories had apparently reached Rome before 64 A.D.[1]

So far, therefore, as the New Testament narrative carries us, we find that Christian communities had been founded in most of the centres of civilisation in the East, and in the principal towns of Macedonia and Achaia; that, starting from a Jewish nucleus, they had in most cases, in the course of a few years, a pre-

---

[1] Cf. 1 Pet. ii. 12. As to the Jewish origin of the stories, see Justin. *Dial. cum Tryph.* c. 16, c. 47, c. c. 96, c. 108, c. 117. Orig.-*contr. Cels.* vi. 27.

ponderance of heathen converts ; that the Jews looked
on them with the bitterest animosity, persecuted them
as far as they had the means, and lost no opportunity
of appealing to the Roman government against
them ; that the Roman officials were rather inclined
to protect them than otherwise, at first looking upon
them as an extreme sect of the Jews, but of necessity
realising by degrees, both from the hostility of the
Jews and from the increasing prevalence of the Greek
nick-name Χριστιανοί, that it was rather a new
religion than an extreme sect; that the heathen
population, while listening not altogether unfavour-
ably or without interest to the religious teaching of
the Christian missionaries, came in the course of time
to be suspicious of Christianity on social and commercial grounds; and finally that this suspicion,
fomented probably by Jewish malevolence, hardened
little by little into the bitter hatred of which we have
abundant evidence in the second century.

IV

CHRISTIANITY IN ROME UNDER NERO

Up to this point we have found no direct collision between the Christians and the Roman government, and the first case of the kind took place in Rome,[1] and is narrated—unfortunately, not with all the clearness that we could wish—by Tacitus. As that historian remarks, in words which he thought appropriate to the Christians, Rome was the place 'quo cuncta undique atrocia aut pudenda confluunt celebranturque;' and with its strangely mixed population, and especially the great influx of Orientals, it was hardly possible that any religion at all widely spread in the East could fail to find its way into Rome, or, having found its way there, to spread at any rate among the lower classes. That the Jewish population there was large we have already seen, though this fact would by no means by itself prove the existence of a Christian community also. Where the apostles or their immediate associates themselves introduced Chris-

[1] The transition at this point from Jewish to Roman persecution is noted by Tertullian, *Apol.* 21: 'Discipuli quoque diffusi per orbem . . . a Judaeis insequentibus multa perpessi . . . Romae postremo per saevitiam Neronis sanguinem Christianum seminaverunt.'

tianity into a city, it was, as all the evidence tends to show, to the Jews that they first appealed, so that the nucleus of the Asiatic Churches was at the outset Judaeo-Christian, though the number of heathen converts very soon in almost all cases preponderated, causing at first modification of the strict Jewish observances,[1] and no doubt gradually almost complete emancipation from them. But in a city like Rome, where a Christian community was founded before the visit of any leader of the sect, the earliest Christians were far more likely to have been heathen converts, immigrants perhaps from some of the Asiatic cities, who would extend the sect in Rome among men of the same class with themselves. This is to a certain extent an *a priori* argument, but it is confirmed by other considerations on which it is not unimportant to dwell. Paul wrote his Epistle to the Roman Church from Corinth in 58 A.D. Putting on one side the question, as too wide to be discussed here, whether the general drift of the epistle is more appropriate to Jewish or heathen Christians,[2] there are several passages which seem to make the latter supposition almost necessary. Δι' οὗ ἐλάβομεν χάριν καὶ ἀποστολὴν εἰς ὑπακοὴν πίστεως ἐν πᾶσι τοῖς ἔθνεσιν ὑπὲρ τοῦ ὀνόματος αὐτοῦ. ἐν οἷς ἐστὲ καὶ ὑμεῖς

---

[1] Acts xv. 18: διὸ ἐγὼ κρίνω μὴ παρενοχλεῖν τοῖς ἀπὸ τῶν ἐθνῶν ἐπιστρέφουσιν ἐπὶ τὸν θεὸν, ἀλλὰ ἐπιστεῖλαι αὐτοῖς τοῦ ἀπέχεσθαι τῶν ἀλισγημάτων τῶν εἰδώλων καὶ τῆς πορνείας καὶ πνικτοῦ καὶ τοῦ αἵματος.

[2] See an article on the question in the *Jahrbücher für deutsche Theol.* 1876, pp. 248–310, 'Ueber die älteste römische Christengemeinde,' by C. Weizsäcker.

κλητοὶ Ἰησοῦ Χριστοῦ.[1] Again: ἵνα τινὰ καρπὸν σχῶ καὶ ἐν ὑμῖν καθὼς καὶ ἐν τοῖς λοιποῖς ἔθνεσιν :[2] and ὑμῖν δὲ λέγω τοῖς ἔθνεσιν.[3] So too the salutations in cap. xvi. 3-16 are clearly almost all of them addressed to Gentile Christians, many of the names, as Lightfoot has pointed out, being found in Roman inscriptions.[4] To this it must be added that the Jewish leaders on Paul's arrival at Rome show no sign of sharing in the hostile feelings shown by the Jews towards Christianity in those places where it was regarded as a secession from Judaism, professing, indeed, to have no personal knowledge of the sect, and only to have heard generally that it was everywhere spoken against.[5] Nor is it unimportant in this connexion to observe that, if we are to believe Tacitus and Suetonius, neither the Roman government nor the Roman populace regarded the Christians as a Jewish sect, and that they were described, not as Nazaraeans—the name by which they were known to the Jews[6]—but as *Christiani*, the nickname conferred by the Hellenistic heathen in the East.

The earliest intimation of a Christian community in Rome is thought to be contained in an obscure passage of Suetonius :[7] 'Iudaeos impulsore Chresto assidue tumultuantes Roma expulit.' This has generally

---

[1] Rom. i. 5, 6.   [2] Rom. i. 13.
[3] Rom. xi. 13. Cf. also xv. 15.
[4] Lightfoot, *Philippians*, p. 171 foll.
[5] Acts xxviii. 21-22.
[6] Acts xxiv. 5; Tert. *contra Marcionem*, iv. 8: 'Unde et ipso nomine nos Judaei Nazarenos appellant.'
[7] Suet. *Claud.* 25.

THE ROMAN GOVERNMENT 57

'been taken to mean that there were riots between the Christians and the Jews similar to those recorded in the Acts, and that the government, regarding the whole matter as a Jewish disturbance, took the measure of temporary expulsion as a police precaution. One can only say that no such meaning can legitimately be drawn from the words 'impulsore Chresto,' and that the reference to the expulsion in the Acts [1] does not in any way bear it out, while the words of Dio Cassius [2] imply that the measure was taken rather to check the Jewish worship than to put down a riot.

In 57 A.D. we apparently have an isolated case of a noble Roman lady, Pomponia Graecina, becoming at Rome a convert to Christianity.[3] She was at any rate 'superstitionis externae rea,' and though the statement of Tacitus is vague, because, to avoid open scandal, she was handed over to her husband's domestic tribunal, the 'continua tristitia,' the 'cultus lugubris,' and the 'non animus nisi moestus' all seem to point to her Christianity; while the discovery of a Christian inscription of the second century in the Catacomb of Callistus mentioning a Pomponius Graecinus does much to confirm the supposition.[4]

By 58 A.D. the community in Rome was sufficiently important for a letter to be addressed to it by Paul, though numerically it must have been still small when 'the brethren' went out to meet Paul on his

---

[1] Acts xviii. 2.
[2] Dio. Cass. lx. 6, quoted on p. 29, note 1.
[3] Tac. *Ann.* xiii. 32.   [4] De Rossi, *Roma sott.* ii. 364.

arrival in Italy to Appii Forum and Tres Tabernae.[1] Here the narrative in the Acts breaks off, and with the exception of the short, but not unimportant, statement that for the next two years Paul was uninterfered with in preaching to all who visited him [2]—from which we may infer (1) the freedom of Christianity from state interference, (2) its still continuing increase—we have no further information about it until it appears in the pages of Tacitus in connexion with the great fire of 64 A.D.[3]

That this fire was deliberately caused by Nero himself there was very great contemporary suspicion, which the emperor was not unnaturally anxious to remove. He did his best to assist the homeless multi-

---

[1] Acts xxvii. 15.

[2] *Ibid.* xxviii. 30 : Ἐνέμεινεν δὲ διετίαν ὅλην ἐν ἰδίῳ μισθώματι καὶ ἀπεδέχετο πάντας τοὺς εἰσπορευομένους πρὸς αὐτόν, κηρύσσων τὴν βασιλείαν τοῦ θεοῦ καὶ διδάσκων τὰ περὶ τοῦ Κυρίου Ἰησοῦ Χριστοῦ μετὰ πάσης παρρησίας ἀκωλύτως.

[3] Tac. *Ann.* xv. 44: 'Sed non ope humana, non largitionibus principis aut deum placamentis, decedebat infamia, quin iussum incendium crederetur. Ergo abolendo rumori Nero subdidit reos, et quaesitissimis poenis adfecit, quos per flagitia invisos vulgus Christianos appellabat. Auctor nominis eius Christus Tiberio imperitante per procuratorem Pontium Pilatum supplicio adfectus erat : repressaque in praesens exitiabilis superstitio rursum erumpebat, non modo per Iudaeam, originem eius mali, sed per urbem etiam, quo cuncta undique atrocia aut pudenda confluunt celebranturque. Igitur primo correpti qui fatebantur, deinde indicio eorum multitudo ingens haud perinde in crimine incendii quam odio humani generis convicti sunt. Et pereuntibus addita ludibria, ut ferarum tergis contecti laniatu canum interirent, aut crucibus adfixi flammandi, ut, ubi defecisset dies, in usum nocturni luminis urerentur. . . . Unde, quamquam adversus sontes et novissima exempla meritos, miseratio oriebatur, tamquam non utilitate publica sed in saevitiam unius absumerentur.'

tude by providing temporary quarters in the Campus Martius and even in his own gardens: his measures for the rebuilding of the city were judicious and not illiberal, while the supposed anger of the gods was appeased by various religious rites. 'But,' says Tacitus, 'neither human assistance in the shape of imperial gifts nor attempts to appease the gods could remove the sinister report that the fire was due to Nero's own order. And so, in the hope of dissipating this rumour, he falsely diverted the charge on to a set of people whom the populace called Christians, and who were detested for the abominations which they perpetrated. The originator of the name, a person called Christus, had been executed by Pontius Pilate in the reign of Tiberius, and the dangerous superstition, though put down for the moment, again broke out, not only in Judaea, the original home of the pest, but even in Rome, where everything horrible or shameful collects and is practised.'

That Tacitus, writing about 120 A.D., and after having himself held the proconsulship of Asia,[1] should have some more or less accurate knowledge of the Christians as a distinct sect, is only natural, but what has seemed to some scholars surprising, and even incredible, is that as early as Nero's time, when Christianity is thought to have been growing up under the toleration extended to the Jews, it should have been singled out for special interference and

[1] This is proved by an inscription recently discovered: see Cagnat, *L'Année Epigraphique*, 1891, p. 29, and *Bull. de Corresp. hellén.* 1890, p. 621.

special repression, especially as a very few years earlier it was certainly uninterfered with. To avoid this difficulty, it has been suggested by Schiller [1] and others that the persecution, if such it can be called, really fell upon the Jews, as the most extreme and fanatical religious sect in Rome, though individual Christians may have been involved in it through being confused with the Jews; and that Tacitus in specifying the former is really antedating the distinction between them, and injecting into the Neronian period a knowledge which was only a reality in his own. That there are difficulties in the account given by Tacitus it cannot be denied, but any such supposition as that given above is rightly regarded by Nissen [2] as a serious impugnment of Tacitus' historical credibility. As a rule he follows, for times anterior to his own, contemporary authorities, and if in this instance he has left them and given a different account, drawn from his own knowledge of the Christians, or even from any tradition which may have been known to have existed among them, he has done what no trustworthy historian ought to do.

Nor is this theory, that the Christians, so far as they were affected by Nero's action, were taken for Jews, without difficulties of its own. If the Roman community had consisted of Judaeo-Christians, either exclusively or preponderatingly, there would have been

---

[1] *Geschichte der röm. Kaiserzeit*, ii. 445–450. Cf. Lipsius, 'Ueber den Ursprung und früheren Gebrauch des Christennamens,' p. 17. A similar view is taken by Hausrath.

[2] *Histor. Zeitschrift*, 1874, p. 340.

the possibility of such confusion, though even so there was the not unimportant distinction between them that whereas the Jews attended the synagogue the Christians did not—a distinction which Mommsen holds was not likely permanently to escape the vigilance of the Roman police.[1] But if the view taken above of the Gentile character of the Roman Christians is correct, there would be very much less chance of any such confusion, and if it had been the Jews who were sought for, there was a very simple, if brutal means of identifying them, from which we know the Roman government did not shrink on other occasions,[2] and which would have at once freed Gentile Christians from implication in a charge against Jews. To this we may add that the theory in question does not really explain the facts. We can understand that if the Christians had really been the victims, but were regarded as a sect of the Jews, an historian not accurately aware of the distinction might describe it as a Jewish persecution; but why, if it really was a Jewish persecution, he should avoid the generic term which was well known, and describe the victims as Christians—a term *ex hypothesi* special and obscure—certainly needs more explanation than

[1] *Histor. Zeitschrift*, No. 64, p. 423 : 'Hierin, in dem Besuch oder Nichtbesuch der Synagoge, wird dem heidnischen Publikum und insbesondere den Stadtrömern der Gegensatz der Juden und der Christen wohl zuerst entgegengetreten sein, namentlich wenn, wie dies wahrscheinlich geschah, die Polizei, welche die Synagogen gewähren lassen musste, gegen die Ekklesien einschritt.'

[2] Suet. *Dom.* 12 : 'Interfuisse me adolescentulum memini cum a procuratore frequentissimoque concilio inspiceretur nonagenarius senex an circumsectus esset.'

this theory gives. Besides, if the Jews had been the victims, would not Josephus have made some mention of the matter ? Would not Dio Cassius have noticed it ? The contemporary historians would, on Schiller's supposition, have rightly described the victims as Jews: would not some tradition, some trace of the incident have remained in connexion with them ? Similar objections might be raised against Merivale's theory that the Jews, who were themselves accused in the first instance, succeeded, possibly through the court influence of Poppaea Sabina, in diverting the accusation from themselves on to the Christians.[1] If this saves the credit of Tacitus to a certain extent, as far as the description of the sufferers as Christians is concerned, it directly contradicts him on another point, for it implies that the Christians—who in this case would certainly have been described as *Nazaraei*—were selected as scapegoats at the suggestion and through the hatred of the Jews, whereas Tacitus expressly says that they were selected as objects of hatred to the populace on account of their abominable crimes.

But in point of fact we are beating the air in combating these theories. I agree with Professor Ramsay[2] that, in the absence of positively conflicting testimony, we must make the best of the account we have. Nor are the difficulties, after all, insuperable. We are apt to forget in picturing to ourselves ancient Rome, with its huge and mixed population, its thoughts and attention fixed on bread and the Circus, and all the morbid excitements which a *régime* like that of

[1] *The Romans under the Empire*, vi. 448-49.   [2] *Op. cit.* p. 229.

Nero provided for them, how thorough and efficient, after all, was the police administration of the city, how strict the surveillance over illicit *collegia*, and above all perhaps how minute and detailed, even in apparently trivial concerns, the despatches must have been from the provincial governors. These arrangements had developed into a system, and it would be a great mistake to suppose that because a Caligula or a Nero spent his time in mad revels or horse-racing or musical performances, the government machinery or the government vigilance was necessarily impaired. Professor Ramsay calls attention to this point in special reference to the Flavian times:[1] he thinks it impossible that the separate existence of Christianity as distinct from Judaism could long have escaped the vigilance of the government in the provinces, and I am disposed to agree with him, and even to throw back the consequences of this vigilance to the time of Nero and to Rome as well as to the provinces. According to Tacitus, the existence of a sect whom they called Christians, and detested for special reasons, was known to the populace of Rome, and at any rate from this point, if not before, to the government. If, as is assumed, the Christians were converts from the heathen population and not from the Jews, and if they were in any degree considerable or increasing in point of numbers; and if—what is an essential point about the sect—they were exclusive and even aggressive, eager to make converts and keeping aloof from the things which most interested their neighbours;

[1] *Op. cit.* p. 267.

above all, if they held secret or nocturnal meetings for the practice of their religious worship—they could hardly fail to become known and to become unpopular. We have already seen that in the Oriental provinces even earlier than this they were mockingly called Χριστιανοί by the Greek populations, and we have seen the social causes at work which were certain to make them in time hated and unpopular. Was Rome likely to be an exception?[1] On the contrary, were not these tendencies likely to become accomplished facts earlier in Rome than in the provinces? If each of the Oriental cities had its own stories about the Christians, *e.g.* Ephesus, or Philippi, or Antioch, these stories might all well find their way to Rome, producing there a cumulative effect. And with regard to the government, probably any sect known to and hated by the populace would become known to it. Then, again, there was every chance that reports from the provincial governors might make some mention of the Christians, while we cannot doubt that a full report of Paul's case must have been sent to Rome by Festus,[2] who certainly knew the term Χριστιανός, and must have arrived at some idea of the distinction between Christianity and Judaism. There is therefore nothing intrinsically impossible or even improbable in the statement of Tacitus, that the Christians of Rome in 64 A.D. were known as a sect distinct from the

---

[1] A mutilated inscription seems to show that the term *Christianus* was known at Pompeii, *i.e.* before 79 A.D. *C. I. L.* iv. 679.

[2] Prof. Ramsay rightly draws attention to the importance of Paul's case. *Expositor*, July 1893, p. 10.

Jews, hated by the populace, not on account of their religion, but owing to certain sinister stories about them, and on this account selected by Nero or Tigellinus as scapegoats on whom the charge of incendiarism might with some probability be fastened.

But purely accidental as was this first contact between the Roman government and Christianity, it might quite possibly lead to results both important and permanent. 'Those,' continues Tacitus, 'who confessed the charge were put upon their trial, and then by information gained from them an immense number of persons was convicted, not so much on the charge of incendiarism as on that of hatred towards civilised society. The victims as they perished were made to afford amusement to the crowd. Some being covered with the skins of wild beasts were torn to pieces by dogs : others were fastened on crosses to be set on fire in order that, when daylight failed, their burning might serve to light up the night.' The general sense of this passage seems perfectly clear, taken in connexion with what has gone before, though there has been some difference of opinion as regards the particular phrases ' qui fatebantur '—' correpti '— 'indicio eorum.' 'Correpti,' from a comparison of its use in Tacitus,[1] certainly means, not 'arrested,' but

---

[1] *Ann.* ii. 84, 4 ; iii. 28, 5 ; iii. 49, 1 ; iii. 66, 2 ; xii. 42, 4. As regards the reading, I have, against Prof. Ramsay, adopted the emendation *convicti*, instead of the MS. *coniuncti*, as making better sense, while the corruption is easily accounted for. The Med. reading— ' aut crucibus adfixi aut flammandi atque ubi defecisset dies,' etc., is certainly to some extent corrupt. Perhaps the simplest alteration is to omit the second *aut*, and to change *atque* into *ut*. There would

F

'put upon their trial,' and this seems to me conclusively to fix the meaning of 'qui fatebantur,' since the confession, whatever it was, came before the trial. Arnold, arguing that *profiteri* or *confiteri* would be the proper words to use of confessing to a religion, explains it as 'confessed to the charge of incendiarism,' supposing that certain members of the Christian body were induced to make this false confession under the influence of torture. That any Christians would have confessed to such a charge without torture is certainly impossible, but how could they be tortured to elicit a confession of incendiarism before they were put on their trial for that crime? On the other hand, what would be the natural course for Nero or Tigellinus to adopt after he, as Tacitus expresses it, 'subdidit reos Christianos'?[1] Surely to arrest all the Christians he could lay hold of. There was, however, no special mark by which Christians were known.

thus be two kinds of punishment only—exposure to wild beasts and crucifixion. Neither of these in themselves involved *ludibrium*, which was added in the one case by dressing up the victims in the skins of wild beasts, in the other by setting fire to them as night came on, clothed possibly in the 'tunica molesta.' It is to the latter punishment that Juvenal probably alludes (*Sat.* i. 159), and I do not with Furneaux see anything inconsistent in the two accounts. Otherwise, the passage would, no doubt, be simplified if with Nipperday we regarded the passage 'aut crucibus ... flammandi' as an interpolation. This is, however, never an altogether satisfactory mode of escaping a difficulty, and in this case the interpolation must have been made earlier than Sulpicius Severus, who evidently found the words.

[1] Arnold, *Die Neronische Christenverfolgung*, p. 20. The interpretation given in the text is supported by Nipperdey (see note *ad loc.*), by Aubé, *Histoire des Persécutions*, i. 92, by Renan, *L'Antéchrist*, p. 162, and by Nissen, *Histor. Zeitschrift*, 1874, p. 340.

Some of those arrested might either not be Christians at all, or not openly professed Christians. A certain number, however, of the bolder sort would at once confess their religion (and as this, by the prejudgment of Nero, was tantamount to confessing the incendiarism, *fateri* was not improperly used), and were accordingly put upon their trial. So far I am in agreement with Professor Ramsay, who adds another argument against Arnold's view which deserves consideration : viz. that ' if so many of the Christians acknowledged the crime . . . . their complicity in it would necessarily have been accepted by the popular opinion,'[1] which, on the contrary, was, as we shall see, still convinced of Nero's guilt. I cannot, however, think that he is justified in translating 'indicio eorum' by 'on the information elicited at their trial.'[2] Of course on Arnold's explanation of 'qui fatebantur' 'indicio eorum' bears its natural meaning, 'on information received from them.' The difficulty is that on the explanation given above, 'qui fatebantur' are the cream of the Christian society, the boldest spirits of the community, and therefore those least likely to incriminate others of the sect. This is clearly the difficulty which has led Professor Ramsay to take these words in a non-natural sense which, I am afraid, they cannot bear. We cannot suppose that the Christians of the first century were all ready to be martyrs, any more than the Bithynian Christians of the second century, many of whom, as we know, seceded under Pliny's treatment. It is clear, there-

[1] p. 238.   [2] p. 233.

fore, that some of those first arrested (not of course necessarily all) furnished the government with the names of those Christians who had so far escaped notice. Possibly they were induced to do this by torture, but more probably the explanation is to be found in the Epistle of Clement to the Corinthian Church, who, clearly alluding to the Neronian persecution, gives it as an instance of the evils arising from strife and jealousy.[1] There were therefore perhaps divisions among the Christians at Rome, as there were at Corinth, and so high did this sectarian spirit run that one party was even willing to denounce the other to the government. The number of Christians who were arrested and put upon their trial by this means was a considerable one, though 'ingens multitudo' is no doubt a rhetorical exaggeration.

The turn, however, which the trial took—a trial conducted in all probability before the *praefectus urbi*—is the most important part of the whole incident. The Christians had originally been singled out, not as members of a 'religio illicita,' but as a set of men, obnoxious to the populace, on whom Nero sought to divert from himself the charge of incendiarism. In the course of the trial the proofs of incendiarism must necessarily to a great extent have broken down, but at the same time a good deal of information would be elicited about the sect, which would answer the purpose of the government just as well; and which would imply a disposition, a state of mind, of which incen-

[1] See the passage quoted on p. 71.

diarism would be a natural result. It would come out, in the first place, that the sect held nocturnal meetings, and the very simplicity of the early Christian worship would have the appearance of mystery and secrecy to the ordinary heathen mind. Then there would be stories which, if we are to believe Tacitus, were already abroad of the Οἰδιπόδειοι μίξεις and the Θυέστεια δεῖπνα: these would, no doubt, be repeated and exaggerated; the stories of child-murder in particular falling in with the current notions about magic and witchcraft,[1] would give some colour to an accusation under that head, while, more important still, the social attitude of the Christians would have at any rate become clear to the government—from one point of view, their isolation and aloofness from all the political and religious interests of the city; from another, their aggressive and proselytising zeal. Isolated members of the sect would be found in almost every large *familia* of slaves; Caesar's own household would be found not to have escaped the taint,[2] and while no doubt the noble and the rich would be conspicuous by their absence, among the lower classes, and especially the servile population, Christianity, with its utter disregard of nationality, would be found a not unimportant element. To crown all, that characteristic of the religion which seemed to Pliny in itself deserving of the severest punishment, its *obstinatio* in the face of interference or repression, the obligation 'to obey God rather than men,'[3] would

---

[1] Cic. *in Vatin.* vi. 14; Hor. *Epod.* 5; Juv. vi. 522.
[2] Philipp. iv. ad fin.   [3] Acts v. 29.

seem to involve an opposition to the omnipotence of the Roman government, which might contain the seeds of real political danger. All these things combined were deemed sufficient to secure a conviction, not so much on the definite charge of incendiarism as of what Tacitus describes as 'odium generis humani'[1] —a wider charge, which might include or might easily be taken to involve the narrower one. That insinuations of magic and witchcraft played, as Arnold suggests,[2] an important part in these trials seems at least possible. The term 'malefica,' used by Suetonius of the new religion, often has this special sense, and it deserves notice that in the Justinian code[3] magicians are described as 'inimici generis humani.'

The result of the trials was naturally the execution of the criminals, and here again the fact must not be passed over—though I think it is possible to make too much of it—that the mode of punishment was that prescribed for those convicted of magic: 'Qui sacra impia nocturnave ut quem obtruncarent, defigerent, obligarent, fecerint facciendave curaverint aut crucibus suffiguntur aut bestiis obiciuntur. . . . Magicae artis conscios summo supplicio adfici placuit,

---

[1] 'Odium generis humani' is explained by Holtzmann as 'völliger Mangel an aller humanen und politischen Bildung;' by Schiller (*Comment. philolog. in hon. Mommsen.* p. 26) as 'Exclusivität gegen Andersgläubige;' by Arnold, much more suggestively, as 'principieller Widerstand gegen die römische Staatsomnipotenz,' p. 23.

[2] Arnold, pp. 65, 66.

[3] Cod. Just. ix. tit. 18 : '[Magi] humani generis inimici credendi sunt.'

id est bestiis obici aut crucibus suffigi : ipsi autem magi vivi exuruntur.'[1] Our conclusion therefore is that the account given by Tacitus is both credible in itself and consistent with all that we are able to infer concerning the Christians at this time. It remains to be added that it receives independent confirmation from other sources. Clement, whose Epistle from Rome to the Church at Corinth is with much probability assigned to the end of Domitian's reign, speaks of a πολὺ πλῆθος whose deaths were connected with the martyrdom of the great apostles Peter and Paul. He mentions particularly the female victims, and describes their punishment in words which at once suggest the *ludibria* of Tacitus : Τούτοις τοῖς ἀνδράσιν οὕτως πολιτευσαμένοις συνηθροίσθη πολὺ πλῆθος ἐκλεκτῶν, οἵτινες πολλαῖς αἰκίαις καὶ βασάνοις διὰ ζῆλος παθόντες ὑπόδειγμα κάλλιστον ἐγένοντο ἐν ὑμῖν. Διὰ ζῆλος διωχθεῖσαι γυναῖκες Δαναΐδες καὶ Δίρκαι αἰκίσματα δεινὰ καὶ ἀνόσια παθοῦσαι ἐπὶ τὸν τῆς πίστεως βέβαιον δρόμον κατήντησαν καὶ ἔλαβον γέρας γενναῖον αἱ ἀσθενεῖς τῷ σώματι.[2] That Nero was fond of horribly realistic representations in the arena we know from Suetonius,[3] and on this occasion not only his own tastes but the desire to amuse and divert the populace from their suspicions against himself, would easily suggest these 'quaesitissimae

---

[1] Paulus, *Sent.* v.
[2] Clem. *Ep. ad Corinth*, c. 6.
[3] Suet. *Ner.* 12 : 'Inter Pyrricharum argumenta taurus Pasiphaen ligneo iuvencae simulacro abditam iniit, ut multi spectantium crediderunt. Icarus primo statim conatu iuxta cubiculum eius decidit ipsumque cruore respersit.'

poenae.' So while the men were made to represent Actaeon torn to pieces by his hounds, or after hanging on crosses during the day were at night clothed in the *tunica molesta*, and so made to illuminate the imperial gardens, the women were, like Dirce, fastened on the horns of bulls, or after figuring as Danaides in the arena, were exposed to the attacks of wild beasts, just as we find Orpheus, without any mythological justification, torn to pieces by a bear.[1]

The Neronian persecution is also alluded to by Melito, bishop of Sardes, in an Apology which he addressed to M. Aurelius about 170 A.D., and in which Nero and Domitian are represented as the only persecutors up to his own time[2]—a view which we cannot regard as historical, though it represents the Christian tradition of sufferings under those emperors. More important evidence is given by Suetonius, who in a list of administrative measures, mostly of the nature of police regulations, says: 'Adflicti suppliciis Christiani, genus hominum superstitionis novae ac maleficae.'[3] I agree with Professor Ramsay to a great extent in his estimate of this evidence. It is clearly independent of Tacitus, but by no means inconsistent with him. The attempt to convict the Christians of burning the city evidently failed; the people saw through it; Tacitus himself

---

[1] Mart. *De Spect.* xxi. 7, 8.
[2] Quoted in Euseb. *H. E.* ix. 26 : Μόνοι πάντων ἀναπεισθέντες ὑπό τινων βασκάνων ἀνθρώπων τὸν καθ' ἡμᾶς ἐν διαβολῇ καταστῆσαι λόγο ἠθέλησαν Νέρων καὶ Δομετιανός.
[3] Suet. *Ner.* 16

implies that Nero was still regarded as the author of the fire;[1] Pliny expressly affirms it,[2] and Suetonius also without qualification;[3] while, as we have seen, in the trial itself, except in the case of those first arrested, the punishment was not for incendiarism so much as for that wider charge of 'odium generis humani.' Hence Suetonius does not think it worth while to disturb his summary of results by bringing the punishment of the Christians into connexion, generally admitted to be fictitious, with the burning of the city. The charge of incendiarism had developed into a general charge of disaffection to the government, resulting from a mischievous and morose superstition. In this aspect only Suetonius mentions it: in the words of Professor Ramsay, which with slight modifications I should accept, 'he merely gives a brief statement of the permanent administrative principle into which Nero's action ultimately resolved itself.'[4] The investigation arising from a purely incidental charge had made the government for the first time

[1] *Ann.* xv. 44: 'Unde quamquam adversus sontes et novissima exempla meritos [*i.e.* on the score of their *flagitia*] miseratio oriebatur tanquam non utilitate publica sed in saevitiam unius absumerentur.' Cf. xv. 67, where Subrius Flavius says: 'Odisse coepi postquam parricida matris et uxoris, auriga et histrio et incendiarius extitisti.'

[2] Plin. *H. N.* xvii. 1: 'ad Neronis principis incendia quibus cremavit urbem;' and xvii. 8: 'ni princeps ille accelerasset etiam arborum mortem.'

[3] Suet. *Ner.* 38: 'Nam quasi offensus deformitate veterum aedificiorum, et angustiis flexurisque vicorum, incendit urbem tam palam ut plerique consulares cubicularios eius, cum stuppa taedaque in praediis suis deprehensos, non attigerint.'

[4] p. 232

acquainted, not with the name—for that was probably known before—but with some of the peculiarities of the sect, and though the numbers were not sufficiently great nor the members of sufficient social importance to make it really a political danger, and though there were certainly no charges amounting to *sacrilegium* [1] or *maiestas*, there were yet suspicions of moral enormities, there were complaints of social isolation on the one side and social interference on another, and lastly, the principles of the religion seemed to involve in the last resort political disobedience, the recognition of an authority which in cases of collision with the state authority was in preference to be obeyed. This, in the somewhat rhetorical language of Tacitus, was 'odium generis humani,' disaffection to the social and political arrangements of the empire,[2] but, as has been already said, not falling

---

[1] The Christians, as Mommsen has shown, could never have been accused of *sacrilegium* in any technical or juristic sense. As a legal offence *sacrilegium* was ἱεροσυλία, *i.e.* stealing from a temple. Cf. *Dig.* xlviii. 13, 11, 1 : ' Sunt autem sacrilegi qui publica sacra compilaverunt.' It was only in a popular sense that it implied ' religious misdemeanour ' generally (cf. Liv. iv. 20, 5), and in this sense no doubt, but in no other, it was often applied to the behaviour of the Christians : as in Min. Fel. 25 and 28, Tert. *Apol.* 2, *ad Scap.* 2 and 4. Tertullian, with his legal knowledge, points out that the Christians were improperly called ' sacrilegi,' *ad Scap.* 2 : ' Nos quos sacrilegos existimatis nec in furto unquam deprehendistis, nedum in sacrilegio.' See *Hist. Zeitschr.* p. 411.

[2] 'Genus humanum' was, as Arnold points out, the civilised population of the empire. So Nero was 'hostis generis humani,' Plin. *H. N.* vii. 8 ; Galba was emperor by the 'consensus generis humani,' Tac. *Hist.* i. 30 ; cf. also *Ann.* xiii. 50, where 'genus mortalium' is similarly used.

under the head of *maiestas*, nor coming within the range of any of the regular *quaestiones*.

The whole thing, indeed, was a matter for police regulation; as such it came, no doubt, in the first instance before the *praefectus urbi*, as the chief police magistrate at Rome, but it could equally well in theory be dealt with by the summary authority or *coercitio* which the executive magistrates at Rome and the proconsuls and legates in the provinces possessed. Mommsen [1] has, indeed, shown conclusively that the repressive measures of the state in the sphere of religious policy belong for the most part to the department of administration, not to the judicial interpretation or enforcement of law, and not even to imperial edicts or constitutions. This *coercitio*, the essential attribute of all the higher magistrates, was

[1] *Histor. Zeitschr.* p. 398: 'Die nicht auf die Ausführung der Strafgesetze gerichtete sondern nach freiem Ermessen ausgeübte obrigkeitliche Fürsorge für die Ordnung und das Wohl des Gemeinwesens kann nicht gedacht werden ohne die Befugniss des Magistrats den widersetzlichen Bürger entweder indirect durch Zufügung von Rechtsnachtheilen oder direct durch Anwendung der Gewalt zum Gehorsam zu zwingen (*coercere*). In dem römischen Gemeinwesen hat dies zu dem Rechtsatz geführt, dass der zur Sache competente Magistrat jedem zum Gehorsam Verpflichteten nach freiem Ermessen und ohne Prozessform jedes nicht durch die Sitte ausgeschlossene Übel zufügen kann . . . Der Gegensatz zu dem eigentlichen Strafverfahren liegt darin dass die Coercition als ausserordentliches Hülfsmittel, gewissermassen als Nothwehr der Gemeinde gegen den Bürger aufgefasst und daher von der Formulirung sowohl des Unrechts wie des Einschreitens dagegen bei ihn abgesehen wird. . . . Die repressiven Massregeln des Staats auf dem Gebiet der Religion gehören überwiegend diesem administrativen Kreise an und sind nothwendiger Weise beherrscht durch die davon untrennbare administrative Willkür.' Cf. *Staatsrecht*, vol. i. pp. 133-153.

for the state an extraordinary means of self-defence: it was not restricted to the regular rule of procedure: the offences or misdemeanours with which it interfered were not defined by any technical nomenclature, and the punishments which it inflicted were, if not arbitrary, at least not specified with any undeviating precision. In Rome from the time of Tiberius this police *coercitio* was mainly vested in the *praefectus urbi*, with the general instructions 'ut servitia coerceret et quod civium audacia turbidum nisi vim metuat.'[1] In the provinces general instructions were given to every governor 'ut pacata atque quieta provincia sit quam regit; quod non difficile obtinebit, si sollicite agat ut malis hominibus provincia careat, eosque conquirat: nam et sacrilegos latrones plagiarios fures conquirere debet et prout quisque deliquerit in eum animadvertere.'[2]

It is in the working out of these general instructions given to the executive magistrates at home and in the provinces, modified and coloured no doubt by the personal characteristics both of the magistrates and of the emperors, that we must look for concrete

[1] Tac. *Ann.* vi. 11.
[2] *Dig.* i. 18, 13. That it was under this general police instruction that the provincial governors could proceed against the Christians receives some confirmation from the part which the εἰρήναρχαι—police superintendents—played in their arrest. The *Digest* describes the 'Irenarchae' as 'disciplinae publicae et corrigendis moribus praefecti' (*Dig.* l. 4, 18, 7): it also proves that it was their duty to arrest 'latrones,' etc., 'ut irenarchae cum adprehenderint latrones,' *Dig.* xlviii. 3, 6. But we also know that it was the Irenarch in Smyrna who sent his *gens d'armes* to arrest Polycarp (Ruinart, p. 39), while Augustine also mentions these officials in connexion with the Christian prosecutions.

examples of any state policy towards the Christians.[1] The first step was taken by Nero's government in 64 A.D. The occasion was purely accidental, but the results were of extreme importance. At the outset the Christians were only known to the government as a small and perhaps fanatical religious sect extremely unpopular with the masses at Rome: as the upshot of the trial they were recognised as a society whose principles might be summarised as 'odium generis humani.' They were therefore punished, not as incendiaries, but as Christians.

[1] So Mommsen points out that this *coercitio*, so far as it has found any entrance into Roman jurisprudence, is not found in the exposition *De publicis Iudiciis*—i.e. in the criminal law—but under the heading *De Officio Proconsulis et Legati*, which treats of extraordinary procedure and police administration. It is under this heading that, according to Lactantius (*Inst.* v. 11, 19), Ulpian had collected the various rescripts referring to the Christians. 'Domitius de officio proconsulis libro septimo rescripta principum nefaria collegit ut doceret quibus poenis adfici oporteret eos qui se cultores Dei confiterentur.'

V

CHRISTIANITY UNDER THE FLAVIAN EMPERORS

THAT the persecution at this time extended beyond Rome to the provinces there is no evidence whatever to show, for the statement of Orosius,[1] unconfirmed by earlier authorities, is naturally worthless. At the same time there is no doubt that, in Professor Ramsay's words, 'the example set by the emperor necessarily guided the action of all Roman officials,' and from this time forward there was always the possibility that similar action would be taken by the governors in the provinces: it was really only a matter of time. Generally speaking, the same causes which made the Christians unpopular in Rome were at work, perhaps not quite so rapidly, in the provinces also, and while Nero for his own ends anticipated popular feeling in the capital, the provincial governors would be far more likely as long as possible to remain behind it, and only to take action against the Christians when popular feeling actually forced it upon them. In all probability this took place in many cases under the Flavian emperors, very probably

[1] *Hist.* vii, 17.

before Domitian. The destruction of the Temple and the consequent disappearance of the Jews as a political unity could hardly fail to have an unfavourable influence on the relations between the Roman government and the Christians. On the one hand, whatever vestige of confusion might still remain between Jews and Christians must have been finally removed now that the former had to register their names and pay their two drachmas to Roman officials; on the other hand, the Jewish war had been a lesson which must have shown the Roman government the political danger of fanatical and aggressive monotheisms. The 'hostile odium contra omnes alios' which was at the root of the Jewish difficulty had already been recognised as involved in the principles of the Christian body. The Jewish religion was now to a certain extent under state surveillance, and cut adrift from all political unity. The Christian religion had no national claim to toleration, and the very absence of a national basis and its claim to universality suggested possibilities of extension of which there had been no fear in the case of the Jews.

The Christian problem, which accident had revealed to the Neronian government at Rome, was one which the Flavian dynasty would certainly have to face in the provinces. Is there any evidence that it was treated in a different manner—that any development took place of what can fairly be called a systematic policy on the part of the Roman government towards the Christians? On this point I feel bound to disagree with Professor Ramsay, who holds that between 64 A.D. and 95 A.D. the principle of the state action was changed, that whereas under Nero the Christians were charged with certain definite offences, such as incendiarism or hostility to society or magic, or the special *flagitia* ascribed to the sect, and were punished for these, they were now, on the contrary, punished for the name only; that Christianity was assumed to be in itself a crime deserving of death; that no questions were asked, no investigation made about crimes committed; that the acknowledgment of the name involved immediate condemnation;[1] that Nero treats a great many Christians as criminals and punishes them for their crimes: Pliny and Trajan treat them as outlaws and brigands, and punish them without a reference to crimes.[2]

As far as Professor Ramsay's arguments depend on the early date of the Pastoral Epistles, which he says confirm his view of the Neronian principle,[3] or on a later date for 1 Peter, which confessedly refers to suffering for the name,[4] I shall not follow him, because all evidence resting on such controverted points must have, *ipso facto*, an element of uncertainty. And it really seems to me to be unnecessary, because, after all, the principle of Nero practically involves, without supposing any development from it, the principle which Professor Ramsay ascribes to the

[1] p. 242.
[2] p. 245.
[3] p. 246, and *Expositor*, July 1893, pp. 20, 21.
[4] Especially 1 Pet. iv. 15: Μὴ γάρ τις ὑμῶν πασχέτω ὡς φονεὺς ἢ κλέπτης ἢ κακοποιὸς ἢ ὡς ἀλλοτριοεπίσκοπος· εἰ δὲ ὡς Χριστιανός, μὴ αἰσχυνέσθω, δοξαζέτω δὲ τὸν θεὸν ἐν τῷ ὀνόματι τούτῳ.

Flavian emperors. If the view which has been taken
above of the Neronian trials is correct, the Christians,
though originally charged with incendiarism, were
not found guilty or punished for that or for any
definitely stated offence. Professor Ramsay speaks
as if 'hostility to society' was one of the particular
charges made against them. On the contrary, the
'odium generis humani' was a summary of the particular charges,[1] a general expression for the contents
of Christianity, and henceforth all Christians in Rome
would be liable to the same treatment, even without
the judicial investigation which had once for all established the criminality of Christianity as involving
this *odium*. Nor need we find anything exceptional
in this, when we remember that the whole matter
was one of police administration, not of judicial procedure against a legally constituted offence. It is this,
of course, which accounts also for the spasmodic
character of proceedings against the Christians, not
only in Rome, but in the provinces as well, a character quite inconsistent with any specific law making
Christianity an illegal society, but completely in
harmony with the nature of police supervision which
took action when action seemed advisable, but might
at any time, without weakening the principle of such
action, allow it to rest either wholly or in part during

[1] Professor Sanday takes this view in the *Expositor* for June
1893. As this was written before I saw his paper, I may cite him
as independently confirming this view of the matter. Cf. how Tertullian (*Apol.* 2) sums up the charge against Christians: 'Christianum hominem omnium scelerum reum, deorum, imperatorum
legum, morum, naturae totius inimicum existimas.'

long intervals of time. The police authorities of Rome, and therefore the imperial government, were convinced that Christianity involved 'odium generis humani.' This was sufficient to justify on the particular occasion a considerable number of executions; it involved the possibility of a continuous series of executions in the future on the ground of information once for all received; and it was almost certain that whenever provincial governors applied for instructions as to their treatment of the new sect, rescripts in accordance with the proceedings in Rome would be sent. In all cases the proceedings would take the form of a *cognitio*; there was in no case any necessity to do more than establish the Christianity of the accused, which, after the investigation in Rome, was in itself criminality deserving execution. On the other hand, it was always open to the magistrates to inquire as much or as little as they liked into the particular charges: the hesitation of Pliny, 'quid aut quatenus puniri soleat aut quaeri,'[1] shows that the procedure varied in this respect. But no doubt, generally speaking, as long as Christianity was comparatively unfamiliar, the special charges would be to a certain extent gone into, while later on this would be thought in fact, as it already was in principle, unnecessary. To sum up: as soon as the Christians were once convicted of an 'odium generis humani,' they were potentially outlaws and brigands, and could be treated by the police administration as such, whether in Rome or the provinces. I cannot, therefore, agree that the

[1] *Ad Trai.* 96, 1.

Flavian emperors introduced any new principle, though I quite admit that under their policy proceedings were from time to time taken against the Christians, possibly in Rome, certainly in the provinces. That Titus at any rate was prepared to sanction a continuation of the policy commenced by Nero is, I think, shown by the report given of his speech before Jerusalem in 70 A.D., by Sulpicius Severus, whose authority was almost certainly Tacitus. In arguing for the destruction of the Temple he is made to say that the religions of the Jews and Christians would be thereby more completely extirpated, for these religions, though opposed to each other, had the same origin: the Christians had arisen from amongst the Jews, and when the root was torn up, the stem would be more easily destroyed.[1] This is a most important passage for proving that as early as 70 A.D. not only the distinction but the opposition between Judaism and Christianity was clearly recognised by the authorities in the Eastern provinces, and that both were regarded as involving possible dangers; but I cannot think, with Professor Ramsay, that Titus thereby pledged himself to any energetic measures of repression against the Christians any more than against the Jews. The Jewish religion, as we know, was tolerated as before, notwithstanding the

---

[1] Sulpic. Sever. *Chron.* ii. 30, 6 : ' Evertendum templum . . . censebant quo plenius Iudaeorum et Christianorum religio tolleretur . . . has religiones, licet contrarias sibi, isdem tamen auctoribus profectas; Christianos ex Iudaeis exstitisse: radice sublata stirpem facile perituram.'

hopes thus expressed by Titus for its extermination; and therefore there seems no reason on this ground, at any rate, to suppose any special interference with the Christians.[1] The fact that we have no extant records of interference with the Christians under Vespasian and Titus is no argument, or a very weak one, against the supposition that they nevertheless took place;[2] but if, as I suppose, they only took place sporadically through some incidental reasons, local or personal, and in the ordinary course of police administration, we can quite understand how they fail to be mentioned both by heathen and Christian writers. In reality, as Mommsen says, 'the persecution of the Christians was a standing one, like that of brigands, though the regulations touching them were applied now mildly and carelessly, now with severity, while every now and then they were stringently and thoroughly enforced.'[3] It was these latter occasions only which attracted the attention of the Christian writers, and which they were apt to represent as isolated and distinct persecutions instead of what they really were—more clearly marked phases of what was constantly going on.

[1] Prof. Ramsay's inference from the mutilated passage of Suetonius, *Vesp.* 15, 'Ceterum neque caede cuiusquam unquam ... iustis suppliciis illacrimavit etiam et ingemuit,' that reference is made to the continued punishment of the Christians in Rome, seems altogether gratuitous: it can neither be affirmed nor denied.

[2] Bishop Lightfoot has a good remark in this connexion: 'This correspondence of a heathen writer is the sole ultimate chronicle of this important chapter in the sufferings of the early Church. What happened in this case is not unlikely to have happened many times.' *Ignatius and Polycarp*, p. 18.   [3] *Röm. Gesch.* v. 523, note.

One of these episodes of increased severity occurred, there can be no doubt, under Domitian, both at Rome and in the provinces; and though, for the reasons given above, I do not think that any new principle was involved, yet undoubtedly certain fresh factors made their appearance which tended to make collisions with the Christians more frequent, while very possibly a new criterion was established, at any rate in the provinces, which made the *cognitiones* more brief, more simple, more summary, and, from the Christian point of view, more unjust. It has already been shown that, apart from political and social considerations, the religious toleration of the Roman government might always conceivably find its limit at the point where Roman citizens were diverted from the national religion by the exclusive claims of one of the monotheistic cults. If actual cases rarely occurred in which the rule of toleration was departed from on these grounds, it was partly because indifference to the national religion was always becoming greater, while the number of citizens attracted by the monotheistic cults was comparatively small; and in the case of men of rank or standing almost infinitesimal. But a revival of the national cult on the one hand, or a secession from it of conspicuous or noble personages on the other, might at any time call down the interference of the state; and if there was added any suspicion of political danger, such interference was almost inevitable. It was such a concurrence of conditions which brought about a spasmodic and temporary persecution of Christians in

Rome under Domitian in 95 A.D. Dio Cassius[1] tells us that Flavius Clemens, a cousin of the emperor, and his wife Domitilla were accused of ἀθεότης: that the former was executed, and the latter banished to an island; that many others also were accused of the same charge, some being executed, others stripped of their property, ὡς ἐς τὰ τῶν Ἰουδαίων ἤθη ἐξοκέλλοντες, Acilius Glabrio being mentioned particularly as charged with the same crime as the rest, and also with having fought with wild beasts in the arena. Suetonius[2] mentions the death of Flavius Clemens—whom he describes as a man 'contemptissimae inertiae'—as arising 'ex tenuissima suspicione,' while he alludes to Acilius Glabrio as a suspected 'molitor rerum novarum.'[3] Eusebius[4] to a great extent confirms the account of Dio Cassius, mentioning no names, but narrating that Domitian killed a considerable number of noble and illustrious men, and

---

[1] Dio Cass. lxvii. 14: Κἂν τῷ αὐτῷ ἔτει ἄλλους τε πολλοὺς καὶ Φλάβιον Κλήμεντα ὑπατεύοντα, καίπερ ἀνεψιὸν ὄντα, καὶ γυναῖκα καὶ αὐτὴν συγγενῆ ἑαυτοῦ Φλαβίαν Δομιτίλλαν ἔχοντα κατέσφαξεν ὁ Δομιτιανός. ἐπηνέχθη δὲ ἀμφοῖν ἔγκλημα ἀθεότητος, ὑφ' ἧς καὶ ἄλλοι ἐς τὰ τῶν Ἰουδαίων ἤθη ἐξοκέλλοντες πολλοὶ κατεδικάσθησαν· καὶ οἱ μὲν ἀπέθανον, οἱ δὲ τῶν γοῦν οὐσιῶν ἐστερήθησαν· ἡ δὲ Δομιτίλλα ὑπερωρίσθη μόνον εἰς Πανδατέρειαν. τὸν δὲ δὴ Γλαβρίωνα τὸν μετὰ τοῦ Τραϊανοῦ ἄρξαντα, κατηγορηθέντα τά τε ἄλλα καὶ οἷα οἱ πολλοί, καὶ ὅτι καὶ θηρίοις ἐμάχετο ἀπέκτεινεν.

[2] Suet. *Dom.* 15: 'Denique Flavium Clementem patruelem suum, contemptissimae inertiae, cuius filios etiam tum parvulos successores palam destinaverat . . . repente ex tenuissima suspicione tantum non in ipso eius consulatu interemit.'

[3] Suet. *Dom.* 10.

[4] *H. E.* iii. 17: Πολλὴν γε μὴν εἰς πολλοὺς ἐπιδειξάμενος ὁ Δομετιανὸς ὠμότητα οὐκ ὀλίγον τε τῶν ἐπὶ Ῥώμης εὐπατριδῶν τε καὶ ἐπισήμων ἀνδρῶν πλῆθος οὐ μετ' εὐλόγου κρίσεως κτείνας, κ. τ. λ.

punished many more with banishment and confiscation; while Melito[1] couples together, as does Tertullian, Nero and Domitian as the earliest persecutors. That Domitian was at any rate to a certain extent inclined to support and revive the national religion is shown by the passages and evidence collected by Schiller;[2] that the principal victims were not only noble Roman citizens but also a possible danger from a political point of view will be clear if we remember that Domitian had no heir of his own, that Flavius Clemens, whose two sons were the destined successors to the empire, was, as the only surviving son of Vespasian's elder brother, Flavius Sabinus, the second personage in the empire, and that Flavia Domitilla, his wife, was a niece of the emperor. That the victims were really Christians is almost certain. Christian tradition, as represented by Eusebius, affirms it,[3] and the words of Suetonius, 'contemptissimae inertiae,' well correspond to the difficulties of a Christian in the position of Flavius Clemens. Dio Cassius, it is true, represents them as living a Jewish life, but in view of the manifest bias which makes this writer consistently avoid all mention of the Christians, this evidence is anything but conclusive, while archaeological discoveries have now established the facts, (1) that Domitilla was the owner of the ground on which one of the catacombs was after-

[1] Euseb. *H. E.* iv. 26.   [2] *Röm. Gesch.* ii. p. 536.
[3] Euseb. *H. E.* iii. 18: ἐν ἔτει πεντεκαιδεκάτῳ Δομετιανοῦ μετὰ πλείστων ἑτέρων καὶ Φλαουΐαν Δομετίλλαν ἱστορήσαντες, ἐξ ἀδελφῆς γεγονυῖαν Φλαουΐου Κλήμεντος, ἑνὸς τῶν τηνικάδε ἐπὶ Ῥώμης ὑπάτων, τῆς εἰς Χριστὸν μαρτυρίας ἕνεκεν εἰς νῆσον Ποντίαν . . . δεδόσθαι.

wards situated,[1] (2) that the family of the Acilii Glabriones were buried in a crypt, the centre of a series of catacombs clustered round the tomb of some saint or martyr,[2] whom, considering the evidence of Dio Cassius, it is not altogether rash to identify with the Acilius Glabrio of Domitian.

The trial, however, under Domitian took a different form from those in 64 A.D. Slaves and freedmen, immigrants from the East, members of the great city proletariate, might be summarily arrested by the *praefectus urbi*, and after scant inquiry executed as members of a sect characterised confessedly by 'odium generis humani.' With Roman citizens of standing and importance a more definite charge was necessary, and this we find from Dio Cassius was primarily $\dot{a}\theta\epsilon \acute{o}\tau\eta s$, *i.e.* not so much *sacrilegium* in any technical sense[3] as a refusal to worship the national gods of the state. In this sense both the Jews and Christians were $\ddot{a}\theta\epsilon o\iota$,[4] though the Jews were tolerated $\ddot{a}\theta\epsilon o\iota$, and the majority of Christians, if this had been the only charge against them, would no doubt have been let alone. But in the case of Roman citizens it was deemed necessary to assert the state right to claim observance on the part of citizens of the national worship. The emperor no doubt tried the case himself. The charge of $\dot{a}\theta\epsilon \acute{o}\tau\eta s$ not being known to Roman law, the case was one for the *coercitio* of the

---

[1] De Rossi, *Bullett. di Archeolog. Cristian.* 1865, 17-24.
[2] De Rossi, cited by Ramsay, p. 262.
[3] See p. 74, *n.* 1.
[4] Mommsen, *Hist. Zeitschr.* p. 407, note 2.

supreme magistrate. But it was one of the peculiarities of the imperial court that, sharing the summary power and lax procedure of police jurisdiction, it could also deal with really legal crimes such as *maiestas* or *repetundae*. Under Tiberius, as we know, *maiestas* was 'omnium criminum complementum,'[1] and very much the same thing became true under Domitian. The charge of *maiestas* was one of very elastic dimensions, and Mommsen has shown that it was quite possible for any dishonour shown to the 'dii populi Romani' to be conceived as a violation of the dignity of the ruling nation, and so brought under the law of *maiestas*.[2] From Suetonius we should infer that this took place on the present occasion. But if it was so, it is important to guard against any language which would seem to imply that henceforth this was the usual mode of dealing with the Christians. Le Blant[3] has no doubt performed a useful work in showing what the usual legal charges were under which the Christians could be proceeded against—how *maiestas* or *sacrilegium* could be brought home to them, or circumstantial evidence produced of magical practices or murder, or how they could be punished as members of an illicit *collegium* under the Lex Iulia. No doubt in particular cases proceedings might be taken under one or other of these forms, but as a rule

[1] Tac. *Ann.* iii. 38.
[2] Mommsen, *Hist. Zeitschr.* p. 396.
[3] Le Blant, 'Sur les bases juridiques des poursuites dirigées contre les martyrs,' Acad. des Inscriptions, *Comptes-rendus*, 1866, p. 358 foll.

the Christian trials are not to be classified in this way. The Christians were punished, not as traitors, nor as magicians, but simply as Christians: *i.e.* as members of a body which was notoriously incompatible with the good order and obedience to existing institutions which an efficient police administration requires from all. It is to this circumstance that the vagueness is due which characterises all that we know of the dealings of the government towards Christianity. It really lay within the discretion of each provincial governor as to how he should deal with the Christians, whether he should hunt them out—a proceeding discountenanced by the emperors, certainly after Trajan—or should wait till information was laid against them by accusers. Again, when accusations were made, it was within his discretion merely to satisfy himself that the accused were really Christians, or to enter into any specific charges made against them. There is no evidence whatever that either by Nero or by any of the Flavian emperors any general instructions were given to provincial governors to put down Christianity.[1] When repressive measures were taken, they would be taken usually, not from any 'Flavian policy,' not because membership in the sect was looked upon as treasonable by the government, certainly not because the Church was looked upon as ' an organised

---

[1] Sulpicius Severus says, *Chron.* ii. 29: 'Hoc initio in Christianos saeviri coeptum. Post etiam datis legibus religio vetabatur palamque edictis propositis Christianos esse non licebat;' but, as Professor Ramsay points out, he uses these terms loosely and inaccurately (p. 255).

unity dangerous to the state,'[1] but in consequence of some manifestation of hostile feeling on the part of the populace, sometimes because their social interests were injured, sometimes because their religious institutions were neglected, sometimes from both causes combined with various other motives for jealousy and dislike.

Practically the Christians were not a danger to the state, and neither Nero nor Domitian could possibly have thought that they were, or have ordered systematic measures of repression on that ground; but nevertheless, since 64 A.D., the principles of the community were known to contain elements inconsistent with that entire obedience which was owed to the state and to state institutions by all well-affected citizens, and on this ground the provincial governors, as guardians of the public peace and acting in the special circumstances of particular cases, could and undoubtedly did from time to time persecute the Christians.

Nor must it be forgotten that in the provinces religious motives had greater weight—not indeed with the government, but with the populace—than at Rome. It has been seen that in the city the police administration always could, though perhaps it seldom did, interfere with citizens who repudiated the national cult, or, in other words, were ἄθεοι. But it would be a mistake to suppose that the populations of the Oriental cities, merely because they were not Roman citizens, were allowed complete liberty in religious

[1] Ramsay, p. 275.

matters, and could adopt Christianity without fear of interference.¹ The national religion had a stronger hold upon the people in the East than in the West,² and it was the manifest policy of the Roman government, which had always tolerated these religions, to give them whatever support against atheists was claimed by popular feeling—so that atheism was a charge with which the imperial police administration in the provinces could always deal, though, as Mommsen points out, the term had reference to different deities from those in Rome. The riot of the artificers at Ephesus shows how easily religious animosity might be aided by motives of another sort, although in this case the populace had not yet fully realised the extent of the opposition between the Christians and their own worship. A more significant example is the attempt of the people of Antioch, after the Jewish war, to enforce their national worship on the Jews resident among them, under the impression that with the destruction of the Temple and the political constitution of the Jews, their religious privileges were also taken away.³

[1] Mommsen, *Hist. Zeitschr.* p. 409 : 'Damit soll keineswegs gesagt sein, dass in dieser Epoche dem Nichtbürger der Übertritt zum Juden- oder zum Christenthum von Rechtswegen freigestanden habe: im Gegentheil konnte dem Athener und dem Antiochener, welcher sich zum Christenthum bekannte, mit demselben Recht wie dem Römer der Atheismus vorgeworfen werden, nur dass die Gottesleugnung hier auf einen anderen Götterkreis bezog.'

[2] Instances are: the credulity of the people at Lystra, who believed that Paul and Barnabas were Hermes and Zeus 'in the likeness of men (Acts xiv. 11-18); and the faith of the Egyptian populace in the healing powers of Vespasian (Suet. *Vesp.* 7). Cf. also Lucian, *Alexand.* 9.   [3] Joseph. *B. J.* vii. 3, 3.

What was unsuccessfully attempted against the Jews must often have met with greater success against the Christians.

But it was not perhaps always easy, when popular feeling or some other occasion made it necessary for the provincial authorities to interfere with the Christians, to identify the members of a sect composed mainly of the humblest and poorest of the population, with no special ritual to attract attention, usually meeting more or less in secret, and by no means all of them ready to profess their Christianity in public. It was apparently in the reign of Domitian that a criterion was established which for the future made the identification of Christians a comparatively simple matter, while it provided the possibility, whenever it was deemed worth while or desirable, of bringing the profession of Christianity, even in the provinces, under the head of *maiestas*. Among other means of establishing some bond of union for the whole empire Augustus had conceived the possibility of a semi-religious bond between Rome and the various provinces, which were otherwise so heterogeneous in worship, language, and institutions. As an outward sign of their common membership in the empire, an organisation was established in the provinces for the worship of 'Rome and Augustus.' For this purpose provincial *concilia* were formed, composed of deputies sent from the various towns or divisions of the province; a provincial temple to Rome and Augustus was built; a provincial *sacerdos* or *flamen* appointed and annual meetings of the *concilia* in connexion with religious services in the temple, and games in honour of the deified emperors were instituted.¹ But nowhere in the whole empire did this institution so flourish or assume such prominence as in the provinces of the East and particularly of Asia Minor. In Asia itself the original temple of Rome and Augustus was established at Pergamus;² here the κοινὸν τῆς 'Ασίας was held, and the games celebrated. But Asia was remarkable not only for the number of its cities, but for the rivalry existing between them, and so we find that in the course of time temples to Augustus grew up in Sardes,³ Philadelphia,⁴ Smyrna,⁵ Ephesus,⁶ and Laodicea,⁷ the κοινὸν being apparently held now in one, now in another. The high priest of Asia was known by the high-sounding title of Asiarch, and the annual religious observances and the richly endowed games attracted the attention of the whole province. How far participation in this cult was expected as a duty or mark of loyalty from individual provincials we have no means of determining.⁸ Under Augustus and Tiberius, after

[1] See my article on the Provincial Concilia, *English Historical Review*, April 1890.
[2] Dio Cass. li. 20. Tac. *Ann.* iv. 37.
[3] *C. I. Gr.* 5918.
[4] *Ibid.* 3428.
[5] *Ibid.* 3208.
[6] Eckhel, ii. 521.
[7] Wood, *Discoveries at Ephesus*, p. 54.
[8] Mommsen (*Röm. Gesch.* v. 321) supposes that the provincial priests of Rome and Augustus—in Asia the Asiarchs—would, as part of their duty, call attention to any neglect of the established cult, and having no power of punishment themselves, would bring the matter before the secular courts: would, in fact, either act as or provide informers: 'Als dann der alte und der neue Glaube im

the first organisation was started, the whole thing was no doubt left to the spontaneous action of the provinces, and the same was probably true of the other emperors, with the exception of Caligula, up to the accession of Domitian. That emperor, however, was much more particular in respect to his own divinity. We know that his procurators had to commence their official instructions with the formula 'Dominus et deus noster hoc fieri iubet,' and that he insisted upon being addressed in a similar way in all communications to himself.[1] That under an emperor with such known proclivities there should have grown up greater strictness and possibly some more express provisions in relation to the observance of the imperial cult in the provinces is extremely likely, and certainly if any such change took place it must have produced an adverse effect upon the position of the Christians. That something of the sort actually did take place is, it seems to me, made extremely probable by the evidence of the Apocalypse. According to the statement of Irenaeus, with which apparently

---

Reiche um die Herrschaft zu ringen begannen, ist deren Gegensatz wohl zunächst durch das provinziale Oberpriesterthum zum Conflict geworden. Diese aus den vornehmen Provinzialen von dem Landtag der Provinz bestellten Priester waren durch ihre Traditionen wie durch ihre Amtspflichter weit mehr als die Reichbeamten berufen und geneigt auf Vernachlässigung des anerkannten Gottesdienstes zu achten und, wo Abmahnung nicht half, da sie selber eine Strafgewalt nicht hatten, die nach bürgerlichem Recht strafbare Handlung bei den Orts- oder den Reichsbehörden zur Anzeige zu bringen, und den weltlichen Arm zu Hülfe zu rufen, vor allem den Christen gegenüber die Forderungen des Kaisercultus geltend zu machen.'

[1] Suet. *Dom.* 13.

all the internal evidence agrees, the date of this book was near the end of Domitian's reign.[1] In it there is distinct and repeated allusion to a persecution of the Christians in Asia:[2] *e.g.* εἶδον ὑποκάτω τοῦ θυσιαστηρίου τὰς ψυχὰς τῶν ἐσφαγμένων διὰ τὸν λόγον τοῦ θεοῦ καὶ διὰ τὴν μαρτυρίαν ἣν εἶχον:[3] and, εἶδον τὴν γυναῖκα μεθύουσαν ἐκ τοῦ αἵματος τῶν ἁγίων καὶ ἐκ τοῦ αἵματος τῶν μαρτύρων Ἰησοῦ:[4] while it is equally clear that the immediate occasion of the execution alluded to was the refusal to worship the emperor:

[1] Cited in Euseb. *H. E.* iii. 18 : οὐδὲ γὰρ πρὸ πολλοῦ χρόνου ἑωράθη [ἡ ἀποκάλυψις] ἀλλὰ σχεδὸν ἐπὶ τῆς ἡμετέρας γενεᾶς πρὸς τῷ τέλει τῆς Δομετιανοῦ ἀρχῆς.

[2] Prof. Ramsay (*Expositor*, July 1893, p. 16) argues from the vehement language of the Apocalypse as compared with the moderate tone of the Apologists of the second century, that the policy of the first century emperors was essentially more severe towards the Christians than that of those in the second. Mommsen speaks of the complaints uttered in the Apocalypse.' Prof. Ramsay says that ' the Apocalypse is not a complaint but a vision of triumph over a cruel and bitter but impotent adversary.' Does he not suggest the answer to his own argument? The intense, exaggerated, visionary tone of the Apocalypse is common to all the productions, mostly Jewish, of the same kind, and while we may accept any historical statements to be found in it, we must discount the general tone of denunciation. On the other hand, if the writer of the Apocalypse overstated the case, the Apologists by the very nature of their task were likely to employ a studied moderation which perhaps understated and mitigated the facts, though there are passages in Tertullian of intense, if repressed, bitterness, which, making allowance for the poetical imagery of the Apocalypse, might almost be compared with the tone of that work. To this it may be added that the Apocalyptic writer thought he was writing on the eve of the second coming of Christ; whereas the Apologists were trying to secure some tolerable *locus standi* for the Christians in an empire of which they no longer looked for a speedy end.

[3] vi. 9; cf. also xx. 4   [4] xvii. 6.

καὶ ἐδόθη αὐτῇ δοῦναι πνεῦμα τῇ εἰκόνι τοῦ θηρίου ἵνα καὶ λαλήσῃ ἡ εἰκὼν τοῦ θηρίου καὶ ποιήσῃ ἵνα ὅσοι ἐὰν μὴ προσκυνήσωσιν τῇ εἰκόνι τοῦ θηρίου ἀποκτανθῶσιν.[1] And, again, εἶδον .... τὰς ψυχὰς τῶν πεπελεκισμένων διὰ τὴν μαρτυρίαν Ἰησοῦ καὶ διὰ τὸν λόγον τοῦ θεοῦ καὶ οἵτινες οὐ προσεκύνησαν τὸ θηρίον οὐδὲ τὴν εἰκόνα αὐτοῦ:[2] while we have the name of one martyr—Antipas—at Pergamus, the seat of the imperial cult at that time, ὃς ἀπεκτάνθη παρ' ὑμῖν ὅπου ὁ Σατανᾶς κατοικεῖ.[3] That it was the rule at the time, or thought to be so by the writer, for all the provincials to worship the emperor's image appears from another passage — προσκυνήσουσιν αὐτὸν πάντες οἱ κατοικοῦντες ἐπὶ τῆς γῆς.[4] It appears from these passages that a number of Christians were executed in Asia during Domitian's reign: a circumstance probably alluded to in the Μαρτύριον Ἰγνατίου[5]—τῶν πολλῶν ἐπὶ Δομετιανοῦ διωγμῶν —some of whom, at any rate, were beheaded,[6] perhaps as belonging to a somewhat higher class,[7] while others were probably sent to Rome to be exposed to wild beasts in the arena there.[8]

[1] Rev. xiii. 15.   [2] xx. 4.   [3] ii. 13.
[4] xiii. 8. Cf. also xii. 11, xiii. 12–14, xiv. 9, xvi. 2, and xix. 20.
[5] Ruinart, Acta Martyrum, p. 696.   [6] Rev. xx. 4.
[7] Paulus, Sent. v. 29, 1.
[8] So Mommsen (Röm. Gesch. v. 522 note) with much probability explains Rev. xvii. 6, καὶ εἶδον τὴν γυναῖκα μεθύουσαν ἐκ τοῦ αἵματος τῶν ἁγίων: and xviii. 24, καὶ ἐν αὐτῇ αἷμα προφητῶν καὶ ἁγίων εὑρέθη. 'Wenn hervorgehoben wird, dass diese Blutgerichte besonders häufig in Rom vollzogen wurden (c. 17, 6; 18, 24), so ist damit die Vollstreckung der Verurtheilung zum Fecht- oder zum Thierkampf gemeint, welche am Gerichtort oft nicht stattfinden konnte

H

From these notices it is not necessary to infer that a formal charge of *maiestas* was brought against the Christians for refusing to worship the emperor. Had this been the case, the persecution would have been much more systematic and general than the evidence gives ground to suppose that it was, while a normal form of *cognitio* would certainly have been established for such cases, which would have made Pliny's hesitation and uncertainty impossible. Much more probably the ordinary charges were laid against the Christians before the proconsul—charges which involved a certain disaffection to the empire and the emperor. In view of the greater importance attached to the imperial cult by Domitian, it might easily suggest itself as a criterion by which the Christianity and consequently the criminality of the accused might be decided, while at the same time an opportunity was afforded them of proving at once their loyalty to the emperor by rendering to him the usual act of worship. If this view is correct, we are not bound with Neumann[1] to suppose the introduction of any new principle in dealing with the Christians at this time, but rather the introduction of a useful test, by which Christians might easily be distinguished from

---

und bekanntlich vorzugsweise eben in Rom erfolgte.' Cf. *Dig.* xlviii. 19, 31 : ' Ad bestias damnare favore populi praeses dimittere non debet : sed si eius roboris vel artificii sint, ut digne populo Romano exhiberi possint, principem consulere debet.' So Ignatius says to the Ephesians, πάροδός ἐστε τῶν εἰς θεὸν ἀναιρουμένων, ad *Ephes.* 12, and cf. 1, 4, ἐλπίζοντα τῇ προσευχῇ ὑμῶν ἐπιτυχεῖν ἐν ‘Ρώμῃ θηριομαχῆσαι.

[1] Neumann, *Der röm. Staat und die allgemeine Kirche*, p. 15.

those who were falsely accused of being so. That this receives much support from Pliny's letter to Trajan will I think appear below.

At Rome the death of Domitian seems at once to have restored the ordinary state of toleration which the Christian community experienced for the most part in the city, and which, as we have seen, was only disturbed by exceptional circumstances.[1] As to what took place in the provinces during the first twelve years or so of Trajan's reign we have no information. If the account given above—an account, be it remembered, which only pretends to rest on probable and indirect evidence—is in any way correct, there was up to this time no general proscription of the Christians, certainly no edict, as some have supposed,[2] forbidding their existence, and there was nothing which can fairly be called an imperial policy towards the Christians. The letter of Pliny, indeed, apart from all other evidence, is by itself a sufficient proof of this. The Christians were as yet too insignificant a body to be seriously regarded as a danger to the state, needing to be met by a definite policy. A purely personal motive had, indeed, thirty years before the death of Domitian brought the Christians of Rome face to face with the police administration of the city, and enough had been then discovered to show that their principles contained elements inconsistent with absolute obe-

[1] Dio Cass. lxviii. 1: τοῖς δὲ δὴ ἄλλοις οὔτε ἀσεβείας οὔτ' Ἰουδαϊκοῦ βίου καταιτιᾶσθαί τινας συνεχώρησε.

[2] See Arnold, *Die Plin. Christenverfolgung*, p. 27, note 3, and Boissier, *Revue Archéologique*, 1876, p. 118 foll.

dience to the state, but, the special occasion over, the persecution apparently ended, and even the populace saw clearly enough that the Christians were not really being punished because they were dangerous, but to satisfy the emperor's personal cruelty.[1] The collisions which had been brought about in Rome by one accidental circumstance might undoubtedly at any time in the provinces be brought about by others, and in particular by the deep and growing hatred with which the sect was beginning to be regarded by the people. In all such cases the provincial governors required no special law to guide their action: they were armed with the supreme police administration of their provinces; if riots took place against the Christians as 'atheists,' deniers or violators of the municipal or provincial cults, it was part of their police duty to protect them and to punish the offenders; if they were accused of forming illegal associations, or of nocturnal meetings, or of immorality, the same authority enabled them to take summary measures. The mere fact that the Christians by their strange doctrines were a cause of popular disturbance and excitement would amply justify police interference.[2] On the other hand, if the governors deemed it necessary to apply to the emperor for instructions, the

[1] Tac. *Ann.* xv. 44: 'tanquam non publica utilitate sed in unius saevitiam absumerentur.'

[2] Paulus, *Sent.* v. 21: 'Qui novas sectas vel ratione incognitas religiones inducunt, ex quibus animi hominum moveantur, honestiores deportantur, humiliores capite puniuntur.' This, as Mommsen points out, only puts in a precise form what was essentially the duty of every police administration.

rescript could only be in effect, 'The Christians are enemies of the human race: it is your duty to insure the tranquillity of your province: if these men interfere with it, they must be punished.' In other words, Christianity by virtue of its inherent disobedience (*obstinatio*, παράταξις [1]) was a criminal offence, but in the eyes of the police administration, not of the law. How far the Christians were actually persecuted under this *régime* would depend not so much on any Neronian or Flavian policy as on the character of the provincial governors, local and particular circumstances, and, above all, on the state of popular feeling in particular districts or provinces.

[1] Cf. the αὐθάδεια which Aristides attributes to οἱ ἐν τῇ Παλαιστίνῃ δυσσεβεῖς (*Orat.* 46).

VI

TRAJAN AND THE CHRISTIANS

APART from a possibly greater insistence on some observance of the imperial cult, which, however, we have seen reason to think was applied more as a test than as a universal obligation, there was probably little to distinguish the government attitude towards Christians in the provinces under Domitian from that under Nerva and Trajan.

For the policy, if it can be called so, of the latter, very important information—though its importance may easily be exaggerated—is afforded us owing to the fortunate circumstance that a literary man was sent out as governor to Bithynia, and that his correspondence with the emperor on a variety of matters relating to the administration of the province was published after his death, together with his other letters. Had this correspondence shared the fate of so many other classical works, or had the governor's inquiry or the emperor's rescript shared the usual fate of similar documents, even more important in themselves, and remained stored away with the other *commentarii principis* in the imperial *scrinia*, we should have had much less clue to the attitude of the government in the second century, and much that is now tolerably clear and consistent would have seemed improbable or obscure.

The province of Bithynia-Pontus had from republican times a considerable Jewish population,[1] probably collected mainly in its large cities, e.g. Nicomedia and Nicaea, Apamaea, and perhaps Sinope and Amisus. It has been already mentioned that it was to places with large Jewish settlements, especially if they lay on important commercial routes rendering communication easy, that the earliest Christian missionaries first betook themselves. Paul himself, in his second missionary journey, had intended to enter Bithynia, but was prevented by the Spirit.[2] Professor Ramsay supposes that Christianity would first enter Bithynia along the trade route from the Cilician gates, by way of Tyana and Caesaraea of Cappadocia to Amisus, and that it probably arrived here between 65 and 75 A.D.[3] There were certainly Christians in the province when 1 Peter was composed;[4] and there were instances of apostasy from it as early as 87 A.D.[5] The province, which together with Asia was the first to have a temple built to Rome and Augustus,[6] was under senatorial administration; but owing to misunder-

[1] Cic. pro Flacc. 28.   [2] Acts xvi. 6.   [3] p. 225.
[4] 1 Pet. i. 1: ἐκλεκτοῖς παρεπιδήμοις διασπορᾶς Πόντου, Γαλατίας, Καππαδοκίας, Ἀσίας καὶ Βιθυνίας.
[5] Ad Trai. 96, 6, where some of the accused assert that they had left the Christian body twenty-five years before.
[6] Dio Cass. li. 20.

standings between proconsuls and provincials,[1] to the prevalence of factions in the cities,[2] and to financial disorders,[3] Trajan found it advisable in 111 A.D. temporarily to take the province into his own administration, and to send out a special *legatus*, with a view to the reformation of abuses[4] and the re-establishment of its financial stability. For this purpose he selected Pliny, as one who had some acquaintance with Bithynian affairs,[5] had had some experience of finance,[6] and also, no doubt, as a man of known moderation and high character.

Pliny reached his province in September, 111 A.D.,[7] and from that time till the beginning of 113 A.D. we have sixty letters written by him to Trajan, asking advice on all sorts of matters connected with the administration of the province—some of them extremely trivial—and forty-eight replies on the part of the emperor. How long Pliny remained in Bithynia we do not know. The letters, which seem to be arranged chronologically,[8] show that during the time mentioned he was passing through the province from west to east,

[1] Plin. *Ep.* iii. 9 and v. 20.
[2] Plin. *ad Trai.* 34: 'Sed meminerimus provinciam istam et praecipue eas civitates eiusmodi factionibus esse vexatas.'
[3] Plin. *ad Trai.* 17 A; 32, 1, etc.
[4] Plin. *ad Trai.* 32, 1: 'Memineris idcirco te in istam provinciam missum quoniam multa in ea emendanda apparuerint.'
[5] He had been counsel both for Julius Bassus and for Varenus Rufus, who were accused by the province of *repetundae*.
[6] He had been *praefectus* both of the *aerarium Saturni*, and of the *aerarium militare*.
[7] Plin. *ad Trai.* 17 A.
[8] *Ibid.* my edition, p. 72.

arranging matters as he went successively at Prusa,[1] Nicomedia,[2] Nicaea,[3] Heraclea,[4] Sinope,[5] and Amisus,[6] while the last letter in which the place is specified is written from Amastris[7]—a city which, on account of its remoteness, Pliny was possibly visiting on his return journey by sea. From the abrupt close of the correspondence it has been conjectured, with some plausibility, that Pliny died before his mission was accomplished.

It is unnecessary to discuss here the question whether in ordinary cases the emperors were consulted by their legates to the same extent that Trajan was by Pliny. Probably the exceptional condition of the province was the cause of an exceptionally frequent and minute correspondence, but in the letter with which we are particularly concerned—that about the Christians—there is nothing that might not with equal appropriateness have come from a proconsul of Asia or a legate of Syria. During the first year of Pliny's administration, apparently, the Christian question had remained dormant; and it was not till he had arrived at the eastern districts of the province— probably Amisus and its neighbourhood—that Pliny was confronted with the problem, which, as we have seen, was certainly no new one either in Bithynia or the eastern provinces generally.[8] Nor at first ap-

[1] Plin. *ad Trai.* 23.
[2] *Ibid.* 33.
[3] *Ibid.* 39.
[4] *Ibid.* 75.
[5] *Ibid.* 90.
[6] *Ibid.* 92.
[7] *Ibid.* 98.
[8] Arnold supposes that the Christian difficulty confronted Pliny first in the neighbourhood of Amaseia and Comana, the centre of the

parently, when certain Christians were brought before his tribunal, did Pliny experience any particular difficulty in dealing with them.[1] It is true that he had

cult of the Cappadocian goddess Enyo, of which Strabo gives an account, xii. 599. But, apart from any other difficulties, Amaseia and Comana were not in Bithynia-Pontus, but in Galatia. See Marquardt, *Staatsverw.* i. 359; Arnold *Studien zur Geschichte der Plin. Christenverfolgung*, pp. 32, 33.

[1] 'Solemne est mihi, Domine, omnia, de quibus dubito, ad te referre. Quis enim potest melius vel cunctationem meam regere, vel ignorantiam instruere? Cognitionibus de Christianis interfui nunquam: ideo nescio, quid et quatenus aut puniri soleat aut quaeri. Nec mediocriter haesitavi, sitne aliquod discrimen aetatum, an quamlibet teneri nihil a robustioribus differant; detur poenitentiae venia, an ei, qui omnino Christianus fuit, desisse non prosit; nomen ipsum, si flagitiis careat, an flagitia cohaerentia nomini, puniantur. Interim in iis, qui ad me tanquam Christiani deferebantur, hunc sum secutus modum. Interrogavi ipsos, an essent Christiani: confitentes iterum ac tertio interrogavi, supplicium minatus: perseverantes duci iussi. Neque enim dubitabam, qualecunque esset, quod faterentur, pertinaciam certe, et inflexibilem obstinationem debere puniri. Fuerunt alii similis amentiae: quos, quia cives Romani erant, adnotavi in urbem remittendos. Mox ipso tractatu, ut fieri solet, diffundente se crimine, plures species inciderunt. Propositus est libellus sine auctore, multorum nomina continens. Qui negabant se esse Christianos, aut fuisse, quum, praeeunte me, deos appellarent, et imagini tuae, quam propter hoc iusseram cum simulacris numinum adferri, thure ac vino supplicarent, praeterea maledicerent Christo, quorum nihil cogi posse dicuntur, qui sunt revera Christiani, dimittendos esse putavi. Alii ab indice nominati, esse se Christianos dixerunt, et mox negaverunt: fuisse quidem, sed desisse, quidam ante triennium, quidam ante plures annos, non nemo etiam ante viginti quinque. Omnes et imaginem tuam, deorumque simulacra venerati sunt, et Christo maledixerunt. Adfirmabant autem, hanc fuisse summam vel culpae suae, vel erroris, quod essent soliti stato die ante lucem convenire, carmenque Christo, quasi Deo, dicere secum invicem, seque sacramento non in scelus aliquod obstringere, sed ne furta, ne latrocinia, ne adulteria committerent, ne fidem fallerent, ne depositum appellati

never personally been present at any of the 'cognitiones de Christianis,' which, as we have seen, must have been frequent enough in the province since 64 A.D., but there were, no doubt, permanent officials who could inform him of the course usually taken; and, as Professor Ramsay points out with great force, Pliny's action presupposes the development of a more or less regular form of procedure.[1] A number of persons were brought before him 'tanquam Christiani.' The course he adopted was to ask them, no doubt singly, whether they were Christians. Being probably the most prominent members of the sect, they seem all to have acknowledged their religion. Pliny asked them the question a second time, and then a third time, threatening death if they persisted. As this had no effect, he ordered their execution, considering that, whatever their confession of Christianity

abnegarent: quibus peractis morem sibi discedendi fuisse, rursusque coëundi ad capiendum cibum, promiscuum tamen, et innoxium: quod ipsum facere desisse post edictum meum, quo secundum mandata tua hetaerias esse vetueram. Quo magis necessarium credidi, ex duabus ancillis, quae ministrae dicebantur, quid esset veri, et per tormenta quaerere. Sed nihil aliud inveni quam superstitionem pravam immodicam. Ideo, dilata cognitione, ad consulendum te decucurri. Visa est enim mihi res digna consultatione, maxime propter periclitantium numerum. Multi enim omnis aetatis, omnis ordinis, utriusque sexus etiam, vocantur in periculum, et vocabuntur. Neque civitates tantum, sed vicos etiam atque agros superstitionis istius contagio pervagata est: quae videtur sisti et corrigi posse. Certe satis constat, prope iam desolata templa coepisse celebrari, et sacra solemnia diu intermissa repeti, pastumque venire victimarum, cuius adhuc rarissimus emptor inveniebatur. Ex quo facile est opinari, quae turba hominum emendari possit, si sit poenitentiae locus.' Plin. *ad Trai.* 96.

[1] p. 217.

involved, their obstinacy and invincible disobedience at any rate deserved punishment. By this simple account of the course taken by him, Pliny makes several things perfectly clear. In the first place, the mere profession of Christianity, if persisted in, was unhesitatingly regarded as a capital offence; no investigation was made into any particular charges; the Christians were clearly not punished as members of an illegal association, nor for refusal of the imperial cult, nor for atheism; they were executed because they avowed themselves Christians. To suppose that Pliny took this perfectly definite and decided course without precedent is quite impossible: there cannot, in my opinion, be the smallest doubt that the course which he pursued had already been pursued—probably not without some sort of guidance from Rome—if not in Bithynia, at any rate in some of the neighbouring provinces. Nor, as we shall see, does Pliny ask for any sort of guidance from Trajan in reference to these cases: he assumes what in fact Trajan's answer fully confirms, that his course was the regular one, and would be approved. It was in fact the logical result, as we have already seen, of the Neronian action. For while with this action it was not in the least degree inconsistent that there should have been for the most part a practical toleration of the Christians in the provinces, as long as public order and the state of popular feeling made this compatible with the police responsibility of the governors, yet, on the other hand, the Christians, insignificant as they were, had been pronounced and were no doubt recognised as 'hostes humani generis,' potentially rebels to the state authority. As such they were always, just as brigands were, liable to punishment, and if their punishment was demanded with any amount of popular insistence, there was certainly no reason why they should not receive it.

But all the cases which Pliny had to decide were not of the same simple character as those above described. The Christians were especially numerous in the district from which he wrote, and proceedings once begun, more complicated cases occurred.[1] An anonymous indictment was put in containing a long list of names. Of these some denied absolutely that they either were or ever had been Christians, and to them Pliny applied certain tests which experience had shown to be conclusive in identifying Christians,[2] requiring them to call upon the gods, to worship Caesar's image,[3] and to curse Christ. On their compliance with these demands he ordered these to be released. Others, however, gave more prevaricating answers, at first confessing their Christianity, then denying it, and finally affirming that they had left the community, some of them for a considerable number of years, one or two alleging that they had

---

[1] 'ipso tractatu plures species inciderunt.'

[2] Plin. *ad Trai.* 96, 5: 'Quorum nihil posse cogi dicuntur qui sunt re vera Christiani.' Cf. Tert. *Apol.* 3: 'Excludimur enim [de nomine] si facimus quae faciunt non Christiani.'

[3] It is perfectly clear that in Bithynia the requirement to worship the emperor was used simply as a test; the refusal of the Christians was not the reason of their punishment. Those originally executed were not required to worship the emperor at all.

ceased to be Christians twenty-five years ago.[1] All of these complied with Pliny's tests, but at this point his course was not so clear. Being no longer Christians, they could no longer be punished as such, *i.e.* as 'hostes humani generis,' but before releasing them Pliny had to consider certain offences which, sometimes in the shape of vague reports, sometimes no doubt in the form of definite charges, had been attributed to the Christian body—charges especially of child-murder at their social meetings, and of incestuous immorality. If the Christians were really guilty of these enormities, it was by no means clear that those who, as Christians, had committed them, even though it was years ago, should be set free merely because they no longer belonged to the body. Pliny accordingly, as all provincial governors by virtue of their police authority could do if they liked, proceeded to more particular investigations, first by cross-examining, either with or without torture, these renegades. What he learnt from them was that the Christians were in the habit of meeting at stated intervals, no doubt on the Lord's day, before dawn for a religious service in which hymns were sung to Christ as to a god, and an oath was taken [2] by the

---

[1] This, as already pointed out, carries us back to 87 A.D., and may point to some action against the Christians in Bithynia under Domitian.

[2] It is interesting to note what Foucart (*Des Associations religieuses chez les Grecs*, p. 182) says of the mysteries at Andania : 'Une certain nombre d'hommes et de femmes . . . s'engagent par un serment solennel à ne pas commettre et à ne laisser commettre aucune action injuste ou honteuse qui puisse ruiner les mystères.'

members to refrain from thefts, robberies, adultery, false swearing, and dishonesty, while later in the day they met again for a common meal, *i.e.* the Agape, at which the food was of the ordinary kind, and the proceedings quite harmless. To confirm the evidence of past members of the sect, Pliny next proceeded to put to the torture two slave women, who were deaconesses in the community, but in spite of the application of torture he could discover nothing further about Christianity except that it was a strange form of religious belief, which distorted the minds of its adherents, and was of an exaggerated and exciting character. There was therefore no reason on the score of these accusations why recantation should not be followed by pardon. We should imagine both on general grounds and from the existence of a test like that of adoring the emperor's image, that this was the course which had usually been pursued, but it would depend on the governor's discretion, and Pliny, who sought for the emperor's guidance and sanction in much more trifling affairs than this, considering also perhaps that the province was in an exceptional state, determined to consult Trajan before he decided these or any fresh cases. He was the more induced to do this as the inquiries already made had revealed to him the fact that the Christians were extremely numerous in Bithynia; that both men and women of every age and of every rank were implicated in the charge, and that not only the large cities but the small country towns and even the villages were infected with the superstition. Nor was this altogether a sudden growth which a little well-timed severity would put down, for Pliny knew quite well that according to Roman law 'grassantibus delictis exacerbanda esse supplicia quoties multis peccantibus exemplo est opus.' The state of things which he describes must have been of fairly long standing, for the temples were almost deserted, the sacred rites had long since been discontinued, and no purchaser could be found for the fodder of the sacrificial victims. Pliny himself is clearly of opinion that a lenient course should be adopted in the case of all who had abjured their Christianity and who complied with the tests he proposed. It was, in fact, the principal object of his letter to obtain Trajan's consent to this course—a course which he believed would soon re-establish religion in the province. But though this was his main object in writing to Trajan, he probably intended to suggest, though he did not venture openly to recommend, further modifications in the procedure against the Christians. His own investigations had apparently convinced him that the Christians were neither dangerous nor immoral: their *obstinatio* no doubt deserved death, but was it necessary to pursue a course which called forth this *obstinatio*? Accordingly, he begins his letter with several general questions, the answers to which would really involve a reconsideration of the attitude taken up by the government towards the sect. Not having been present at any of the trials, he does not understand 'quid et quatenus aut puniri soleat aut quaeri?' As we have seen, there was little precision in these matters; the magisterial *coercitio* was not marked in any case by a formal procedure, and with regard to the Christians the governors had probably accommodated their proceedings to the local circumstances, sometimes punishing members of the sect (as they always could do) merely as Christians, sometimes as 'atheists,' sometimes perhaps as belonging to a *collegium illicitum*, sometimes even as child-murderers. Similarly the judicial investigation would take now a wider now a narrower scope, sometimes merely seeking to establish the fact of Christianity, sometimes entering into a variety of particular charges. In view of what he had himself discovered about the religion, this vagueness appeared unsatisfactory to Pliny, and he asks for a definite answer to the question whether the mere profession of Christianity ('nomen ipsum'), even if no definite acts of immorality could be proved ('si flagitiis careat'), was what deserved punishment, or whether it was the abominable crimes which were supposed to be involved in the profession ('flagitia cohaerentia nomini'). Pliny's own prompt and unhesitating punishment of those first brought before him proves him to have been not unaware that the 'nomen ipsum' was, as matters stood, deserving of death; and the fact that he nevertheless asks the question shows his own leanings towards a less summary course—a leaning which he still further emphasises by his second question whether some difference should not be made in respect to age,[1] so that

---

[1] If the charge had been technically one of *sacrilegium*, there would have been no need to ask the question, for Ulpian says (*Dig.*

young boys and delicate maidens, who, as we know from other sources, often figured among the martyrs, might be treated with less rigour than those of more mature age.

Such, as I conceive it, was the point of view from which Pliny wrote his famous letter. Trajan's reply is brief and decisive: 'You have adopted the proper course, my dear Pliny, in distinguishing between the cases of the Christians who have been brought before you. For no general or definite rule can be laid down. They need not be hunted out, but if brought before you and convicted, they must be punished. Those, however, who deny their Christianity, and prove their denial by an act of worship to our gods, may wipe out past suspicions and secure a free pardon by recantation. Anonymous accusations of all sorts are inadmissible: they are the worst possible precedents, and contrary to the spirit of our time.'[1] In this rescript Trajan does not directly touch on any of the humanitarian considerations which Pliny had somewhat covertly suggested. The vague procedure of which

---

xlviii. 13, 7): 'Sacrilegii poenam debebit proconsul pro qualitate personae, proque rei conditione et temporis et aetatis et sexus vel severius vel clementius statuere.'

[1] 'Actum quem debuisti, mi Secunde, in excutiendis causis corum, qui Christiani ad te delati fuerant, secutus es. Neque enim in universum aliquid, quod quasi certam formam habeat, constitui potest. Conquirendi non sunt: si deferantur et arguantur, puniendi sunt: ita tamen, ut, qui negaverit se Christianum esse, idque re ipsa manifestum fecerit, id est, supplicando diis nostris, quamvis suspectus in praeteritum fuerit, veniam ex poenitentia impetret. Sine auctore vero propositi libelli, in nullo crimine locum habere debent. Nam et pessimi exempli, nec nostri saeculi est.'

Pliny complained was necessary: cases must be taken as they come: no general rule and no formal procedure can be laid down. The profession of Christianity is in itself a criminal offence, and persons convicted of it are to be executed. But two concessions are made: (1) there is no need for the police authorities to take the initiative and to search for offenders; as by the general instructions given to provincial governors they are bound to do in the case of *latrones, sacrilegi, plagiarii*,[1] etc.; clearly because, though like these they were outlaws and liable to punishment, unlike them they were not active enemies of society, and the peace of the province did not require their extermination: in other words, Trajan did not regard them as a political danger; (2) and, directly in answer to Pliny's appeal, the denial of Christianity was to be followed by pardon on compliance with the usual tests: in other words, Trajan was willing with Pliny to give them the benefit of any doubt there might be as to their alleged *flagitia*,[2] which, as already stated, could by no means be condoned by a simple withdrawal from the Christian body. A further decision on the inadmissibility of anonymous accusations had nothing specially to do with the Christians, though it included their case.

[1] *Dig.* i. 18, 13: 'Congruit bono et gravi praesidi curare ut pacata atque quieta provincia sit quam regit, quod non difficile obtinebit, si sollicite agat ut malis hominibus provincia careat, eosque conquirat: nam et sacrilegos, latrones, plagiarios, fures conquirere debet, et prout quisque deliquerit in eum animadvertere.'

[2] Cf. Min. Fel. *Octav.* 28: 'Et si qui infirmior malo pressus et victus Christianum se negasset, favebamus ei, quasi eierato nomine iam omnia facta sua illa negatione purgaret.'

This rescript of Trajan has, as is well known, been regarded from two opposite points of view. By the Christian Apologists it was looked upon as a measure favourable to the Christians, mitigating and discountenancing their persecution, and practically acquitting them of the charges made against them.[1] On the other hand, many modern writers, especially German scholars,[2] regard it as the first legal authorisation of persecution: as the virtual proscription of Christianity. From all that has been already said it will be clear that the latter view is absolutely groundless. Trajan, with certain modifications, not touching the principle of persecution, confirms Pliny's action, and Pliny's action was based on precedents, either in his own or in other provinces, which had certainly been directly or indirectly sanctioned from Rome. The former view is much nearer the truth, though it is undoubtedly coloured by the tendency common to all the Apologists to represent the 'good emperors' as favourable to Christianity. Trajan was not favourable to Christianity, the principles of which he recognised, as his predecessors since Nero must have done, to involve disobedience and therefore disaffection to the state. But the question was, apart from danger to the empire which was not worth con-

[1] See especially Tertullian, *Apol.* 5 : 'Quales ergo leges istae quas adversus nos soli exsequuntur impii, iniusti, turpes, truces, vani, dementes? quas Traianus ex parte frustratus est vetando inquiri Christianos.'

[2] *E.g.* Overbeck, *Studien zur Geschichte der alten Kirche*, 1875, pp. 93–157. The same view is taken by Aubé, and by Dierauer, *Zur Geschichte Trajans*, p. 118.

sidering, whether the peace and good order of the provinces would be best promoted by insisting on this disaffection and waging a war of extermination with the Christians—a course which was seldom or never rigorously pursued even in the case of brigands—or, without giving up the principle of their criminality, by allowing the governor at his discretion to extend a practical toleration to the sect, and to encourage secession from it by holding out the hope of pardon to seceders. This may be called a half-measure by those who criticise Trajan's action in the light of subsequent events, or a compromise by those who credit him with an insight into the meaning of the Christian development which it is extremely unlikely that he possessed. As a matter of fact, it was the decision of a practical statesman, who declined on the one hand to be led into severe repressive measures against a body which was only remotely and theoretically dangerous to the state, while he on the other refused to give up on humanitarian grounds the claim of the state to absolute obedience on the part of all its subjects.[1] Tertullian's rhetorical dilemma, 'negat inquirendos ut innocentes et mandat puniendos ut nocentes,'[2] rests on a not unnatural misunderstand-

---

[1] As Mommsen says (*Histor. Zeitschr.* p. 417), 'wenn für die römische Nationalität der römische Glaube nur ein anderer Ausdruck war, so hat der römische Staat gegenüber einem Proselytismus, der den römischen Glauben aufhebt, in Selbstvertheidigung gestanden, und auch die Geschichte erkennt das Recht der Nothwehr an.'

[2] Tert. *Apol.* 2: 'O sententiam necessitate confusam! Negat inquirendos ut innocentes, et mandat puniendos ut nocentes. Parcit et saevit, dissimulat et animadvertit. Quid temet ipsum censura circumvenis? Si damnas, cur non et inquiris? si non inquiris, cur

ing of the government point of view. That point of view, indeed, from which the name of Christian was by itself deserving of punishment, from which Christians as such were regarded as *hostes publici*, as imbued with an 'odium generis humani,' as characterised by an *obstinatio* which was the negation of complete political obedience—a point of view dating, as we have seen, from 64 A.D.—rested as yet on somewhat abstract grounds.

To the political government and administration of the empire the Christians were never anything but loyal subjects: 'Fear God and honour the king,' was the maxim which expressed clearly enough their relationship to the secular and political life around them. But in practice it was impossible to separate the political from the religious life of the empire, and in regard to the latter the Christian maxim had from the first been stated in a form which by its implied reservation meant passive resistance, if no more, to the omnipotence of the state: 'Render unto Caesar the things that be Caesar's, and to God the things that be God's.' The state religion, quite apart from any belief or disbelief in it on the part of either the ruler of the empire or its subjects, was nevertheless, at any rate since Augustus—sometimes with more insistence, as under Domitian and M. Aurelius; sometimes with greater laxity, as under Nero and perhaps

non et absolvis? Latronibus vestigandis per universas provincias militaris statio sortitur: in reos maiestatis et publicos hostes omnis homo miles est: ad socios, ad conscios usque inquisitio extenditur. Solum Christianum inquiri non licet, offerri licet: quasi aliud esset actura inquisitio quam oblationem.'

under Hadrian—always regarded as a part of the imperial organisation,[1] the chief pontificate being as necessary and universal, if not as important, a part of the attributes of the *princeps* as the tribunician power or the 'imperium proconsulare.' Outward respect to this state worship of the national gods, if not regular conformity with its public ceremonials, was expected, not only from all Roman citizens, but from all subjects of the empire.[2] But respect for and conformity with what was to them the worship of idols the Christians absolutely and always refused: this refusal was *obstinatio* or political disobedience, and political disobedience was the attribute of a 'publicus hostis.'[3] The outlawed position, therefore, of the Christians, that which made the 'nomen ipsum' deserving of punishment, was primarily their religion, their Christianity *per se*; and yet, if we interpret the situation into modern language, they were punished on political and not on religious grounds,

[1] Professor Ramsay, approved by Mommsen, says the 'keystone' of it. This may have been intended by Augustus, but it seems to me that this was a part of the Augustan system which was never fully worked out by his successors. Mommsen's own language is less open to objection when he says that the national religion was 'the spiritual symbol of the political union.' *Expositor*, July 1893, p. 3.

[2] See the *Acta Cypriani* (praef. p. cx in Hartel): 'Imperatores ... praeceperunt eos qui Romanam religionem non colunt debere Romanas caerimonias recognoscere.'

[3] Tertull. *Apol.* 35: 'Proptereaigitur publici hostes Christiani quia imperatoribus neque vanos neque mentientes neque temerarios honores dicant,' etc. Cf. 37: 'Sed hostes maluistis vocare generis humani.' Cf. 6: 'In quo principaliter reos transgressionis Christianos destinatis, studium dico deorum colendorum.'

because it was not the slight to the national religion which the government really cared about, but the disobedience shown through the religion to the imperial government. It is on this account that I describe the opposition supposed to exist by the government between itself and Christianity as a somewhat abstract and shadowy one. It is inconceivable to me that either Nero or Domitian or Trajan saw in Christianity anything more than an abstract danger. Not till the Christian bodies became a Church organised throughout the empire with bishops at their head, one of whose duties it may have been to bring the scattered communities into a more living touch with one another; not till Christianity became what Judaism had been before the great war on a smaller scale and within national limits—a state within the state—was the abstract danger developed into a real one, recognised as such, and met by systematic measures of repression.[1]

This development, however, had not taken place when Trajan sent his rescript to Pliny, and for more than a century after this the persecution of the Christians, though 'permanent, like that of brigands,' was probably never systematic nor general, proceeding as it did, not from a deliberately hostile policy on the part of the government, which, on the contrary, tolerated the Christians as far as it could consistently with the peace and good order of the provinces, but from the bitter and rancorous hatred of the provincial populations, to which concessions had to be made—a

[1] See below on p. 165.

hatred which, as we have seen, was partly, especially in the fanatical East, a religious hatred against 'atheists' as deniers of the local divinities, partly a social hatred against the disturbers of trade interests, and the despisers and denouncers of so many features in social life, partly a would-be-moral loathing against the practising of immoral abominations—abominations which were morbidly believed in, as such things usually are, with a credulity which neither needs nor heeds corroboration or refutation.[1] 'If,' says Tertullian, 'the Tiber floods the city, or the Nile refuses to rise, or the sky withholds its rain, or disasters occur in the shape of earthquake or famine or pestilence, the cry is raised at once "Christianos ad leones."'[2]

Had the imperial policy worked with the popular hatred instead of checking it, the systematic persecution of the third century would have been anticipated in the first and second; the whole tone of the Apologists of the second century would have been too absolutely out of harmony with the facts of the situation, and the statement of Origen[3]—a statement the

[1] The resemblance, such as it is, to Mommsen's language in the *Expositor*, p. 2, is accidental. 'The conviction that the Christian conventicles were orgies of lewdness and receptacles of every crime got hold on the popular mind with all the terrible vehemence of aversion that resists all argument and heeds not refutation.'

[2] Tertull. *Apol.* 40.

[3] Orig. *contra Celsum*, iii. 8: ὑπομνήσεως χάριν . . . ὀλίγοι κατὰ καιροὺς καὶ σφόδρα εὐαρίθμητοι ὑπὲρ τῆς Χριστιανῶν εὐσεβείας τεθνήκασι. No doubt the number of those punished short of death may have been greater; cf. Tert. *Apol.* 12: 'In metalla damnamur... in insulas relegamur.'

importance of which, it seems to me, it is impossible to explain away—that the victims up to his own time were few and far between, could not have been made.

It has been already said that the importance of Trajan's rescript may easily be exaggerated. It was originally a rescript to the particular governor of a particular province, and as such had directly no wider application,[1] though we cannot doubt that the course which Trajan recommended in Bithynia he would also wish to be pursued in other provinces. In all probability, indeed, Pliny was not the only governor who consulted Trajan on the subject: the collection and publication of Pliny's letters has preserved this particular rescript, which may well have been only one among many, just as the persecution in Bithynia almost certainly had its counterpart in other provinces.

To speak of Trajan's letter, therefore, as an edict either of proscription or toleration is a complete misconception of the facts. Undoubtedly, however, though a recommendation given under particular circumstances, it may safely be regarded as an index of the imperial policy.

Before passing from this correspondence, one or two smaller points must be noticed. In a former publication I expressed the view that Pliny punished

[1] Professor Mayor makes the somewhat astonishing assertion that 'the *corpus iuris* and Haenel's collection have no meaning except by virtue of the supposition' that rescripts to particular governors had a general application throughout the empire. See *Class. Rev.* iv. 120 *ad fin.*

the Christians as members of a *collegium illicitum*.[1] The bearing of the law regarding *collegia* upon the Christian communities will need some discussion further on, but I am certainly convinced that Professor Ramsay is right in denying all connexion between the application either of the general law about *collegia*, or Pliny's edict about *hetaeriae* and the prosecution of the Bithynian Christians. Pliny would have enforced his own edict without any need to consult the emperor, and Trajan would certainly have shown no forbearance, toleration, or indulgence to the Christians if he had regarded them as members of a *collegium* or *hetaeria*.

Another point regards the source from which the original charges before Pliny's tribunal and the subsequent anonymous accusation-list proceeded. The latter in particular points to some special and personal motives of malevolence and ill-will. A possible explanation of this is suggested by the last paragraph of Pliny's letter, when he says that already as the result of the measures he had taken, the temples hitherto deserted were again becoming visited by worshippers, ceremonies long since discontinued were resumed, and the fodder of the sacrificial victims was once more finding purchasers. Here, as at Ephesus, special trades depended on the local cults: Christianity threatened and injured these by diminishing the number of their worshippers, and this special cause of hatred added to the general ill-odour in which the Christians everywhere stood—an ill-

[1] *Pliny's Correspondence with Trajan*, pp. 61, 243.

odour which, Mommsen has pointed out, was partly an inheritance from their original Jewish antecedents—caused one of those temporary manifestations of popular feeling which were usually the cause of any decided or severe action on the part of the governors.

VII

PERSECUTION FOR THE NAME

It appears conclusively, both from the letter of Pliny and the rescript of Trajan, that the Christians could be punished for the *nomen* alone, or the mere profession of Christianity, apart from the specification or proof of definite crimes. Professor Ramsay thinks that this was the case only from about 80 A.D. To me it seems that it might have happened at any time since 64 A.D., and since writing the preceding pages I have seen that Mommsen and Professor Sanday both take the same view.[1] Professor Ramsay, as I understand, proposes to show from the Pastoral Epistles, assumed as belonging to a date earlier than 80 A.D., that the Christians were before that time condemned on the ground of specific charges.[2] Surely this, even granting the early date of the Epistles, will be far from conclusive of the question. If the whole matter was one for the police administration of the empire, the proceedings in particular cases would be essentially vague, and would

---

[1] Mommsen in the *Expositor*, July 1893, pp. 5, 6; Prof. Sanday in the *Expositor* for June 1893.

[2] *Expositor*, July 1893, p. 31.

admit of many variations from and modifications of anything like an established precedent. The Neronian trials at Rome no doubt furnished such a precedent, and in them, while probably several specific charges came into consideration, the condemnation was not on the ground of any of them, but of a summary of them all amounting to 'odium generis humani:' in other words, the Christians were condemned for what was involved in the name or profession of their sect. Provincial governors could take the same course, and no doubt some of them did, 1 Peter, if we assume its early date, being evidence for it.[1] But, on the other hand, it was quite within their discretion to inquire into and punish specific charges, and in the early days, when Christianity was still a strange and unfamiliar appearance, they would be likely to do this, and any cases which Professor Ramsay may adduce out of the Pastoral Epistles would belong to this category. Indeed, this uncertainty of procedure, though more likely to occur in the early relations between government and Christianity, was apparently a characteristic of it all through. Tertullian complains that the whole matter was 'confessio nominis non examinatio criminis,'[2] and yet he also says 'sacrilegii et maiestatis rei convenimur,'[3] and *maiestas* was surely as specific a charge as could be made.

But the language of Tertullian suggests a more important question than that of the precise date at which the 'nomen ipsum' became punishable—a

---

[1] Especially 1 Peter iv. 15, quoted on p. 80.
[2] Tert. *Apol.* 2. [3] *Ibid.* 10.

question which, as far as I can judge, Mommsen's utterances both in the 'Historische Zeitschrift' and in the 'Expositor' still leave a little uncertain—viz. whether those who were punished as 'rei maiestatis' were or were not punished for the name. To all appearance Mommsen answers this question in the affirmative. In the earlier article, after speaking of the conception of the Christian belief as in itself a capital crime, and quoting such well-known passages as 1 Peter iv. 15, and Just. 'Apol.' i. 11 in support of it, he goes on to say that this conception could not have depended on the edict of this or that particular emperor, but must have been grounded in the essence of the Roman criminal law, and we can see from Tertullian—*i.e.* in the passage about *maiestas*—how it was juristically to be explained.[1] Still more plainly in the 'Expositor:'[2] 'The Christian atheism, the negation of the national gods, was the contempt of the " dii publici populi Romani," in itself high treason, or, as the Christians express it ... the mere Christian name, the testimony of such atheism, constituted a crime in the eyes of the law.' It seems to follow from this that when Christians were condemned as Christians διὰ τὸ ὄνομα, on account of the 'nomen ipsum,' they were punished as 'rei maiestatis.' If Mommsen affirms this, that the mere confession 'Christianus sum' was tantamount to a conviction under the 'lex majestatis,' I do not know who could venture to contradict him; but one would have supposed that no one

---

[1] *Histor. Zeitschr.* p. 396.   [2] July 1893,

could be convicted of a definite legal offence like *maiestas* without regular procedure and definite evidence, the absence of which is just what Tertullian and others complain of in the ordinary Christian trials. Again it is just the absence of these points which characterises what Mommsen in the 'Historische Zeitschrift'[1] describes as by far the most common form of state repression in religious matters, the magisterial *coercitio* or general police administration. From this a considerable discretionary power on the part of the magistrate was inseparable, and as soon as ever Christianity was recognised as involving something less than absolute obedience to the state, it is quite conceivable—and the procedure of Pliny is a conclusive case in point—that the confession 'Christianus sum,' if persisted in, could be followed by a capital sentence. It is possible that I have misunderstood Mommsen's meaning, and found a difficulty where none exists, but at any rate it seems to me that there were at least three, and possibly four, ways in which Christianity might be visited with capital punishment:

(1) On the ground of the *obstinatio* which characterised all Christians as such: the refusal to worship the state gods, the disobedience to the state authority. This rendered all Christians outlaws—'hostes publici'—liable to summary punishment at the hands of the police authorities, either in Rome or the provinces. This was punishment for the name only, and under

[1] pp. 410 foll

this head by far the majority of cases of persecution fell.¹

(2) The refusal to worship the state gods, which from the first point of view was *obstinatio*, from another was ἀθεότης, and this, involving as it did contempt for the 'dii publici populi Romani,' though apparently not originally falling under it, could be, and in some cases certainly was, brought under the head of *maiestas*. This is the 'crimen laesae Romanae religionis,' the 'irreligiositatis elogium' of Tertullian,² and it is quite possible that recourse was had to this more formal procedure oftener in Tertullian's time than in Pliny's, and in the western more than in the eastern provinces.

(3) The refusal to worship the emperor might be taken, not simply as a proof of Christianity, as in the Bithynian cases, but as violating the *maiestas* of the emperor. That is what Tertullian describes as 'secundus titulus laesae augustioris maiestatis.'³

(4) The Christians might in certain cases be proceeded against as homicides, or *incesti*, or magicians. Those cases, however, would certainly be rare, such charges being usually rather thrown in informally to create a prejudice against the Christians than put forward as substantial accusations.⁴

---

¹ It was, beyond controversy, under this head that the action of Pliny would fall.

² Mommsen, *Hist. Zeitschr.* p. 396; Tert. *Apol.* 24.

³ Tert. *Apol.* 28 and 10 : ' Deos, inquitis, non colitis, et pro imperatoribus sacrificia non impenditis.'

⁴ Tert. *Apol.* 2 : ' Quando si de aliquo nocente cognoscitis non statim confesso eo nomen homicidae vel sacrilegi vel incesti vel

If the rescript of Trajan is not important as laying down a new or imperial policy with regard to the Christians, it nevertheless furnishes us with the first authentic evidence as to the view taken of Christianity by the supreme government. Trajan clearly did not regard the religion as a political danger within the range of practical politics: he does not forbid prosecution—he, in fact, in certain cases authorises it—but he evidently wishes to confine it within the narrowest limits consistent with the peace of the province, the governor undoubtedly having a very great discretionary power allowed him, since he could always invite accusations, though he could not initiate them. Eusebius seems very correctly to sum up the situation when he says [1] that those who wished to injure the Christians had no more difficulty in finding excuses than before; that sometimes the populace, sometimes particular governors, contrived means of attacking them, though these attacks were always partial, confined to particular provinces, and not open and public prosecutions. There seems good

---

publici hostis (ut de nostris elogiis loquar) contenti sitis ad pronuntiandum, nisi et consequentia exigatis.' Cf. c. 4: 'Incestus sum, cur non requirunt? infanticida, cur non extorquent? in deos, in Caesares aliquid committo, cur non audior, qui habeo quo purger?' Cf. Athenag. *Supplic.* 3 : τρία ἐπιφημίζουσιν ἡμῖν ἐγκλήματα, ἀθεότητα, Θυέστεια δεῖπνα, Οἰδιποδείους μίξεις.

[1] Euseb. *H. E.* iii. 33 : οὐ γενομένου ποσῶς μὲν τοῦ διωγμοῦ σβεσθῆναι τὴν ἀπειλὴν σφοδρότατα ἐγκειμένου, οὐ χείρονάς γε μὴν τοῖς κακουργεῖν περὶ ἡμᾶς ἐθέλουσι λείπεσθαι προφάσεις, ἔσθ' ὅπῃ μὲν τῶν δήμων, ἔσθ' ὅπῃ δὲ καὶ τῶν κατὰ χώρας ἀρχόντων τὰς καθ' ἡμῶν συσκευαζομένων ἐπιβουλὰς, ὡς καὶ ἄνευ προφανῶν διωγμῶν μερικῶς κατ' ἐπαρχίαν ἐξάπτεσθαι.

reason to suppose that this state of things—a general indulgence and toleration on the part of the emperors, occasionally interrupted by violent manifestations of popular feeling, which provincial governors had either not the will or not the strength to resist—continued throughout the second century: that the Christians were still punished for the name, but that the initiative in the way of searching them out was not taken by the governors, while accusers had to come forward in their own name; and finally, that the number of victims was on the whole a comparatively small one. It must be admitted that the evidence for this state of things comes for the most part from the Christian Apologists: from Justin Martyr, from Melito, from Athenagoras, from Minucius Felix, and especially from Tertullian. It cannot be denied that there were to a certain extent two streams of tradition in the early Church, one exoteric, the other esoteric.[1] In the latter the standing opposition between the Church and the world tends to be represented as a practically standing persecution of the Church by the state. This was not altogether an unnatural view, and, as we have seen, was not without some elements of historic truth—elements which, fused with much later tradition, nevertheless form some groundwork for the criticism of the 'Acta Martyrum.' On the other hand, the Apologists were men of culture and education above the majority of Christians: they were to some extent scholars and philosophers, students of history, acquainted, some of them, even

[1] Overbeck, *Studien zur Geschichte der alten Kirche.*

with the principles of Roman law.¹ Their Apologies were intended, not for their fellow-Christians, but to reach the ears of the Roman government. It is therefore impossible to suppose that the representation which they give of the state of affairs is entirely unhistorical, or that they could possibly describe the emperors of the second century, their own contemporaries, as tolerant and indulgent, if in reality they were the authors and promoters of a definite policy of persecution. But while the general *bona fides* of Apologists must thus be admitted, it is none the less true that the tradition to which their writings gave rise was from its very nature an exoteric one. It was to the interest of Christianity, of which they stood forward as the Apologists, to accentuate and in a measure to exaggerate the indulgent attitude of the government, especially in the period preceding their own, or at any rate to omit anything unfavourable to their own cause. Thus Justin draws attention to the favourable rescript of Hadrian,² but says nothing of the isolated cases of persecution, such as that of Telesphorus at Rome, which undoubtedly took place under that capricious emperor. Melito, while mentioning the same rescript of Hadrian,³ and some letters written to various cities by Antoninus Pius forbidding any violent or riotous behaviour against the Christians,⁴ makes no mention of the martyrdom of

¹ Thus Eusebius (*H. E.* ii. 2) says of Tertullian: τοὺς 'Ρωμαίων νόμους ἠκριβωκὼς ἀνήρ.
² Justin. *Apol.* i. 68.   ³ Quoted in Euseb. *H. E.* iv. 26, 10.
⁴ *Ibid. loc. cit.*: ὁ δὲ πατήρ σου, καὶ σοῦ τὰ σύμπαντα διοικοῦντος αὐτῷ, ταῖς πόλεσι περὶ τοῦ μηδὲν νεωτερίζειν περὶ ἡμῶν ἔγραψεν, ἐν οἷς καὶ

Polycarp; while Tertullian considers M. Aurelius as a protector rather than otherwise of Christianity [1]— a view, as Mommsen points out, not without some historical foundation [2]—while making no reference to the severe and widespread persecution which took place in his reign. Taking, therefore, the evidence of the Apologists, and remembering that antecedent and *a priori* objections to it are to a very great extent removed by the undisputed evidence afforded by the rescript of Trajan, we may regard the following points as established.

(1) The Christians subsequently to as before the rescript of Trajan were punished generally for the name, *i.e.* not on the technical ground of *maiestas* (though this may have been the charge in particular cases, especially since the rescript of Hadrian), but for the inherent disloyalty to the state involved in their ἀθεότης, and manifested in the *obstinatio* with which they clung to it. The following passages, among many others, are sufficient to establish this. Justin says: ἐφ' ἡμῶν δὲ τὸ ὄνομα ὡς ἔλεγχον λαμβάνετε . . . Χριστιανοὶ γὰρ εἶναι κατηγορούμεθα . . . ἐὰν δέ τις ὁμολογήσῃ εἶναι, διὰ τὴν ὁμολογίαν κολάζετε: [3] and again, ὡς καὶ ἐκ τοῦ ἀνεταζομένους

πρὸς Λαρισσαίους καὶ πρὸς Θεσσαλονικεῖς καὶ 'Αθηναίους καὶ πρὸς πάντας Ἕλληνας.

[1] Tert. *Apol.* 5 : 'Ceterum de tot exinde principibus usque ad hodiernum divinum humanumque sapientibus, edite aliquem debellatorem Christianorum. At nos e contrario edimus protectorem si litterae M. Aurelii gravissimi imperatoris requirantur,' etc.

[2] *Histor. Zeitschr.* p. 400, note 3.

[3] Justin. *Apol.* i. 4.

ὑφ' ὑμῶν ὁμολογεῖν εἶναι Χριστιανοὺς, γιγνώσκοντες τῷ ὁμολογοῦντι θάνατον τὴν ζημίαν κεῖσθαι:[1] and once more, καίπερ θανάτου ὁρισθέντος κατὰ τῶν διδασκόντων ἢ ὅλως ὁμολογούντων τὸ ὄνομα τοῦ Χριστοῦ.[2] Similarly, in the account of the trial of Ptolemaeus, at Rome:[3] Τελευταῖον δὲ ὅτε ἐπὶ Οὔρβικον ἦλθεν ὁ ἄνθρωπος ὁμοίως αὐτὸ τοῦτο μόνον ἐξητάσθη εἰ εἴη Χριστιανός . . . καὶ τοῦ Οὐρβίκου κελεύσαντος αὐτὸν ἀπαχθῆναι Λούκιός τις καὶ αὐτὸς ὢν Χριστιανὸς ὁρῶν τὴν ἀλόγως οὕτως γινομένην κρίσιν πρὸς τὸν Οὔρβικον ἔφη Τίς ἡ αἰτία; . . . ὀνόματος Χριστιανοῦ προσωνυμίαν ὁμολογοῦντα τὸν ἄνθρωπον τοῦτον ἐκολάσω. In the same way Tertullian says, 'illud solum expectatur . . . confessio nominis non examinatio criminis:'[4] and 'non scelus aliquod in causa esse sed nomen . . . ut nomen . . . de sua sola confessione damnetur . . . Christianus si nullius criminis reus est, nomen valde infestum, si solum nominis crimen est.'[5]

(2) Recantation was followed by pardon. Thus

[1] Justin. *Apol.* i. 11. [2] *Ibid.* i. 45.
[3] *Ibid.* ii. 2. He expressly says, ii. 1, that this procedure was universal: τὰ πανταχοῦ ὁμοίως ὑπὸ τῶν ἡγουμένων ἀλόγως πραττόμενα.
[4] Tert. *Apol.* 2.
[5] *Ibid.* 2 ad fin. Cf. also Hermas, *Simil.* 9, 28: ὅσοι ποτὲ ἔπαθον διὰ τὸ ὄνομα ἔνδοξοί εἰσι παρὰ τῷ θεῷ . . . ὅτι ἔπαθον διὰ τὸ ὄνομα τοῦ υἱοῦ τοῦ θεοῦ . . . ὅσοι . . . ἐπ' ἐξουσίαν ἀχθέντες ἐξετάσθησαν καὶ οὐκ ἠρνήσαντο κ. τ. λ. Athenagoras, ii. 3: καὶ γὰρ οὐ πρὸς τῆς ὑμετέρας δικαιοσύνης τοὺς μὲν ἄλλους, αἰτίαν λαβόντας ἀδικημάτων μὴ πρότερον ἢ ἐλεγχθῆναι κολάζεσθαι, ἐφ' ἡμῶν δὲ μεῖζον ἰσχύειν τὸ ὄνομα τῶν ἐπὶ τῇ δίκῃ ἐλέγχων. Tert. *Apol.* 2: 'Denique quid de tabella recitatis illum Christianum, cur non et homicidam?' 44: 'Aut cum Christiani suo titulo offeruntur.'

Justin says : [1] ἐὰν μέν τις τῶν κατηγορουμένων ἔξαρνος γένηται, τῇ φωνῇ μὴ εἶναι φήσας, ἀφίετε αὐτὸν, ὡς μηδὲν ἐλέγχειν ἔχοντες ἁμαρτάνοντα. In the persecution at Lugdunum under M. Aurelius, perhaps in consequence of the incriminating evidence of slaves with regard to the Θυέστεια δεῖπνα and Οἰδιπόδειοι μίξεις, the governor took a different course, and those who denied their religion were shut up in prison.[2] This action, however, was due to the arbitrary conduct of an unusually hostile governor, and was not sanctioned by the emperor, whose rescript was to the effect that those who persisted were to be put to death, while those who recanted should be released.[3] In most cases, indeed, the governors were not only willing but anxious to avoid harsh measures against the Christians by obtaining a recantation from them. We have already seen that by Pliny's time the custom had grown up of giving the Christians three chances of abjuring their religion before executing punishment, and this before long developed into the regular practice of torturing the accused in order to force from them, not the confession of their religion, but the denial of it. 'Ceteris negantibus,' says Tertullian, 'adhibetis tormenta ad confitendum, solis

[1] Justin. *Apol.* i. 4. Cf. Orig. *Contra Cels.* ii. 13 : Χριστιανοὶ δὲ μόνοι μέχρι τελευταίας ἀναπνοῆς ὑπὸ τῶν δικαστῶν ἐπιτρέπονται ἐξομοσάμενοι τὸν Χριστιανισμὸν καὶ κατὰ τὰ κοινὰ ἔθη θύσαντες καὶ ὀμόσαντες οἴκοι γενέσθαι καὶ ζῆν ἀκινδύνως.
[2] Euseb. *H. E.* v. 1, 33 : οἱ γὰρ κατὰ τὴν πρώτην σύλληψιν ἔξαρνοι γενόμενοι συνεκλείοντο καὶ αὐτοὶ καὶ μετεῖχον τῶν δεινῶν, οὐδὲ γὰρ ἐν τῷ καιρῷ τούτῳ ὄφελός τι αὐτοῖς ἡ ἐξάρνησις ἐγίνετο.
[3] *Ibid.* v. 1, 47 : ἐπιστείλαντος γὰρ τοῦ Καίσαρος τοὺς μὲν ἀποτυμπανισθῆναι, εἰ δέ τινες ἀρνοῖντο, τούτους ἀπολυθῆναι.

Christianis ad negandum.'[1] In all probability the practice was originally a rough and ready means of saving the Christians from the results of their own obstinacy, and Tertullian tells us of a Cincius Severus who 'ipse dedit remedium quomodo responderent Christiani ut dimitti possent.'[2] But under tyrannical governors it might easily be turned into the means of gratuitous and abominable cruelties,[3] as in the case of the martyrs at Lugdunum—cruelties which have been perpetuated with all the ingenuity of pious invention in the 'Acta Martyrum.' The fact that a mere lip-denial, whether voluntary or enforced by means of torture, was for the most part during the second century followed by liberation and pardon is a clear proof, if one were wanted, that the contest between Christianity and the state was far from having become at this period an internecine struggle, since the possibility that one 'compulsus negare non

---

[1] Tert. *Apol.* 2; Cf. *ad Scap.* 4: 'Quid enim amplius tibi mandatur quam nocentes confessos damnare, negantes autem ad tormenta revocare? Videtis ergo quomodo ipsi vos contra mandata faciatis ut confessos negare cogatis. Adeo confitemini innocentes esse nos, quos damnare statim ex confessione non vultis.'

[2] Tert. *ad Scap.* 4: 'Quanti autem praesides et constantiores et crudeliores dissimulaverunt ab huiusmodi causis: ut Cincius Severus qui Thistri ipse dedit remedium quomodo responderent Christiani ut dimitti possent : ut Vespronius Candidus qui Christianum quasi tumultuosum civibus suis satisfacere dimisit,' etc.

[3] *Ibid. loc. cit.*: 'Claudius Herminianus Cappadocia cum ... Christianos crudeliter tractasset ... postea cognito errore suo quod tormentis quosdam a proposito suo excidere fecisset, pene Christianus decessit.' Cf. Justin, *Dial. c. Tryph.* 110 : κεφαλοτομούμενοι γὰρ καὶ σταυρούμενοι καὶ θηρίοις παραβαλλόμενοι καὶ δεσμοῖς καὶ πυρὶ καὶ πάσαις ταῖς ἄλλαις βασάνοις ὅτι οὐκ ἀφιστάμεθα τῆς ὁμολογίας.

ex fide negarit et absolutus ibidem post tribunal de vestra rideat aemulatione, iterum Christianus,' must have been as obvious to the government as to Tertullian, who describes the practice as a 'praevaricatio in leges.'[1]

(3) The Christians were apparently, in conformity with Trajan's recommendation, not sought out. This is, indeed, rather a general inference from the reluctance of the provincial governors to deal harshly with the Christians, as evidenced in instances given by Tertullian, and in many of the 'Acta Martyrum' themselves,[2] and also from the comparatively small number of victims to the state persecution as evidenced by Origen.[3] This was necessarily a point as to which the governors had a certain amount of discretion. The *legatus* of Gallia Lugdunensis apparently gave orders for the Christians to be sought out,[4] though the very statement seems to imply that this was an unusual proceeding. It was, however, by no means without parallel, as the words of Celsus prove: ὑμῶν δὲ κἂν πλανᾶταί τις ἔτι λανθάνων ἀλλὰ ζητεῖται πρὸς θανάτου δίκην.[5] On the other hand, Pudens (probably a governor of Crete under M. Aurelius[6]), on discovering that a certain Christian

[1] Tert. *Apol.* 2.
[2] See the *Acta Martyrum Scilitanorum*: ἐπεὶ καὶ χαρισθείσης αὐτοῖς προθεσμίας τοῦ πρὸς τὴν τῶν Ῥωμαίων ἐπανέλθειν παράδοσιν ἀκλινεῖς τὴν γνώμην διέμειναν κ. τ. λ.
[3] See p. 121, note 3.
[4] Euseb. *H. E.* v. 1, 14: ἐπεὶ δημοσίᾳ ἐκέλευσεν ὁ ἡγεμὼν ἀναζητεῖσθαι πάντας ἡμᾶς.
[5] Orig. *Contra Cels.* viii. 69.
[6] He was formerly held to be a proconsul of Africa under Com-

who was sent to him was really the victim of a conspiracy to extort money, tore up the *elogium*, as the charge-sheet was technically called, and then dismissed the prisoner 'sine accusatore negans se auditurum secundum mandatum.'[1]

(4) The prosecutions were in the provinces generally due to the hatred and violence of the populace, or to the antipathy of some particular class among them. Of this there seems to be no doubt. The Bithynian persecution may probably, as we have seen, have been due to commercial losses caused by the Christians. Hadrian's rescript [2] distinctly implies that the governors often gave way to popular clamour. The letters of Antoninus Pius to the cities in Greece [3] distinctly forbid rioting against the Christians. The letter written by the Church at Lugdunum to those in Asia or Phrygia clearly attributes the commencement of the persecution there to the clamours, outrages, and attacks of the infuriated populace,[4] while Eusebius states that the persecutions

---

modus or Septimius Severus, but our only authentic knowledge of him is from an inscription, *C. I. L.* viii. 5354, where he is proconsul of Crete and Cyrene, a praetorian post, and therefore earlier than his consulship in 166 A.D. See Neumann, page 33, note 1.

[1] Tert. *ad Scap.* 4: 'Pudens etiam missum ad se Christianum cum elogio, concussione eius intellecta dimisit scisso eodem elogio, sine accusatore negans se auditurum secundum mandatum.'

[2] See below, p. 141, note 1.

[3] See p. 132, note 4.

[4] Euseb. *H. E.* v. 1, 7: καὶ πρῶτον μὲν τὰ ἀπὸ τοῦ ὄχλου πανδημεὶ σωρηδὸν ἐπιφερόμενα γενναίως ὑπέμενον, ἐπιβοήσεις καὶ πληγὰς καὶ συρμοὺς καὶ διαρπαγὰς καὶ λίθων βολὰς καὶ συγκλείσεις καὶ πάνθ' ὅσα ἠγριωμένῳ πλήθει ὡς πρὸς ἐχθροὺς καὶ πολεμίους φιλεῖ γένεσθαι.

of this time resulted ἐξ ἐπιθέσεως τῶν κατὰ πόλεις δήμων.[1] Similarly in the 'Acta' of Polycarp the proconsul urges the martyr, 'Satisfac populo.'[2] 'Quotiens etiam,' asks Tertullian, 'praeteritis vobis suo iure nos inimicum vulgus invadit lapidibus et incendiis?'[3] and, again, 'Nec ulli magis depostulatores Christianorum quam vulgus,'[4] and still more definitely, 'De qua iniquitate saevitiae non modo caecum hoc vulgus exsultat et insultat, sed et quidam vestrum, quibus favor vulgi de iniquitate captatur, gloriantur.'[5] Tertullian's evidence on this point is, indeed, summed up in his address to the provincial governors as 'boni praesides, meliores multo apud populum si illis Christianos immolaveritis.'[6]

(5) The emperors themselves, when appealed to by the governors, were more inclined to check than to encourage persecution, though their policy in this was purely utilitarian, based on no sort of approval of or sympathy with the Christians, to whose execution they assented without scruple whenever the

---

[1] Euseb. *H. E.* v. 5, *prooem.* 1.
[2] *Acta Polycarpi*, Ruinart, p. 31. Cf. Euseb. *H. E.* iv. 15, 6: τὸ πᾶν πλῆθος ἀποθαύμασαν τῆς ἀνδρείας τὸν θεοφιλῆ μαρτύρα καὶ τὴν καθόλου τοῦ γένους τῶν Χριστιανῶν ἀρετὴν ἀθρόως ἐπιβοᾶν ἤρξασθαι ' αἶρε τοὺς ἀθέους ;' and 26 : πᾶν τὸ πλῆθος τῶν ἐθνῶν τε καὶ Ἰουδαίων πρὸς τὴν Σμύρναν κατοικούντων ... μεγάλῃ φωνῇ ἐβόα ... οὗτός ἐστιν ὁ τῆς Ἀσίας διδάσκαλος, ὁ πατὴρ τῶν Χριστιανῶν, ὁ τῶν ἡμετέρων θεῶν καθαιρέτης.
[3] Tert. *Apol.* 37.
[4] *Ibid.* 35.
[5] *Ibid.* 49. Cf. Justin. *Apol.* ii. 3, who says that Crescens, the philosopher, accused the Christians as ἄθεοι καὶ ἀσεβεῖς ... πρὸς χάριν καὶ ἡδόνην τῶν πολλῶν τῶν πεπλανημένων ταῦτα πράττων.
[6] Tert. *Apol.* 50.

advantages of such a course seemed to preponderate, but simply on the supposition that the Christians were harmless and somewhat contemptible enthusiasts, of whose *obstinatio* it was hardly worth while to take notice, while the disturbances caused by popular outbreaks against them were not consistent with the good order of the empire.

VIII

ATTITUDE OF HADRIAN, PIUS, AND MARCUS AURELIUS

THIS certainly seems to have been the attitude of Hadrian in his rescript to Minucius Fundanus, proconsul of Asia, in about 124 A.D., the full text of which I append below in a note.[1] Asia was undoubtedly the province in which the Christian difficulty was most urgent and most persistent. Here

---

[1] The rescript is found in Greek appended to Justin's *First Apology*, and in Eusebius *H. E.* iv. 9, and in Latin in Rufinus' translation of Eusebius. As Eusebius expressly states that Justin gives the Latin version (*H. E.* iii. 8, 7), Bishop Lightfoot, with much probability, supposes that Rufinus did not translate it into Latin but substituted the original rescript.

'Accepi literas ad me scriptas a decessore tuo, Sereno Graniano, clarissimo viro, et non placet mihi relationem silentio praeterire, ne et innoxii perturbentur, et calumniatoribus latrocinandi tribuatur occasio. Itaque si evidenter provinciales huic petitioni suae adesse volent adversum Christianos, ut pro tribunali eos in aliquo arguant, hoc eis exequi non prohibeo: precibus autem in hoc solis et adclamationibus uti eis non permitto. Etenim multo aequius est, si quis volet accusare, te cognoscere de obiectis. Si quis igitur accusat et probat, adversus legem quicquam agere memoratos homines pro merito peccatorum etiam supplicia statues. Illud mehercule magnopere curabis ut si quis calumniae gratia quemquam horum postulaverit reum, in hunc pro sui nequitia suppliciis severioribus vindices.'

probably the Christians were most numerous, the populace most hostile, and accusers most plentiful; here, too, all the social conditions most repugnant to and most impatient of Christian ideas of morality were most pronounced and most deeply rooted. Here certainly, sometimes in one city, sometimes in another, persecution must have been almost continuous and permanent. The proconsuls may have observed, and probably they did so, the principle of Trajan, not to search out offenders, but this in a province so full of sycophants, sophists, and *delatores*, was but scant protection.[1] And not only were real Christians brought before the tribunal of the proconsul. In a case where so little had to be substantiated, where the mere 'nomen Christiani' was the gist, nay the whole, of the charge, there was every inducement to make a trade of this sort of delation, to accuse or to threaten with accusation those who were not Christians, and then to exact money for letting proceedings drop. That non-Christians were sometimes accused we know from Pliny's letter; that attempts to extort money were sometimes made we know from a case already alluded to as mentioned by Tertullian.[2] But clearly such unprincipled conduct, besides running counter to the spirit of the times, destroyed whatever value there was in the police repression of Christianity, and introduced a spirit of terrorism into the province. It was, I conceive, in some such circumstances as these, that Licinius Silvanus Granianus, the proconsul, con-

---

[1] Mommsen, *Röm. Gesch.* v. 333 foll.
[2] See p. 138, note 1.

sulted Hadrian, who sent the well-known rescript, for the genuineness of which Mommsen has authoritatively pronounced, to his successor, Minucius Fundanus.[1] The general object of the rescript is clearly enough stated at the outset, 'ne et innoxii perturbentur, et calumniatoribus latrocinandi tribuatur occasio.' To prevent this, the emperor lays it down that accusers are not to be allowed to make use of any mob-influence against the Christians, and that they must do more than prove the 'nomen Christiani'—they must prove that the accused have acted against the law : ' si quis igitur accusat et probat, adversus legem quicquid agere memoratos homines, pro merito peccatorum etiam supplicia statues ; ' while, finally, accusers who failed to make good their charges were to be themselves severely punished. It seems to me that this rescript was intended, as indeed it naturally would be, for the special circumstances of Asia : it does not in any way, as I interpret it, rescind the decision of Trajan that the 'nomen' was a crime, but to avoid any miscarriage of justice, such as, with a summary procedure, a large number of accused, a hostile pressure exercised by the mob, might very easily occur, it lays down more stringent conditions for the proof of punishable crime. It is possible, as Professor Ramsay says,[2] that there is a studied vagueness in this rescript.

[1] Licinius Silvanus Granianus was consul in 106 A.D., C. Minucius Fundanus in 107 A.D. (Klein, *Fasti Consulares*, p. 56), and according to Waddington (*Fastes Asiatiques*, p. 197 sq.) they would naturally have reached the proconsulship of Asia about 123-4 and 124-5 respectively.

[2] p. 323.

I doubt whether this would be reflected in the actions depending on it.[1] The ἀθεότης of the Christians as well as their refusal to worship the emperor could, as has already been shown, be brought under the law of *maiestas*, and it was no doubt to this procedure, in which more definite proof was required and a stricter investigation pursued, that Hadrian's rescript pointed. Though intended primarily for Asia, it may quite possibly have had some influence on the governors of other provinces. It was of course always possible for the Christians to be accused and convicted of *maiestas*. Justin Martyr affirms that they were accused as ἄθεοι and ἀσεβεῖs,[2] and Tertullian in a passage already referred to speaks of them as 'rei maiestatis.' Punishment for the name only, as there is abundant evidence to show, was executed after Hadrian's rescript just as much as before, but it is quite possible that it gave a certain stimulus towards the employment of the more definite and regular legal procedure.[3]

---

[1] The suspicions cast upon this rescript by Keim (*Rom und das Christenthum*, p. 553), Overbeck (*Studien zur Geschichte der alten Kirche*, p. 134), Aubé (*Persécutions de l'Eglise*, p. 261), and Baur (*Die drei ersten Jahrhunderte*, p. 442) are met once for all by Mommsen, who declares that its 'grundlose Verdächtigung der beste Beweise ist wie wenig sich die Neueren in den Standpunkt der römischen Regierung dem Christenthum gegenüber zu finden vermögen.'

[2] Note that ἀσέβεια is technically *maiestas* and not *sacrilegium*.

[3] Hadrian's own liberalism and freedom from prejudice in religious matters are exemplified in the story told of him by Lampridius (*Vit. Alex. Sev.* 43): 'Christo templum facere voluit, eumque inter deos recipere, quod et Hadrianus cogitasse fertur, qui templa in omnibus civitatibus sine simulacris iusserat fieri quae hodieque

Under Antoninus Pius there is reason, as Bishop Lightfoot has shown,[1] to believe that there was by no means that complete peace to the Church which Sulpicius Severus ascribes to his reign,[2] and the cases of Ptolemaeus and Lucius, executed at Rome by the *praefectus urbi*, Lollius Urbicus, cannot have been unknown to the emperor,[3] while the martyrdom of Polycarp at Smyrna is proved by the exhaustive arguments of M. Waddington to have belonged to this reign.[4] But if we are to believe the evidence of Melito, as quoted by Eusebius, he, like Hadrian, discouraged the riotous behaviour of the mob, sending letters to the authorities at Larissae, Thessalonica, and Athens, and to all the Hellenes (a term which is understood by Professor Ramsay as including Greek cities like Smyrna on the Aegean coast), forbidding any such conduct.[5]

With regard to M. Aurelius, the case is somewhat more doubtful, and he is usually considered a severe persecutor of the Christians, and, indeed, the contrast between his reign in this respect and that of his degenerate son and successor, Commodus, has partly

idcirco quia non habent numina dicuntur Hadriani, quae ille ad hoc parasse dicebatur: sed prohibitus est ab iis qui consulentes sacra reppererant omnes Christianos futuros si id fecisset et templa reliqua deserenda.' Tertullian calls him 'omnium curiositatum explorator,' *Apol.* 5 ; cf. Dio Cass. lxix. 5 and 11.

[1] Lightfoot, *Apostolic Fathers*, Part II. vol. i. p. 493.
[2] Sulp. Sev. *Chron.* ii. 31, 32.
[3] Justin, *Apol.* ii. 2.
[4] Waddington's arguments are summarised by Lightfoot, *Apostolic Fathers*, Part II. vol. i. p. 639 foll.
[5] See p. 132, note 4.

led to the general inference that the better the emperor, the greater his severity towards the Christians. It certainly cannot be denied that the Christians were persecuted, and with some severity, in several different parts of the empire during this reign, but I cannot think that there is any evidence which justifies Neumann [1] in ascribing to the emperor a new policy different from, and severer than, that of Trajan, or which can lead us to suppose that the persecutions, such as they were, arose from imperial initiative rather than from the general circumstances of the time and local conditions. In the first place, it must be remembered that as time went on, the practice increased among the Christians of recording the deaths or sufferings of their members—a practice which, when the Churches were less organised, and the consciousness of a common history less pronounced, had either not been commenced or was less completely carried out. Hence we should expect that, quite apart from the actual frequency of persecutions, the number of those recorded would tend to become greater. In the next place, we entirely fail in the records belonging to this reign to find evidence for anything like a general persecution. The evidence of Melito proves a certain amount of persecution in Asia; [2] the martyrdom of Justin shows that the Christians in Rome were still liable to be brought before the jurisdiction of the *praefectus urbi*, while it is known that a number of Christians from the city

---

[1] p. 28 foll.
[2] Euseb. *H. E.* iv. 26, 5.

or Italy were condemned to the mines of Sardinia.[1] The letter of the Churches of Lugdunum and Vienna to those in Asia and Phrygia[2] furnishes authentic evidence for a severe, though not widespread, persecution in Gaul; and, finally, the first Christian blood was shed in this reign in the province of Africa at Medaura,[3] while the martyrdoms at Scili, in the same province, though occurring a few months after the death of M. Aurelius, must still be virtually ascribed to his reign.[4]

What strikes us, however, most in this list, is neither the extent of the persecutions (which would surely have been much greater if they had resulted from any deliberate policy) nor the number of the victims (which even at Lugdunum apparently did not exceed forty-eight)[5] but rather the fact that instances of collision between Christianity and the government are now found in the Western as well as the Eastern provinces. This, however, would more naturally be ascribed to the recent growth of Christianity in those parts, and the consequent excitement of the populace against it, than to a new policy on the part of the government. As to the earliest rise of the religion in the Western provinces, we are unfortunately very

[1] Hippolyt. *Haer.* ix. 12: μετὰ χρόνον δὲ ἑτέρων ἐκεῖ ὄντων μαρτύρων, ἡ Μαρκία ... προσκαλεσαμένη τὸν μακάριον Οὐίκτορα ... ἠρώτα, τίνες εἶεν ἐν Σαρδονίᾳ μάρτυρες.

[2] Euseb. *H. E.* v. 1.

[3] Augustin. *Epist.* xv. and xvi. Cf. Tert. *ad Scap.* 3: 'Vigellius Saturninus qui primus hic gladium in nos egit.'

[4] The date is now fixed to the year 180 A.D. See Lightfoot, p. 508, and Neumann, p. 284.

[5] Gregory of Tours, *Glor. Mart.* 49.

imperfectly acquainted, but that Christianity could be described in Lugdunum as καινή τις θρησκεία[1] more than 100 years after the Neronian persecution in Rome seems to point either to a late introduction or to a late extension.

That there was, to a certain extent, under M. Aurelius, and not without his own approval and perhaps his own initiation, a reactionary tendency towards a stricter observance of the national religion in the face of desperate wars with barbarians, and the widespread horrors of a devastating pestilence, is no doubt true, and this might easily cause more frequent cases of collision in the provinces between either the populace or the governors on the one side and Christianity on the other. As Tertullian in a memorable passage points out, it was just such calamities which occasioned the unreasoning cry 'Christianos ad leones.'[2] But this fact by itself is far from constituting M. Aurelius as a persecutor of the Christians, and still further from assisting Neumann's theory that the persecution in his reign resulted from certain definite rescripts, primarily aimed at Christianity, and seriously modifying the general toleration of the previous reigns. Modestinus, no doubt, reports a rescript of the emperor :[3] 'Si quis aliquid fecerit quo leves hominum animi superstitione numinis terrentur, huiusmodi homines in insulam relegari;' while Paulus lays down the rule, 'qui novas sectas vel ratione incognitas religiones inducunt ex quibus animi

---

[1] Euseb. *H E.* v. 1 [2] Tertull. *Apol.* 40.
Dig. xlviii. 19, 30.

hominum moveantur, honestiores deportantur, humiliores capite puniuntur.'[1] To the effect of these rescripts, only the former of which has any direct connexion with M. Aurelius, Neumann ascribes the persecutions in this reign, and in particular that (of which we have the fullest information) at Lugdunum.[2] On several grounds this seems to be an entirely mistaken view. In the first case the rescript, as Mommsen points out, was merely the precise expression— called forth probably by some particular and local circumstances—of a duty imposed by self-defence upon every efficient government.[3] It had no direct reference to the Christians, though it might of course be applied to them if necessary, but its retention in the 'Digest' under the Christian emperors is a proof of its general and not particular application. Nor was there the slightest need of a rescript of this kind. If there was any reason to deal more severely with the Christians, there was a summary police jurisdiction which could at any moment be applied to them, by which the mere establishment of their Christianity could be followed by capital punishment. As Christians, they were in theory in the position of outlaws : it was only necessary to discard the somewhat illogical toleration which usually prevailed, and to bring practice into accord with theory, and a general persecution of the Christians as such was possible. To have punished them merely as the causes of public excitement, when they might have

[1] Paul. *Sent.* v. 21, 2.   [2] p. 29.
[3] *Hist. Zeitschr.* p. 400.

been treated as 'hostes publici,' would have been a step backward rather than forward.

Nor do the records which remain of the persecutions support Neumann's theory. No doubt at Lugdunum the immediate occasion of the persecution was an outbreak of popular hatred and fury; but we have seen reason to suppose that this, so far from being exceptional or needing the explanation of a special rescript, was what in the Eastern provinces had happened again and again, the reasons for the popular hatred, as well as its intensity, varying in different cases and localities. When the accused were brought before the legate, there was no question of particular charges; there was no accusation of ἀθεότης or ἀσέβεια, not a word to imply that the charge was disturbance of the public peace. In fact, no question was asked except whether they were Christians,[1] and the account says explicitly that no other charge was made against them.[2] Finally, the punishments inflicted on those condemned were not those specified in the rescript—*relegatio, deportatio*, or decapitation—but in the majority of cases exposure to wild beasts.[3] There seems, therefore, no reason to suppose that the persecutions at Lugdunum were due to any increased severity on the part of the central government. The

---

[1] Euseb. *H. E.* v. 1, 10: ἀλλὰ μόνον τοῦτο πυθομένου εἰ καὶ αὐτὸς εἴη Χριστιανός, τοῦ δὲ λαμπροτάτῃ φωνῇ ὁμολογήσαντος, ἀνελήφθη καὶ αὐτὸς εἰς τὸν κλῆρον τῶν μαρτύρων.

[2] Euseb. *H. E.* v. 1, 33: ἀλλ' οἱ μὲν ὁμολογοῦντες ὃ καὶ ἦσαν, συνεκλείοντο ὡς Χριστιανοί, μηδεμιᾶς ἄλλης αὐτοῖς αἰτίας ἐπιφερομένης.

[3] Euseb. *H. E.* v. 1, 47: καὶ ὅσοι μὲν ἐδόκουν πολιτείαν Ῥωμαίων ἐσχηκέναι τούτων ἀπέτεμνε τὰς κεφαλάς, τοὺς δὲ λοιποὺς ἔπεμπεν εἰς θηρία.

action of the legate in ordering all the Christians to be searched out was evidently taken on his own responsibility, while the further innovation of retaining in custody those who had seceded was due to the accusations of Θυέστεια δεῖπνα and Οἰδιπόδειοι μίξεις which were made by heathen slaves, and was disallowed by the emperor when his rescript came ordering εἴ τινες ἀρνοῖντο τούτους ἀπολυθῆναι.[1]

There is nothing, therefore, in the evidence to show that the persecution at Lugdunum was anything more than a repetition of that in Bithynia, the greater cruelty associated with it being due partly to the personal character of the legate, partly to the fact that our account of the one comes from a heathen, of the other from a Christian, source.

In the province of Asia there was, according to Melito, some fresh access of persecution under M. Aurelius, and he speaks of certain καινὰ δόγματα or διατάγματα in consequence of which through the action of συκοφάνται the godly race—τὸ τῶν θεοσεβῶν γένος—is persecuted.[2] What these καινὰ διατάγματα were it is quite impossible to say. It is certain from Melito's language that they were edicts of the proconsul; they may have been more stringent regulations about the imperial cult, or the observance of the national worship, but there is not the smallest evidence

[1] Euseb. *H. E.* 1, 47.
[2] Euseb. *H. E.* iv. 26, 5 : τὸ γὰρ οὐδὲ πώποτε γενόμενον, νῦν διώκεται τὸ τῶν θεοσεβῶν γένος καινοῖς ἐλαυνόμενον δόγμασι κατὰ τὴν Ἀσίαν. οἱ γὰρ ἀναιδεῖς συκοφάνται καὶ τῶν ἀλλοτρίων ἐρασταὶ τὴν ἐκ τῶν διαταγμάτων ἔχοντες ἀφορμὴν φανερῶς ληστεύουσι νύκτωρ καὶ μεθημέραν διαρπάζοντες τοὺς μηδὲν ἀδικοῦντας.

of any connexion with the rescript in the 'Digest,' but rather the contrary, for the rescript in question, though its application might be vexatious to the Christians, was certainly not cruel and could hardly have been described by Melito as ὁ μηδὲ κατὰ βαρβάρων πρέπει πολεμίων.[1] Professor Ramsay, while dissenting from Neumann's view as to a special rescript against the Christians, still thinks that ' new methods were introduced by M. Aurelius, at least in the sense that proceedings against the Christians were enforced more actively,'[2] by which he means that they were in this reign sought out even when no accusers came forward. I do not think that the documents relating to the time bear out this view. In Asia, Melito distinctly mentions συκοφάνται;[3] at Lugdunum, as we have seen, the legate orders all the Christians to be searched out, but it deserves notice that this is the second stage in the proceedings and not the first. The persecution commenced with the usual manifestations of popular feeling, and, there is no reason to doubt, with the usual accusations more or less definite; then the legate arrived, and apparently in consequence of the charges made ordered a general search for the Christians. If any previous rescript was disregarded, it was rather that

[1] Euseb. *H. E.* iv. 26, 6.   [2] p. 338.

[3] One of the passages usually quoted to prove that the Christians were sought out, really, if taken with the context, proves the contrary. Athenagoras, *Supplic.* i. 2, says: συγχωρεῖτε δὲ μηδὲν ἀδικοῦντας... ἐλαύνεσθαι καὶ φέρεσθαι καὶ διώκεσθαι ἐπὶ μόνῳ ὀνόματι προσπολεμούντων ἡμῖν τῶν πολλῶν : but here the quotation usually ends, but Athenagoras adds: καὶ δεούμεθα ὑμῶν καὶ περὶ ἡμῶν τι σκέψασθαι ὅπως παυσώμεθά ποτε ὑπὸ τῶν συκοφάντων σφαττόμενοι, which shows that accusations were made according to Trajan's rescript.

of Hadrian than that of Trajan, by which popular acclamations were forbidden to be taken as formal accusations. Another proof that in this reign the Christians were hunted out is often found in the statement of Celsus: ὑμῶν δὲ κἂν πλανᾶταί τις ἔτι λανθάνων ἀλλὰ ζητεῖται πρὸς θανάτου δίκην.[1] But in addition to the uncertainty as to the exact date of Celsus, the statement seems altogether too vague and too general to warrant the conclusion which Professor Ramsay draws from it. Finally with regard to the 'Acta Justini' (which, by the way, belong to quite the beginning of the reign, whereas the harsher policy of Aurelius is usually ascribed to the end of it), I cannot agree with Professor Ramsay that the implication is in favour of the criminals being searched out rather than accused. If the tradition mentioned by Eusebius is untrustworthy, that Justin's death was due to the accusation of Crescens the philosopher,[2] at least we should expect that any searching out of the Christians, especially in Rome, would have resulted in the death of more than one or two individuals.

It seems, therefore, that the prosecutions under M. Aurelius were essentially of the same description as those under his predecessors. He has no hesitation in ordering the execution of those who when accused refused to recant; but on the other hand, like previous emperors, he seems to have discouraged the severity of provincial governors as at Lugdunum, as well as the eagerness and greed of informers. Tertullian, who does not hesitate to call him a 'protector'

[1] Orig. *Contra Cels.* viii. 69.   [2] Euseb. *H. E.* iv. 16, 7, 8.

rather than a 'debellator Christianorum,' says definitely enough: 'qui sicut non palam ab eiusmodi hominibus poenam dimovit ita alio modo palam dispersit, adiecta etiam accusatoribus damnatione.'[1] The view taken above as to the attitude of the emperors towards the Christians differs to a certain extent from that of Professor Ramsay, who thinks that there was a definite and hostile policy towards the Christians from the time of the Flavian emperors; that they were recognised as a dangerous element in the state, and that no mere pressure of popular feeling could affect the action of a strong government like the Roman. He, however, at the same time admits ' that a wider and more generous policy was adopted, though in a very hesitating and tentative way, by the second century emperors, who did not fear the current of the times as the older empire had done.'[2] I think we hardly have the material for drawing any such contrast between the emperors of the first and second century in their attitude towards the Christians. It is true that in the case of the Flavian emperors we have no evidence of any action on their part tending to check the severity of persecution, as we have in the case of Trajan, Hadrian, and Antoninus Pius, but, on the other hand, we are equally (except perhaps in the case of Domitian) without positive evidence that they directly encouraged or instituted persecution. It seems to me that the empire, in the sense of the central government, was all this time without a permanent or steady policy towards the Christians: it had not yet

---

[1] Tert. *Apol.* 5.   [2] *Expositor*, July 1892, p. 15.

made up its mind. It was of course aware of the general hatred against the sect; it was aware that Christianity was at variance with some of the essential features of Roman society; it was aware of the suspicions or reports of gross immorality practised at midnight meetings; it knew the intolerant and exclusive attitude of the sect towards the national religion, and it did not shut its eyes to the fact that this *obstinatio* constituted logically potential disobedience or disloyalty to the state. This principle was asserted and occasionally acted upon from the first; but a policy implies something more than occasional action, and this was wanting throughout the first two centuries. If the emperors had made up their minds that Christianity was a political danger, they would have developed a policy and the treatment of the Christians would have been very different from what it was; there would have been a serious attempt to put the new religion down; the persecutions would have been general and continuous, and the imperial edicts clear and precise. We should not have found Pliny at the close of what Professor Ramsay thinks was the severer period, in any uncertainty about the course to be pursued, and, above all, we should not have found Trajan deciding ' conquirendi non sunt.'

The emperors clearly did not think Christianity, in spite of the logical results of its principles, a practical danger to be reckoned with by the state, and in consequence their attitude towards it was not definite but opportunist. It differed at different times and in different provinces, sometimes even in different parts of the same province, and sometimes peace and tranquillity would be best consulted by protecting the Christians against the hatred of the populace, sometimes by practically sacrificing them to it; but the whole question was as yet not an imperial concern—'neque enim in universum aliquid quod quasi certam formam habeat constitui potest'[1]—it formed part of the police administration of each provincial legate and proconsul to whose discretion in the ordinary course of things the treatment of the Christians was left. No doubt tolerably frequent appeals were from time to time made to the emperors for their advice in particular cases. We cannot believe that the letter of Pliny was an isolated case, and we know from Lactantius that a collection was made in the seventh book 'De Officio Proconsulis' of the various rescripts issued by the emperors against the Christians.[2] The list would have been an invaluable one, but we can hardly doubt that all these rescripts, like that of Trajan, had reference primarily to particular localities and circumstances, and that while Christianity was recognised as a penal offence, there was no general edict of proscription and no encouragement of a systematic persecution.

I cannot help thinking, therefore, that Professor Ramsay has to some extent antedated the existence of anything like a policy of proscription on the part

[1] Plin. *ad Trai.* 97.
[2] Lactant. *Inst.* v. 11, 19: 'Domitius de officio proconsulis libro septimo rescripta principum nefaria collegit, ut doceret quibus poenis adfici oporteret eos qui se cultores dei confiterentur.'

of the Roman government; and he does this because he antedates the time when Christianity was regarded as a serious and practical danger to the social and political foundations of the empire. No doubt there came a time when this was the case, but it did not come within the first two centuries, with which alone Professor Ramsay deals. To a certain extent, if I may presume to say so, he argues in a circle on this subject. Speaking of what he describes as the 'Flavian policy,' he says:[1] 'But soon the Flavian government recognised that the united organisation of the Christians was no whit weakened by the destruction of the Temple. The Christians still continued no less than before to maintain a unity independent of and contrary to the imperial unity, and to consolidate steadily a wide-reaching organisation.' What evidence, we may ask, is there of any wide-reaching organisation between 70 and 80 A.D. ? However, it is from the assumption of this organisation that Professor Ramsay draws a general inference as to the hostile policy of the imperial government. 'Either Rome,' he says, 'must now compel obedience, or it must acknowledge that the Christian unity was stronger than the empire;'[2] and so, quite in accordance with this, he says 'the Flavian action was directed against the Church as an organised unity.'[3] In another passage, however, we find Professor Ramsay arguing that there must have been a Christian organisation in order to explain the persecution of the Christians. 'An organisation strong, if only rudimentary, is

[1] p. 356.   [2] p. 356.   [3] p. 274.

required to explain the imperial history, and such an organisation is attested by the Christian documents.'[1] That is to say: there was a far-reaching organisation, therefore a strong government must have inaugurated a policy of persecution; and there is evidence of persecution, therefore we must assume some Christian organisation to explain it. However, putting on one side what is no doubt only a seeming inconsistency, I quite admit that from the time when the government became convinced that Christianity was developing into a widespread organisation—was, in fact, becoming a state within the state—its action approached more and more to being a policy in the proper sense of the word, and a policy definite, permanent, and hostile to Christianity.

I do not propose, and I am not competent, to enter here into the question of Church organisation, either its nature or the steps by which it was accomplished, but merely to point out very briefly that as far as our evidence goes, the unity of Christianity was almost up to the end of the period treated by Professor Ramsay a unity of idea, of belief, of doctrine, and of hope, but not a unity of organisation: though it was only the latter kind of unity which would seem a practical danger to a government like that of imperial Rome. We are unfortunately very much in the dark as to the numbers of the Christians, not only during the first two centuries, but even up to the so-called conversion of the empire. In some of the provinces, and especially in the great centres of

[1] p. 372.

Hellenic civilisation, such as Antioch, Ephesus, Smyrna, they were probably a numerous body at a tolerably early period, though not so numerous as to be in themselves a political danger. In Bithynia we have the evidence of Pliny—which, however, may be variously interpreted. In Rome the numbers of the Christians must have received a considerable check by the Neronian persecution, and there can hardly be a doubt that during the whole of this period they were quite an insignificant body, amid the numerous population of the capital. When we remember that even in the time of Theodosius, seventy years after the conversion of Constantine, the Christians numbered no more than one-fourth or one-fifth of the population in a city like Antioch,[1] it is quite impossible to imagine that, as far as numbers went, the Christians would have been a serious political danger in the first two centuries. Tertullian, no doubt, in a rhetorical and characteristic passage,[2] seems to assert that the Christians formed the greater part of the population, but the exaggeration is so flagrant and apparent as to deprive the statement of all statistical value.

[1] Friedländer, *Sittengeschichte*, iii. 598.
[2] Tert. *Apol.* 37: 'Hesterni sumus et vestra omnia implevimus, urbes, insulas, castella, municipia, conciliabula, castra ipsa, tribus, decurias, palatium, senatum, forum: sola vobis relinquimus templa. Possumus dinumerare exercitus vestros: unius provinciae plures erunt.' Cf. c. 1: 'Obsessam vociferantur civitatem, in agris, in castellis, in insulis Christianos; omnem sexum, aetatem, conditionem, etiam dignitatem, transgredi ad hoc nomen.' *Ad Scap.* 2: 'Tanta hominum multitudo, pars pene maior civitatis cuiusque;' *ibid.* 5: 'Quid facies de tantis milibus hominum, tot viris ac feminis, omnis sexus, omnis aetatis, omnis dignitatis?' etc.

But a comparatively small numerical strength might very conceivably, with the help of organisation and common action, become, if not politically dangerous, at least a force to be reckoned with and looked at with suspicion.

Of this wide-spread organisation I do not know what proof can be adduced. That during the earlier years of Christianity there was a certain intercommunication between the principal Churches through the apostles to whose preaching they owed their origin; that the apostles, while sojourning in one part of the empire, sent letters of admonition and encouragement to the Christians in another; that on occasions alms might be sent from Philippi to Rome, or from Rome to Philippi; that, somewhat later, letters were written in the name of one congregation by its bishop to another, like that of the Roman Clement to the Corinthians under Domitian, are, of course, well-known and indisputable facts. The Christians all over the empire were the 'brethren' with common hopes, common beliefs, and to a certain extent common sufferings. The splendid system of military and commercial roads which formed a network over the empire made communication comparatively easy, and a fraternal hospitality was one of the distinguishing features of the early Christians. Hence, to a certain extent, the various congregations, even after the apostles had ceased to wander from one to another, were *en rapport* with one another, sympathising with one another in time of persecution, and sending accounts to one another of the way in which their several martyrs witnessed to the common faith. Thus the Church at Smyrna sends a letter to the brethren in Pontus, describing the martyrdom of Polycarp;[1] Ignatius, on the eve of his own martyrdom, sends letters of comfort and encouragement to various cities in Asia and Europe;[2] while our knowledge of the persecution at Lugdunum is gained from a letter of the Churches of Lugdunum and Vienna to the Christians of Phrygia.[3] Thus, in a sense, the Christians were conscious of their own unity, but this is by no means the same thing as the development of a widespread organisation. The several communities were of course becoming organised; the episcopal constitution was developing, but the unity of which they were conscious was still an ideal unity: intercommunication was casual, occasional, and informal. It is often said, and no doubt with truth, that the Gnostic heresies did much towards bringing out the unity of the Church; but still, even this was a unity resting, not upon organisation, but upon the preaching of the same doctrine and community in the same belief; this was the aim, the essential unity of the Christian body, and the outer sign or manifestation of this unity was as yet nothing more definite than what Tertullian calls 'communicatio pacis et appellatio fraternitatis et contesseratio hospitalitatis.'[4]

---

[1] Euseb. *H. E.* iv. 15, 2; cf. Lightfoot, vol. i. p. 588 foll.
[2] *Ibid.* iii. 36, 4, and 15; iii. 38, 1.
[3] *Ibid.* v. 1.
[4] Neumann, p. 53: 'Ihre Einheit ruht auf der Predigt derselbe Lehre und dem Besitz desselben Glaubens.' Tert. *De Praescript. Haereticor.* 20.

We shall perhaps be less surprised at the absence for so many years of any common organisation, if we remember that it was not till the middle of the second century that the belief in the imminent second coming of Christ and the establishment of his millennium upon earth ceased to be the general Christian belief—a belief which left no room for questions of common organisation. As Neumann very well says,[1] 'Even a considerable number of people, scattered in different places, united only by a common belief, and expecting the speedy end of all things, though they might be a source of annoyance to the state by their refusal of divine honours to the emperors, were nevertheless no source of danger, so long as no common action was to be feared from them.' This seems correctly enough to describe the state of affairs till nearly the close of the second century. The troubles connected with the Christians were local and provincial, and though, like other provincial matters, they were from time to time referred to the emperors, they were still merely part of the police administration of the various governors. It is inconceivable to me how Professor Ramsay can say 'that Trajan found himself unable to resist the evidence that this organisation was illegal and dangerous.'[2] Illegal he no doubt recognised it as being in the sense that the Christian *obstinatio* involved disobedience to the omnipotent state, and on

---

[1] p. 57. Cf. Mommsen, *Histor. Zeitschrift*, p. 419: 'Den Christen dieser Epoche vor der Entwickelung der Episkopalordnung und der ökumenischen Concilien die Centralisation und damit die Staatsgefährlichkeit abging.'

[2] p. 372.

that ground he could not but sanction the extreme punishment in the extreme resort, but he also saw that this disobedience was an abstract and not a concrete or practical danger, and gave expression to this discernment in the order 'conquirendi non sunt.'

But, of course, there came a time when the scattered communities of Christians cemented their ideal unity of belief by a system of common organisation, out of which emerged the Catholic Church, an organised body, within but not connected with the organisation of the empire, embracing under it the particular communities, subdivided into provinces, dioceses, churches, holding from time to time synods or councils, in which several communities (sometimes more, sometimes fewer) met together for consultation or common action, and above all claiming for the common Christian principles an authority which was to override, in case of collision, the law of the state.[1] It is not my purpose to trace the growth of this organisation, but only to point out (1) that it gave an entirely different aspect to the Christian question, which from being a local and provincial difficulty came to be an imperial problem; (2) that it was not till the close of the second century that this change

[1] Cf. Tert. *Apol.* 45: 'Deum non proconsulem timentes;' also c. 4: 'Si lex tua erravit, puto, ab homine concepta est, neque enim de caelo ruit.' Celsus calls this (Orig. *C. Cels.* viii. 2) the 'voice of insurrection,' στάσεως φωνή. Cf. Orig. *C. Cels.* i. 1: οἱ νόμοι τῶν ἐθνῶν οἱ περὶ ἀγαλμάτων καὶ τῆς ἀθέου πολυθεότητος νόμοι εἰσὶ Σκυθῶν καὶ εἴ τι Σκυθῶν ἀσεβέστερον. So a distinction is made between οἱ κείμενοι ἐν ταῖς πόλεσι νόμοι and οἱ θεῖοι νόμοι. Orig. *C. Cels.* viii. 26: the former were οἱ ἄνομοι νόμοι, *ibid.* v. 37. See Neumann, p. 234.

could have manifested itself to the Roman government. The development towards common action among the Churches commenced, as was natural, in the Eastern provinces, where the frequent meetings of the provincial *concilia* in connexion with the imperial worship, with delegates from the most important cities, may well have suggested the idea of organisation, and where the Montanist heresy made some common action on the part of the orthodox Churches almost a necessity. The phrase μεγάλη ἐκκλησία is found in Celsus,[1] ἐκκλησία καθολική in one of the Ignatian letters;[2] but in both cases it seems to be used of the orthodox Christians as opposed to the various heretical sects, and to imply the ideal unity of belief rather than any unity of organisation. In the last years, however, of M. Aurelius, we find informal meetings of 'the faithful' within the province of Asia, with a view to oppose the Montanist heresy.[3] Ten years later synods are held in Palestine under the presidency of the bishop of Caesaraea, in Pontus under that of Palmas, bishop of Amastris; in Gaul under Irenaeus of Lugdunum, to come to some agreement on the question of the Easter festival.[4] On this occasion the common action goes still further, for the decrees of the several synods are apparently sent to

---

[1] Orig. *C. Cels.* v. 59. [2] *Ad Smyrn.* 8.
[3] Euseb. *H. E.* v. 16, 10: τῶν γὰρ κατὰ τὴν Ἀσίαν πιστῶν πολλάκις καὶ πολλαχῇ τῆς Ἀσίας εἰς τοῦτο συνελθόντων, καὶ τοὺς προσφάτους λόγους ἐξετασάντων καὶ βεβήλους ἀποφηνάντων καὶ ἀποδοκιμασάντων τὴν αἵρεσιν, οὕτω δὴ τῆς τε ἐκκλησίας ἐξεώσθησαν καὶ τῆς κοινωνίας εἴρχθησαν.

Euseb. *H. E.* v. 23, 2-4: σύνοδοι δὴ καὶ συγκροτήσεις ἐπισκόπων ἐπὶ ταὐτὸν ἐγένοντο, κ. τ. λ.

Victor, the bishop of Rome, who attempts to excommunicate as heterodox the Churches of Asia, which under the presidency of Polycrates, bishop of Ephesus, had passed a dissentient resolution of their own.[1]

These are the unmistakable beginnings of an organisation which would inevitably soon be co-extensive with the empire—a state within the state—the existence of which was certainly opposed to the most essential and characteristic principles of the Roman government. With the organisation of the Catholic Church began the real struggle between the empire and Christianity, which could only have one of two issues—the suppression of the religious organisation, or its acceptance by and incorporation in the empire.

It was not immediately, however, that any distinct change of policy took place. Partly the new union of the Churches was concealed by the noisy disputes which were, after all, the occasion of their coming together; partly the empire was concerned with great wars, as under Severus, or was passing through a period of reaction and conservatism as under Alexander.[2] But still Severus, who in Rome was quite inclined to follow the example of his predecessors, and to protect the Christians against mob-

---

[1] Euseb. *H. E.* v. 24, 9 : ἐπὶ τούτοις ὁ μὲν τῆς Ῥωμαίων προεστὼς Βίκτωρ ἀθρόως τῆς Ἀσίας πάσης ἅμα ταῖς ὁμόροις ἐκκλησίαις τὰς παροικίας ἀποτέμνειν ὡσὰν ἑτεροδοξούσας τῆς κοινῆς ἑνώσεως πειρᾶται.

[2] Cf. *Vit. Alex. Sev.* 22 : 'Iudaeis privilegia reservavit, Christianos esse passus est'—a statement which of course implies no formal recognition of Christianity, but merely practical toleration.

violence,[1] must have received some impressions during his passage through Syria in 202 A.D., which caused him to take a more serious view of the dangers inherent in Christianity, for his decision that no fresh converts were to be allowed to join that body[2]—even though it may have been, as Neumann supposes, a local rescript, and not, as has often been assumed, a general edict—still makes indisputably a step in advance: a remark which may be made with equal truth, though with the same limitations, of the persecution instituted by Maximin the Thracian, and which was directed, not against the Christians generally, but against the clergy, or, in other words, against the growing organisation of the Church.[3] It must suffice to conclude this part of the subject by saying that these tendencies on the one side and the other received their completion by the series of general and systematic persecutions which commenced with the reign of Decius.

The general result of the previous discussion has been to show that during the first two centuries there was in no sense any systematic persecution of Christianity. It is true that a rigorous and logical application of the principles of the Roman government

---

[1] Tert. *ad Scap.* iv.: 'Sed et clarissimas feminas et clarissimos viros Severus sciens huius sectae esse non modo non laesit verum et testimonio exornavit, et populo furenti in nos palam restitit.'

[2] Spart. *Vit. Sever.* 17: 'Iudaeos fieri sub gravi poena vetuit; idem etiam de Christianis sanxit.'

[3] Euseb. *H. E.* vi. 28: διωγμὸν ἐγείρας τοὺς τῶν ἐκκλησιῶν ἄρχοντας μόνους ὡς αἰτίους τῆς κατὰ τὸ εὐαγγέλιον διδασκαλίας ἀναιρεῖσθαι προστάττει.

would have resulted in a proscription of Christianity, but in view of its practically harmless character, and the absence of any dangerous or widespread organisation, cases of interference with its members were only intermittent and spasmodic. As we have seen, the Christians might have been proceeded against under the law of *maiestas*: practically, as far as we can judge, this happened comparatively seldom. A case might have been made out against them on a charge of magic : we should find it hard, however, to show any distinct instance of it. Vague charges of homicide and gross immorality were made and believed even by men of culture and education like Fronto,[1] but, as a rule, no serious attention could have been paid to these reports, the evidence for which, so far as there was evidence at all, came from tortured slaves.[2]

[1] Minuc. Fel. *Octav.* 9, 6 : 'Haec sacra sacrilegiis omnibus taetriora. Et de convivio notum est ; passim omnes loquuntur, id etiam Cirtensis nostri testatur oratio.' Cf. 31, 2.
[2] Euseb. *H. E.* v. 1, 14. Tert. *Apol.* 7 : ' Tot hostes eius quot extranei . . . ex natura ipsi domestici nostri.'

IX

CHRISTIANITY AND THE COLLEGIA

THERE still remains, however, one question to be asked and answered: how the Christians were able to exist uninterfered with, to so great an extent as our evidence shows that they were, in the face of the imperial policy in regard to associations (*collegia, sodalitates, hetaeriae*).[1]

We know that the imperial government, with its increasingly bureaucratic organisation and its centralisation in Rome and the emperor, was essentially hostile to all free and spontaneous organisation among the people. Combination for a single object might easily develop into a combination for other objects. Not only was this almost self-evident, but the history of the republic had repeatedly proved its truth. Julius Caesar in this as in so many other directions initiated the policy which marked the empire of which his brief tenure of power laid the

---

[1] Liebenam, *Zur Gesch. und Organis. des römischen Vereinswesen*, p. 267, puts the question so: 'In welcher äussern Form haben die ersten christlichen Gemeinden, zu einer Zeit wo genossenschaftliche und Vereinsbildungen strenger Aufsicht unterlagen, im Staate Fuss fassen können?'

foundation. Suetonius says briefly[1] and insufficiently: 'Cuncta collegia praeter antiquitus constituta distraxit.' This, I imagine, points, not to any general measure, but to his personal action as dictator in the city, and by edict in the provinces. The same policy seems to have been developed and to a certain extent systematised by Augustus. Of him Suetonius says: 'Plurimae factiones titulo collegii novi ad nullius non facinoris societatem coibant; igitur . . . collegia praeter antiqua et legitima dissolvit.'[2] This statement is partly illustrated and explained by an inscription in which a *collegium symphoniacorum* is mentioned 'quibus senatus coire, convocari, cogi permisit e lege Iulia ex auctoritate . . . . Augusti ludorum causa.'[3] The Augustan regulation, therefore, took the form of a Lex Iulia, which not only dissolved a large number of existing *collegia*, but provided that for the future every *collegium* before being recognised as legitimate had to receive a licence from the senate. No doubt the law at first had reference to Rome only, or perhaps to Italy also, which, like the capital, was by the arrangement of 27 B.C. assigned to senatorial administration. The principle, however, would certainly be transferred more or less completely to the provinces, and we may with some safety assume that from this time in theory new *collegia* in the senatorial provinces were supposed to receive a licence from the senate, those in the imperial provinces from the emperor, probably

---

[1] Suet. *Caes.* 42. [2] Suet. *Aug.* 32.
[3] *C. I. L.* vi. 2193.

through his legates. As illustrative of this we find the following expressions: 'corpus cui coire licet,'[1] 'collegia quibus ius coeundi lege permissum est,[2] 'collegium dendrophororum Romanorum quibus ex senatus consulto coire licet,'[3] 'corpus fabrum navalium Ostiensium quibus senatus consulto coire licet;'[4] in Gallia Lugdunensis: 'corpora omnia Lugduni licite coeuntia;'[5] in the Alpes Maritimae: 'collegia tria quibus ex senatus consulto coire permissum est;'[6] in Asia at Cyzicus: 'ut corpus quod appellatur neon . . . . in civitate sua auctoritate amplissimi ordinis confirmetur.'[7] So, too, Marcian in the 'Digest' says:[8] 'Nisi ex senatus consulti auctoritate aut Caesaris collegium vel quodcunque tale corpus coierit, contra senatus consulta et mandata et constitutiones collegium celebrat.' *Collegia* which were not so licensed were *illicita*, and in the extreme resort membership in a *collegium illicitum* came under the head of *maiestas*: 'Quisquis illicitum collegium usurpaverit, ea poena tenetur qua tenentur qui hominibus armatis loca publica vel templa occupare iudicati sunt.'[9] We shall have to return to these regulations later on in order to detect, if we can, their practical working, but meanwhile, if we add to what has been cited the action of Trajan—who distinctly refused to sanction the institution of a *collegium fabrum*, to consist of only 150 members, for

[1] *Dig.* xxxiv. 5, 20.
[2] *Dig.* xl. 3, 1.
[3] Orell. 4075.
[4] *C. I. L.* xiv. 168.
[5] Wilm. 2224.
[6] *C. I. L.* v. 7881.
[7] *Ephem. Epigraph.* iii. 156.
[8] *Dig.* xlvii. 22, 3.
[9] *Dig.* xlvii. 22, 2.

the purpose of a fire-brigade in Nicomedia, on the ground that all such organisations tended to become *hetaeriae*,[1] *i.e.* social and political clubs, and who only reluctantly and on the score of vested interests allowed the existence of an *eranus* at Amisos, laying it down 'in ceteris civitatibus quae nostro iure obstrictae sunt res huiusmodi prohibenda est,'[2] and, finally, who ordered Pliny to proscribe *hetaeriae* generally in his province [3]—enough will have been said to show generally the hostile and suspicious attitude of the government towards associations and *collegia* of all kinds and in all parts of the empire.

Now to casual observers at any rate the Christian communities must have presented many external resemblances to the numerous θίασοι or religious associations with which the Eastern provinces more especially were honeycombed,[4] and must, indeed, have been ranked among them. That the Jews were ranked among them we know expressly from Josephus,[5] and there are not wanting indications (to be noticed later on) that the Christians were regarded in the same light. The Jews, however, were expressly excepted from the regulations which limited or forbade these θίασοι: the Christians were not. There is therefore *prima facie* some difficulty in understanding how the Christians were enabled to develop

[1] Plin. *ad Trai.* 34 : 'Quodcunque nomen ex quacunque causa dederimus iis qui in idem contracti fuerint . . . hetaeriae aeque brevi fient.'
[2] *Ibid.* 93.   [3] *Ibid.* 96, 7.
[4] See Foucart, *Des Associations religieuses chez les Grecs.*
[5] Joseph. *Ant. Iud.* xiv. 10, 6, cited on p. 23.

as they did in spite of the fundamental illegality in their external organisation. But, in the first place, this difficulty is far from being unique or limited to the Christians. Inscriptions prove to us the existence in immense numbers, and in every part of the empire, of *collegia* of every sort and kind, with regard to only a very small minority of which there is any sign that they were licensed either by the senate or by the emperor. When we regard this fact, which a reference to the index of any volume of the 'Corpus Inscriptionum' will abundantly verify, and then turn to such statements in the 'Digest' as the following, 'Mandatis principalibus praecipitur praesidibus provinciarum ne patiantur esse collegia sodalicia;'[1] or 'collegia si qua fuerint illicita mandatis et constitutionibus et senatus consultis dissolvuntur'[2]—and regard these as precise statements of the imperial practice—we seem involved in a difficulty and contradiction at least as great as that which confronts us in dealing with the Christian communities. Nor is this difficulty entirely met by supposing that a large number of these inscriptions are subsequent either to the time of Severus, who, as we shall see, facilitated the existence of the so-called *collegia tenuiorum* in the provinces, or to that of Alexander Severus, who did something towards impressing the *collegia* into the service of the state,[3] for, after all deductions on these grounds, the number of

---

[1] *Dig.* xlvii. 22, 1. [2] *Ibid.* xlvii. 22, 3.
[3] *Vit. Alex. Sev.* 33: 'Corpora omnium constituit vinariorum, lupinariorum, caligariorum, et omnino omnium artium, idemque ex sese defensores dedit et iussit qui ad quos iudices pertineret.'

known *collegia* would still remain a very large one. Unfortunately, a thorough examination of this question is impossible, because literature is practically silent on the subject; and though the inscriptions are very numerous, the light which we gain from them concerns mainly the organisation of the *collegia*, and not the circumstances of their origin, nor to any great extent their functions as a social or political force.[1] We shall, however, perhaps be able to discover that there are certain considerations, which, if they do not entirely explain the difficulty presented by these two opposite sets of circumstances—the stringent regulations against *collegia* on the one hand, and on the other their wide extension in spite of these—may yet point out the way to their partial reconciliation.

The reason of the state hostility to *collegia* is to be found in the dread of any combination for political purposes in the subject populations of the empire; but the reality and imminence of this danger varied in different parts of the empire, in different classes of society, and perhaps above all in the different characters of the associations themselves. The policy of the Roman state in such matters was usually more or less opportunist: it was too wise to work an abstract principle of policy to death for the sake of mere consistency; it much more frequently allowed its action to be modified by circumstances; its general enactments were regulative, and pointed in a certain direction, but it was not considered necessary

[1] The most thorough information on the subject is to be gained from Liebenam in the work referred to on p. 168, note 1.

to follow up the course indicated beyond the limit which the circumstances of a particular case required. And this was particularly the case in matters which belonged, as the collegial question did, to the police administration of the city and the provinces, being under the charge of the *praefectus urbi* [1] in the former, and the legates and proconsuls in the latter.

In republican times the right of association had in all probability been free and unimpeded with the simple qualification 'dum ne quid ex publica lege corrumpant,'[2] and originally there seems to have been a religious root to them all, although this in many cases tended to retire into the background. When a foreign cult was adopted by the state, *sodalitates*, originally perhaps composed of the compatriots of the new deity, were established by the senate for the due observance of the cult. Thus Cato is made to say by Cicero, ' Sodalitates autem me quaestore constitutae sunt sacris Idaeis Magnae Matris acceptis,'[3] and similarly the introduction of other new cults not authorised by the state was accompanied by the growth of similar *collegia*. So we find *collegia*[4] and *sodalicia*[5] of Isis, just as in much later times there were *collegia* of Serapis,[6] of Sol Invictus,[7] of Jupiter Heliopolitanus, composed of the Berytenses inhabiting Puteoli,[8] and many others. But while many of these *collegia* and *sodalitates* retained their primarily

---

[1] *Dig.* i. 12, 1, 14.
[2] *Dig.* xlvii. 22, 4.
[3] *Cat. Mai.* xiii. 45.
[4] *C. I. L.* iii. 882, vi. 355.
[5] *Ibid.* ii. 2730.
[6] *Ibid*, ix. 3337.
[7] *Ibid.* vi. 734.
[8] *Ibid.* x. 1634.

religious character, many others, as, *e.g.*, the 'collegia compitalicia' of the time of Cicero and Clodius, tended to be used either for political ends or at any rate to lead to political results, and by the end of the republic the numerous *collegia* of the city contributed not a little towards the anarchy which characterised the senatorial *régime*.

It was not, however, only in Rome and Italy that the existence of these associations made itself felt in matters with which professedly they had nothing to do, though, as being nearer to the seat of government, they were perhaps here more dangerous. In the Hellenised provinces of the East there had been for centuries an immense number of religious associations, which, however they may have escaped the notice of the republican governors, whose year of office was usually occupied with matters of more personal importance to themselves, would certainly, under the empire, be dealt with on the same principles as the Roman and Italian *collegia*. And, indeed, what had been allowed and endorsed under the senatorial government, from the first, as we have seen, attracted the attention and excited the suspicions of the emperors. The principle of the empire in this respect is clearly enough expressed in the words which Dio Cassius puts into the mouth of Maecenas:[1] τὸ μὲν θεῖον πάντῃ πάντως αὐτός τε σέβου κατὰ τὰ πάτρια, καὶ τοὺς ἄλλους τιμᾶν ἀνάγκαζε· τοὺς δὲ δὴ ξενίζοντάς τι περὶ αὐτὸ καὶ μίσει καὶ κόλαζε, μὴ μόνον τῶν θεῶν ἕνεκα, ἀλλ᾽ ὅτι καὶ καινά τινα δαιμόνια οἱ τοιοῦτοι

[1] Dio Cass. lii. 36.

ἀντεισφέροντες πολλοὺς ἀναπείθουσιν ἀλλοτριονομεῖν · κἀκ τούτου καὶ συνωμοσίαι καὶ συστάσεις ἑταιρεῖαί τε γίγνονται. It was this principle which was embodied in the Lex Iulia, a law which, as we have already suggested, primarily concerned only Rome and Italy, though it soon came to be regulative of the action of the provincial governors as well. But there are certain social tendencies which legislation finds it impossible to overcome, and which it is the part of wise statesmanship only to repress when the public interests imperatively demand it. The imperial government had certainly enough statesmanship to realise this, and therefore while the Lex Iulia expresses the general attitude of the government towards associations, it can hardly be taken as a stringent rule, literally observed, admitting of no exceptions and enforced with equal rigour in all parts of the empire.

The Lex Iulia, as we have seen, consisted of two parts: the dissolution of existing *collegia* 'praeter antiqua et legitima,' and a provision for the licensing of new ones by the senate or the emperor. Only those *collegia* therefore, strictly speaking, were *legitima* or *licita* which were either specially exempted from the action of this law, like the Jewish communities, or θίασοι,[1] or those, the constitution of which had been specially licensed, and we should probably be tolerably safe in assuming that this licence would only be allowed to those *collegia* which were (1) non-political, and (2) which served some public utility, 'si . . . idcirco instituta sunt ut necessariam operam publicis utilita-

[1] *Ant. Iud.* xiv. 10, 6.

tibus exhiberent.'[1] So we find among the *collegia* expressly licensed by the senate *dendrophori*,[2] *fabri*[3] and *centonarii*[4] for the extinguishing of fires; *symphoniaci ludorum causa;*[5] *mensores machinarii frumenti publici*,[6] *fabri navales* at Ostia,[7] etc., while Pliny expressly bases his request for a *collegium fabrum* at Nicomedia on the need of a public fire-brigade.[8]

But without a special staff of officials to see that the provisions of the law were carried out, it was quite impossible among the multiplicity of associations all over the empire, and especially in the great cities, to insure the 'legitimate' character of all or even most of them. At ordinary times and as a general rule there was, no doubt, considerable laxity in this respect, and a very large number especially of the religious *collegia*, but probably of funeral and mutual-assistance clubs as well, had received no licence and were therefore, strictly speaking, *illicita*. Most of them were probably too insignificant to attract notice, or if noticed, too obviously harmless to call for interference. And therefore, at ordinary times, when there was no special cause to look askance at associations in a particular province, most of these *illicita collegia* were let alone, especially as most of them were composed of the lowest classes of society, and to a great extent of slaves, against whose combination there was no objection, if their masters consented.[9]

[1] *Dig.* l. 6, 6, 12.
[2] Liebenam, p. 105.
[3] *C. I. L.* vi. 3678, cf. 9405-9415.
[4] Liebenam, p. 102.
[5] *C. I. L.* vi. 2193.
[6] Liebenam, p. 75-78.
[7] *C. I. L.* xii. 256.
[8] *Ad Trai.* 33, 3.
[9] *Dig.* xlvii. 22, 3, 2.

Sometimes, of course, the action of the government was more stringent than at others, and Caligula apparently removed all restrictions—a policy which Claudius did not continue.[1] Trajan set his face, at any rate in Bithynia, against the whole system of *collegia*. Severus again showed himself more indulgent.[2] Nor was it only the varying policy of the emperors themselves which made the treatment of *collegia* now more lax, now more severe. Much also would depend upon particular governors. Thus we hear that Flaccus, praefectus of Egypt under Tiberius, τὰς ἑταιρείας καὶ συνόδους αἳ ἐπὶ προφάσει θυσιῶν εἱστιῶντο τοῖς πράγμασιν ἐμπαροινῆσαι διέλυε,[3] and what he did, no doubt other governors may have done from time to time in other provinces. Still it is quite certain that numerous *collegia*, which were unlicensed or *illicita*,[4] existed, though their existence was always precarious, and they might at any moment be put down. 'Nulla dubitatio est,' says the Digest, 'quod si corpori cui licet coire legatum sit, debeatur; cui autem non licet, non valebit nisi singulis legetur, hi enim non quasi collegium sed quasi certi homines admittentur ad legatum.'[5] In other words, the only *necessary* disadvantage suffered by a *collegium illicitum* was its non-recognition by law as a juristic person. Similarly Tacitus, in describing some disturbances which had taken place at Pompeii, says,

[1] Dio Cass. lix. 28.   [2] *Dig.* xlvii. 22, 1.
[3] Phil. *Adv. Flacc.* p. 966: Mang. p. 518.
[4] ἀθέμιτον δὲ σύστημα ἢ σωμάτειόν ἐστι τὸ μὴ ἀπὸ νόμου ἢ βασιλέως συστάν. *Basilica*, lx. 32.
[5] *Dig.* xxxiv. 5, 20.

'collegia quae contra leges instituerant dissoluta;'[1] *i.e.* certain *collegia illicita* were in existence at Pompeii which were now dissolved, not because they were *illicita*, but because disturbances had been caused. So at Amisus, the *eranus* about which Pliny inquires, had clearly had no licence, but it was nevertheless left untouched out of respect to vested rights.[2]

When, however, there was any suspicion of political danger, these *collegia illicita* were at once put down, as by Flaccus in Egypt, by the senate in Pompeii, by Pliny in Bithynia; and as it was this political character and not the mere want of a licence which brought down state interference, in course of time the term 'illicitum' came to get the meaning of 'political' rather than 'unlicensed'—a distinction which is more clearly marked in the Greek translation by the substitution of παράνομα for ἀθέμιστα. It is in this sense of the word that such statements in the 'Digest' as the following are to be explained: 'Quisquis illicitum collegium usurpaverit ea poena tenetur qua tenentur homines qui hominibus armatis loca publica vel templa occupare iudicati sunt,'[3] and 'sed permittitur tenuioribus stipem menstruam conferre dum tamen semel in mense coeant, ne sub praetextu huiusmodi illicitum collegium coeat.'[4] So Trajan reluctantly sanctions the *eranus* at Amisus, provided that it does not tend 'ad turbas et inlicitos coetus,'[5] where the word must mean 'political.'

---

[1] Tac. *Ann.* xiv. 17.   [2] Plin. *ad Trai.* 94.
[3] *Dig.* xlvii. 22, 2.   [4] *Dig.* xlvii. 22, 1.   [5] *loc. cit.*

It results from what has been said that the practice of the government in regard to unlicensed *collegia* was not by any means so strict and stringent as by the letter of the law it might have been. It has been very truly said: 'Der Caesarismus nahm den obern Classen das Associationsrecht und liess es den andern.'[1] It seems to me that this explains a good deal. Apart from the purely religious associations which were generally speaking tolerated,[2] there was a distinction more or less broad between the *collegia opificum* and the *collegia sodalicia* (ἑταιρικὰ συστήματα, *hetaeriae*). About the former we unfortunately know very little. Some of them were of extremely ancient date, and on that ground were expressly exempted from the Lex Iulia. But what seems to have characterised them is the fact that their members either belonged to the same trade or calling, such as the *pistores*, the *fabri navales*, the *caudicarii*, etc., or at least combined for some definite public object, such as the purpose of a fire brigade, *e.g.* the *fabri, centonarii, dendrophori*. On the other hand, the *collegia sodalicia* seem to have been more social in their character, to have had no special public utility in view, but to have had common meetings for feasting and recreation, and to have combined either for the special object of a burial club[3] or of a mutual

---

[1] Rodbertus, Hildebrand's *Jahrb.* v. 299, cited by Liebenam, p. 32.

[2] *Dig.* xlvii. 22, 1: 'Sed religionis causa coire non prohibentur, dum tamen per hoc non fiat contra senatus consultum quo illicita collegia arcentur.'

[3] 'Qui stipem menstruam conferre volent in funera.' Wilm. 319.

assistance society,[1] or of both combined.[2] Probably these two classes frequently overlapped, but still we find that Trajan drew a sharp distinction between them, in refusing to license a fire brigade—*collegium fabrum*—on the express ground that it might degenerate into an *hetaeria*: 'Quodcunque nomen ex quacunque causa dederimus iis qui in idem contracti fuerint, hetaeriae aeque brevi fient.'[3]

While the *collegia opificum* would probably all be found among the lower classes, this would not be so necessarily the case with the *collegia sodalicia*, and no doubt from the first the practical policy of the government would be to enforce the law in the case of those who from wealth or social position might have political influence which combination might make dangerous, but to tolerate the harmless associations composed of poor people and slaves.[4] In the course of time this practical policy appears to have crystallised itself in legislation. Thus Marcian states in the 'Digest:' 'Mandatis principalibus praecipitur praesidibus provinciarum ne patiantur esse collegia sodalicia, . . . sed permittitur tenuioribus stipem menstruam conferre, dum tamen semel in mense coeant, ne sub praetextu huiusmodi illicitum collegium coeat.'[5] The *collegia* among the lower classes and slaves, alluded to in the last clause, were technically known as *collegia tenuio-*

[1] 'Ad sustinendam tenuiorum inopiam.' Plin. *ad Trai.* 94.
[2] 'Egenis alendis humandisque.' Tert. *Apol.* 39.
[3] Plin. *ad Trai.* 34.
[4] As the Christian communities usually were; cf. Min. Fel. *Octav.* 'de ultima faece collectis imperitioribus.'
[5] *Dig.* xlvii. 22, 1.

rum.¹ Mommsen supposes that they were *collegia funeraticia*, and that they were especially exempted from the provisions of the Lex Iulia by a *senatus consultum* at some time between Augustus and Hadrian.² In the inscription relating to the 'Collegium Dianae et Antinoi'—a funeral club at Lanuvium, dating from 133 A.D.—we have apparently a clause from the preamble of this *senatus consultum*: 'Kaput ex s. c. populi Romani—Quibus coire, convenire collegiumque habere liceat—qui stipem menstruam conferre volent in funera, in it collegium coeant, neque sub specie eius collegii nisi semel in mense coeant conferendi causa unde defuncti sepeliantur.'³ The *collegium* in question was apparently a purely funeral club, though its members were allowed to have common dinners five times a year, but the statement of the 'Digest' seems to show that there were probably at least two other clauses in the *senatus consultum*, one giving a qualified sanction to religious associations ('sed religionis causa coire non prohibentur,' etc.), and another sanctioning *collegia tenuiorum* for somewhat wider objects than burials alone. By this *senatus consultum*—which could have had reference at widest to the city, Italy, and senatorial provinces—a legal sanction was given to existing tendencies, and the senate was perhaps relieved from the constant business of licensing these numerous *collegia*.⁴ At what precise time the general exemption

---

¹ *Dig.* I. 6, 'tenuiores per collegia distributi;' cf. also xlvii. 22, 3.
² See Liebenam, p. 39 foll.   ³ Wilm. 319.
⁴ Cf. Plin. *Panegyr.* 32.

from the Lex Iulia was extended to the provinces we do not know. The action of Pliny in consulting Trajan about a *collegium* of this description at Amisus shows that it was not in force at that time in Bithynia, and it was possibly not till the time of Severus that it was a general rule throughout the empire —' quod non tantum in urbe sed in Italia et in provinciis locum habere divus quoque Severus rescripsit.'[1]

The general result of what has been said is to show that within the restrictions laid upon *collegia* and associations there was still in practice room for Christianity to develop, though it was quite possible at various times for collisions to occur between it and a specially vigilant executive. In this connexion there is no necessity to enter into the question of the early Christian organisation. The growth of πρεσβύτεροι as an order in the community, the differentiation of ἐπίσκοποι and their original functions, and the development from an aristocratic to a monarchical form of government, concern the history of Christianity, and not the history of the Roman policy towards it. Whatever was the exact constitution of the early communities, it is beyond all doubt that they had certain general and external resemblances to the *collegia* or θίασοι, or religious associations around them. If they were in any way affiliated to the Jewish synagogues, these latter were certainly regarded as θίασοι, and the Christians would therefore be ranked among them too: or again, if

[1] *Dig.* xlvii. 22, 1.

Weingarten[1] is right in supposing that the earliest communities grouped themselves round some leading family, it is still easy to find analogies in the heathen world, where we have a 'collegium quod est in domu Sergiae Paullinae'[2]—a 'collegium quod consistit in praedis Larci Macedonis,'[3] etc. The term ἐκκλησία itself was used of Greek associations,[4] while conversely Eusebius uses the terms συναγωγή, σύνοδος and τὸ κοινόν of the Christian Church.[5] To this it may be added that Lucian describes the president of a Christian community as θιασάρχης,[6] that Celsus speaks of Christians as ἴδιοι θιασῶται of Jesus,[7] and finally that a Christian inscription in Africa uses the terms *ecclesia fratrum, cultor, area, cella*,[8] all of them familiar enough in heathen *collegia*. In any case, merely as religious associations, the Christians might well, either 'sub umbraculo religionis certe licitae'[9] or in common with many other externally similar bodies, have escaped under ordinary circumstances interference from the government.

There were, however, certain features about Christianity which might bring it into occasional conflict with the Roman policy towards *collegia*. In one

---

[1] *Histor. Zeitschr.* xlv. 401 foll., 'Die Umwandlung der ursprünglichen christlichen Gemeindeorganisation zur katholischen Kirche,' 201. Cf. 1 Cor. xvi. 19; Rom. xvi. 3-16.

[2] *C. I. L.* vi. 9148. [3] *C. I. L.* vi. 404.

[4] Le Bas-Waddington, 1381-2. *C. I. Gr.* 2271.

[5] Euseb. *H. E.* vi. 19, 16, and vii. 32, 27.

[6] Lucian, *De Mort. Peregr.*; with which cf. ἀρχιθιασίτης, *C. I. Gr.* 2271.

[7] Orig. *Contr. Cels.* iii. 22. [8] *C. I. L.* viii. 9585.

[9] Tert. *Apol.* 21.

respect especially these communities resembled the *hetaeriae* of which Trajan had so much suspicion in Bithynia, in that they met, not only for purely religious purposes, but also for common meals, paid for by contributions from each member (ἔρανος), or by a common fund (*arca*). At first these common meals, the breaking of bread, were of daily occurrence.¹ At a later time, as the immediate expectation of the Second Advent grew fainter, they were held once every week.² While the religious services took place in the morning, these *Agapae* or Love-Feasts, at which what was later developed into the Eucharist was combined with an ordinary supper, were held in the evening,³ and while at the former strangers were admitted, and even welcomed, at the latter no one was allowed to be present except baptised members of the community.⁴ As long as the communities were small or undistinguishable from the Jewish, or consisted solely of the very poor and humble, these social meetings might for the most part escape notice and interference. But still, apart from the general principles of the Christians, of which we have already treated, it was here that occasion might always be found against them by a suspicious governor. These common meals constituted them ἑταιρεῖαι, or *sodalitates*, and these if unlicensed, as the Christian bodies were, might at any time be put down in the same way that the religious associations in Egypt were by Flaccus.⁵ Nor are there wanting indications that the Christians were

---

¹ Acts ii. 46, but cf. xx. 7.   ² 'Stato die.' Plin. *ad Trai.* 96.
³ *Ibid.*   ⁴ Justin. *Apol.* i. 65.   ⁵ See p. 177.

actually to some extent affected by their existence as *sodalitates*, and that they occasionally laid themselves open to the suspicion of violating the conditions under which religious associations were tolerated: 'dum tamen per hoc non fiat contra senatus consultum quo illicita collegia arcentur.' At the same time, incidents of this kind could never amount to anything like a proscription of Christianity.[1]

In Bithynia *factiones* or clubs were a crying danger in Trajan's time. The disturbances caused by them were one of the reasons why Pliny was sent out,[2] and we have already several times noticed Trajan's refusal to sanction a *collegium fabrum*, lest it should become an *hetaeria*. At one time I was inclined to hold the view that Pliny's action against the Christians was on the score of their being a *collegium illicitum*. This view I have now given up. Pliny would have had no

[1] 'Bishop Lightfoot says (*Apostolic Fathers*, Part II. vol. i. p. 11): 'The mere negative fact that the Christian religion had not been recognised as lawful would be an ample justification for proceeding against the Christians, as soon as it came to be recognised that Christianity was something distinct from Judaism. No positive prohibition was needed. Here was a religion rampant which had never been licensed by the state, and this fact alone was quite sufficient to set the law in motion.' This is an altogether misleading and inaccurate statement. The law might in certain cases be set in motion against the Christians as an *illicitum collegium*. As a religion, its *unlicensed* character would only come into consideration when it drew Roman citizens away from the national cult. What is the authority for the statement on p. 20 that 'lawful religions held a licence from the state for worship or for sacrifice, and thus their gatherings were exempted from the operation of the law against clubs'?

[2] Plin. *ad Trai.* 34: 'Meminerimus provinciam istam eiusmodi factionibus esse vexatam.'

need to consult the emperor on a matter about which his views had been already so clearly expressed, nor would Trajan have uttered his famous decision, 'conquirendi non sunt,' if he had regarded them as members of an *hetaeria*. But still, the incident shows that the Christians might have been affected in this way. They, as Pliny discovered, contained among their members some of the better classes of society,[1] and these, according to the Christian principles, would take part in whatever of common life there was in the community;[2] and one of the features of this common life was a weekly meeting for the purpose of a common meal. If the view taken above is correct, this would have rendered the Christians liable to interference. Bithynia, too, was in an exceptional state, and the ordinary toleration of unlicensed *collegia* was at any rate for the time replaced by a stringent enforcement of the provisions of the Lex Iulia. Pliny, by Trajan's order, had issued an edict forbidding *hetaeriae*.[3] This did not, indeed, actually affect the Christians. But the reason why it did not is almost more striking than if it had. For in consequence of this edict we find that the Christians gave up their common meal,[4] and so became a purely religious association, and not an *hetaeria*: 'quod ipsum facere desisse post edictum meum quo secundum mandata tua hetaerias esse vetueram '—a

[1] 'Multi omnis ordinis.'
[2] Lactant. *Divin. Inst.* v. 14, 15: 'Apud nos inter pauperes et divites, servos et dominos interest nihil.'
[3] Plin. *ad Trai.* 97, 7: 'Post edictum meum quo secundum mandata tua hetaerias esse vetueram.'
[4] *Ibid.*: 'Quod ipsum facere desisse post edictum meum,' etc.

step which of course left the general position of the Christians *qua* potentially 'hostes publici' as it was before, though it made them safe from interference on a particular point.

There is no reason to suppose that this edict was anything more than a local one, but still there were always similar dangers in other provinces, and probably in Rome. Nor is it altogether an improbable conjecture that in certain parts of the empire the Agapae were given up in consequence of similar edicts against *hetaeriae*; and the Eucharist in consequence made a part of the morning religious service. At any rate, we find Justin Martyr in his first Apology[1] giving an account of the Eucharist as a separate religious service unconnected with the Agape. We are not without evidence, too, that in the course of the second century the Christians were occasionally regarded as belonging to a secret and illegal association. Celsus seems to have placed this accusation in the forefront of the indictment which he drew up against them: πρῶτον τῷ Κέλσῳ κεφάλαιόν ἐστι διαβαλεῖν Χριστιανισμὸν ὡς συνθήκας κρύβδην πρὸς ἀλλήλους ποιουμένων Χριστιανῶν παρὰ τὰ νενομισμένα.[2] Similarly in Minucius Felix they are spoken of as 'homines deploratae inlicitae ac desperatae factionis,' as holding 'nocturnae congregationes' as a 'latebrosa et lucifuga natio.'[3] It is probable that by about the middle of the second century the Eucharist was generally separated from

---

[1] Justin. *Apol.* i. 65 foll. [2] Orig. *C. Cels.* i. 1.
[3] Min. Fel. *Octav* 8.

the Agape, the latter being given up or maintained according to times and circumstances, but always liable to bring the Christians into trouble as an *hetaeria*. Tertullian is a not unimportant witness on this point. We infer from his words that the Eucharist was celebrated in the morning, and as a religious service,[1] but that the Agapae, in the African Church at any rate, were still celebrated; and though Tertullian is conscious of the charge of illegality made against them, he attempts to remove the prejudice and to find with his legal knowledge a legal basis for the social meetings of the Christians. 'Proinde . . . . inter licitas factiones,' he says, 'sectam istam deputari oportebat a qua nihil tale committitur quale de illicitis factionibus timeri solet.'[2] The object of prohibiting associations was 'ne civitas in partes scinderetur,' but to attain this end completely it would be necessary to put down the *comitia*, the *concilia*, the *contiones*, and even the *spectacula*. The bases of the Christian union were 'conscientia religionis, disciplinae divinitas, et spei foedus.'[3] The Christians should be judged by facts, not theories: 'haec coitio Christianorum merito sane illicita si illicitis par, merito damnanda si non dissimilis damnandis.'[4] And he finally exclaims: 'Quum probi, quum boni coeunt, quum pii, quum casti congregantur, non est factio dicenda sed curia.'

[1] Tertull. *de Cor.* 3: 'Eucharistiae sacramentum et in tempore victus et omnibus mandatur a Domino, etiam antelucanis cœtibus, nec de aliorum manu quam Praesidentium sumimus.'
[2] Tert. *Apol.* 38.   [3] *Ibid.* 39.
[4] *Ibid.* 39 *ad fin.*

All this clearly enough implies that, in spite of the innocent and harmless nature of the Christian gatherings, they were as a matter of fact regarded as a *factio illicita*. In another passage he asserts this explicitly: 'forte in senatus consulta et in principum mandata coitionibus opposita delinquimus.'[1] But it is not only on the general harmlessness of the Christian meetings, and on the innocence of their feasts, which, as he says, 'de nomine rationem sui ostendunt,' that Tertullian bases his defence of the Christian communities. The 'Apologeticus' was written very shortly after the rescript of Severus, by which the formation of *collegia tenuiorum* was allowed generally throughout the provinces, and there seems to be no doubt that Tertullian attempted to take advantage of this rescript and to vindicate the meetings of the Christians as a 'collegium tenuiorum.' After saying that the meetings were presided over by 'probati quique seniores,' he goes on: 'etiam si quod arcae genus est, non de honoraria summa quasi redemptae religionis congregatur: modicam unusquisque stipem menstrua die vel cum velit et si modo velit et si modo possit apponit: nam nemo compellitur sed sponte confert . . . Nam inde non epulis nec potaculis nec ingratis voratrinis dispensatur, sed egenis alendis humandisque et pueris ac puellis re ac parentibus destitutis' etc.[2] There are so many technical terms here, such as *arca, honoraria summa, stips, menstrua die*, and so much similarity to the words in the 'Digest' already cited, that we have really no

[1] Tert. *Adv. Psychicos*, 13. [2] Tert. *Apol.* 39.

alternative but to suppose that Tertullian is referring to the rescript in question. The Christians, in his view, had the right to be regarded as 'licitae factiones,' because their objects were the same, though with less admixture of luxury and social enjoyment, as those of the *collegia tenuiorum*. Nor does there seem any reason to suppose that such a claim on the part of the Christian communities to be regarded as in the eye of the law a *collegium tenuiorum*' would be disallowed by the authorities. Such a recognition would not in the slightest degree affect the general relations of the Christians and the government: it was no recognition of Christians and Christianity. In all probability the Christians would describe themselves as 'fratres cultores dei,'[1] or in some such way : at any rate the designation of *Christiani*, in face of the name being a punishable offence, would be avoided. And therefore their position as a recognised or tolerated *collegium* would in no way prevent persecution 'for the name' or accusation under the law of *maiestas*.[2] It would merely give the various Christian

[1] Cf. *C. I. L.* viii. 9585. Tert. *Apol.* 39 : 'Quod fratrum appellatione censemur.' Just. *Apol.* i. 65 : ἐπὶ τοὺς λεγομένους ἀδελφούς. De Rossi, *Rom. sotter.* i. 105 ; Liebenam, p. 273. See also Acts xv. 23 and 36, xxi. 7 and 18, xxviii. 14. Min. Fel. *Oct.* 31 : 'Sic nos ... fratres vocamus ut unius dei parentis homines.'

[2] So it is quite a mistake to suppose that Gallienus in desisting from the persecution set on foot by Valerian acknowledged Christianity as a 'licita religio.' All that he did was to restore to the Christian communities the possession of their burial-grounds (Euseb. *H. E.* vii. 13, 3), which had been taken away by his predecessor (*H. E.* vii. 11, 10). Naturally, in times of persecution even *licita collegia* would not be safe from interference if they were known to consist of Christians, and at times apparently the popular

communities a certain *locus standi* for their ordinary meetings; it would facilitate their combination for charitable purposes, making it more possible for them to approximate, without the suspicion of dangerous or anti-social communism, to their principle of having all things in common ('omnia indiscreta sunt apud nos'[1]); and finally it would secure to them the right of common burial, and the possibility of possessing common burial-places, which the vast system of the Catacombs round Rome proves to have been so essential an element of early Christianity. Indeed, the undoubted possession by the Christians at the end of the second century of *areae* or *coemeteria* of their own seems necessarily to imply that in some way or other they had corporate rights, that their communities ranked as juristic persons—a result which could only follow from their being generally or specially licensed.

It was M. Aurelius who first granted these corporate rights to licensed *collegia*. Thus they had the right of manumitting slaves,[2] and of receiving legacies,[3] and no doubt, either then or little later, of owning land.[4] From the first the Christians, like the Jewish

hatred of the Christians, instead of expressing itself by the cry 'Christianos ad leones,' substituted that of 'areae non sint.' Tertull. *ad Scap.* iii. 2: 'Sub Hilariano praeside cum de areis sepulturarum nostrarum adclamassent: Areae non sint.'

[1] Tert. *Apol.* 39.

[2] *Dig.* xl. 3, 1: 'Divus Marcus omnibus collegiis quibus coeundi ius est manumittendi potestatem dedit.'

[3] *Dig.* xxxiv. 5, 20.

[4] Cf. *Dig.* iii. 4, 1: 'Quibus autem permissum est corpus habere collegii societatisve sive cuiusque alterius eorum nomine, proprium est ad exemplum reipublicae habere res communes, arcam communem,' etc.

communities at Rome, would if possible be buried together, but this would only be possible if the richer among them who owned burial-places of their own, allowed members of the sect to be buried there too along with their own families. Thus it is proved by inscriptions that Flavia Domitilla owned land which was used as an early Christian burial-place,[1] and in which there were in later times extensive catacombs. There is similar evidence to support the view that the Acilii Glabriones owned a burial-place in which Christians were buried together,[2] while smaller family burial-places limited to Christian members of the *familia* are also exemplifications of the same tendency.[3]

No doubt, one of the first uses which the Christians would make of their *de facto* recognition as *collegia tenuiorum*, would be the purchase of

[1] Lightfoot, *Clement*, i. 35 foll.; De Rossi, *Rom. sotter.* i. 306, ii. 280 and 360; *C. I. L.* vi. 948, 8942, 16246. See also De Rossi, *Bullet. di Archeol. cristian.* 1865, pp. 17 foll., 33 foll., 41 foll., 84 foll.; 1874, pp. 5 foll., 68 foll., 122 foll.; 1875, pp. 5 foll., 46 foll.; 1877, pp. 128 foll. etc. From De Rossi's investigation it seems that the 'coemeterium Domitillae' is to be identified with the Catacombs of the Tor Marancia near the Ardeatine Way. A plot of ground was granted to P. Calvisius Philotas 'ex indulgentia Flaviae Domitillae.' A tablet is put up to herself and her freed-people by Tatia 'nutrix septem liberorum Divi Vespasiani atque Flaviae Domitillae Vespasiani neptis' on land belonging to Flavia Domitilla.

[2] See De Rossi, cited by Ramsay, p. 262.

[3] De Rossi, *Rom. sotter. cristian.* i. 109: 'M. Antonius Restitutus fecit ypogen sibi et suis fidentibus in Domino.' Also *Bullet. di Archeol. cristian.* 1865, p. 54: 'Monumentum Valeri Mercuri et Iulittes Iuliani et Quintilies Verecundes libertis libertabusque posterisque eorum ad religionem pertinentes meam.'

O

ground for burial-places. It is not material to our present subject to decide at what date this took place. We know that Pope Zephyrinus, at about 199 A.D., put Callistus over the cemetery at Rome, *i.e.* probably made him curator of it;[1] and Neumann[2] has inferred partly from this that Pope Victor was the first to register the Christian communities at Rome as *collegia funeraticia*. His argument seems to me far from convincing. The general licence given to *collegia* of this kind in Rome dates back at least as far as to Hadrian's reign, and if we find the African Christians within a very few years of its extension to the provinces by Severus taking advantage of it, we may surely suppose with some reason that the Roman Christians had long since set the example of doing this.

However this may be, the organisation of the Christian communities as *collegia tenuiorum* or *funeraticia*, and their recognition as such by the state, would only remove, as has already been shown, one particular ground on the score of which they might have been interfered with—an interference which, however frequent, could never have been described as religious persecution on the part of the state. It would, however, give a certain protection and sanction perhaps to the Christian meetings, certainly to the Christian burial-places, which might probably remain unviolated and secure to them in any but a general and systematic persecution. But when this has been said,

---

[1] Hippolyt. *Haer.* ix. 12: μεθ' οὗ [Victor] κοίμησιν Ζεφυρῖνος τοῦτον μεταγαγὼν ἀπὸ τοῦ Ἀνθείου ἐς τὸ κοιμητήριον κατέστησεν.

[2] p. 108.

all has been said: there was nothing in the partial recognition by the state which would in any way exempt or help to exempt the Christians from whatever measure of persecution they were subject to from the Roman government on more general grounds, as ἄθεοι, as *rei maiestatis*, or as *hostes publici*.

APPENDIX ON TWO 'ACTA MARTYRUM.'

IT was one of the causes of Pliny's hesitation in Bithynia that he had never been present at any of the 'cognitiones de Christianis.' Our knowledge of the Christian question suffers from the same cause. If we only had accounts of one or two Christian trials similar to those given by Tacitus of the cases of Piso[1] and Libo Drusus,[2] or by Pliny of those of Marius Priscus[3] or Caecilius Classicus,[4] we should be in a position to form much clearer ideas of the relations between the Christians and the government. Still there are two documents which at least deserve to be mentioned in this connexion, and which, so far as they go, give some kind of confirmation to the views which have been expressed above. In all cases, civil and criminal, both at Rome and in the provinces, official protocols were made of the cases which came before the judicial magistrates. Instances of such protocols or 'Acta' in civil cases are found in the 'Digest' in reference to a case tried before a procurator[5] and to a case in the emperor's court,[6] while the general rule is stated in the Justinian code from an edict of 194 A.D.:[7] 'Is ad quem res agitur acta

[1] Tac. *Ann.* iii. 10–18. [2] Tac. *Ann.* ii. 27–32.
[3] Plin. *Ep.* ii. 11. [4] Plin. *Ep.* iii. 9.
[5] *Dig.* xxvi. 8, 21. [6] *Dig.* xxviii. 4, 3.
[7] *Cod. Just.* ii. 1, 2.

publica tam criminalia quam civilia exhiberi inspicienda ad investigandam veritatis fidem iubebit.' That this rule was extended to such trials as those of the Christians we have positive evidence. Dionysius of Alexandria gives an account drawn from such official 'Acta' of a Christian trial under Valerian before the praefectus Aegypti;[1] and Cyprian's profession of faith was read by his disciples in the 'Acta Proconsulis:' 'Quid nos discipuli secuti apud praesidem dicere deberemus prior apud acta proconsulis pronuntiasti.'[2] That the Christians, in cases where they had no opportunity of themselves taking notes at the trials of their martyrs, would gladly avail themselves of these official protocols, is what we should naturally expect; and, as a matter of fact, many instances, according to Professor Ramsay,[3] are recorded in which they purchased from the clerks (*commentarienses*) copies of the official shorthand reports of the proceedings. That there was a collection of such accounts before the time of Eusebius we know from several passages of his 'Ecclesiastical History.'[4] In the course of time these authentic 'Acta' developed or degenerated into the kind of legend with which such collections as that of Ruinart make us familiar. Miraculous incidents of all kinds were added, and in most cases almost every trace of the original account is lost, though Le Blant and Ramsay have shown that careful criticism may occasionally detect a substratum of authentic fact. In striking contrast to these miraculous legends are two documents to which attention has recently been called, and which, by the

---

[1] Euseb. *H. E.* vii. 11, 5 : αὐτῶν δὲ ἐπακούσατε τῶν ὑπ' ἀμφοτέρων λεχθέντων ὡς ὑπεμνηματίσθη.

[2] Cyprian, *Ep.* lxxvii. 2, p. 834.

[3] p. 330.

[4] Euseb. *H. E.* iv. 15, 47 : τοῖς τῶν ἀρχαίων συναχθεῖσιν μαρτυρίοις. v. 4, 3 : τὸν ἐν τῇ δηλωθείσῃ γραφῇ τῶν μαρτύρων κατάλογον. v. 21, 5 : ἐκ τῆς τῶν ἀρχαίων μαρτυρίων συναχθείσης ἡμῖν ἀναγραφῆς.

absence of miraculous features and of exaggeration generally, as well as by their consistency with what we know of the period, seem to be early, if not contemporary, records of Christian trials.

Both of them relate to the reign of Commodus: one of them to the trial of the martyrs of Scili, in Numidia, under the proconsul Saturninus in 181 A.D., the other to the trial of Apollonius in Rome between 180–184 A.D.

The 'Acta' of the African martyrs were discovered in Greek, probably translated from an original Latin account,[1] in a Parisian MS. of the tenth century,[2] and may profitably be compared with the later version of the martyrdom given in Ruinart.[3] The trial took place before Saturninus, the proconsul, in the βουλευτήριον at Carthage. The proconsul said to them: 'Ye can find indulgence with our emperor, if ye call to your aid a prudent consideration.'[4] The holy Speratus answered and said: 'We have never injured nor cursed any man: nay, we rather give thanks if any entreat us evil, for we serve our Lord and King.' The proconsul said: 'But we also worship God, and our worship is simple. We swear by the genius of our lord the emperor, and we pray for his safety. Ye must do the same likewise.' The holy Speratus answered: 'If ye will vouchsafe us a favourable hearing, I will reveal to you the mystery of true simplicity.' The proconsul said: 'So soon as you utter any word disrespectful to our worship I will allow you no further hearing. Swear rather by the safety of our lord the emperor.' The holy Speratus answered: 'I recognise not the kingdom of this present

[1] They are published by Usener—*Acta Martyrum Scilitanorum Graece edita*, Bonn, 1881—who points out such expressions as πιθανότης = *persuasio* and διαμεῖναι πορεύομαι = *perseveratum eo* as indicating a Latin original.

[2] *Cod. Par. Graec.* No. 1470.

[3] pp. 84–89.

[4] ἐὰν σώφρονα λογισμὸν ἀνακαλέσησθε.

world. I praise my God and serve him, whom no man hath seen, for that is impossible to the eye of flesh. Robbery have I never committed. Contrariwise, in all my business I render the tax due, for I recognise our Lord the King of kings and the Ruler over all peoples.' The proconsul said to the others: 'Abjure the faith which this man hath professed.' The holy Speratus answered: 'To commit murder and to bear false witness is a dangerous persuasion.' The proconsul said: 'Take no part in such folly and obstinacy.' The holy Cittinus took up the word and said: 'There is no one whom we can fear save the Lord our God, who dwells in heaven.' The holy Donata said: 'We give honour to the emperor as the emperor, but fear we render to our God.' The holy Hestia said: 'I am a Christian.' The holy Secunda added: 'What I am, that will I also remain.' Then said the proconsul to the holy Speratus: 'Dost thou likewise continue a Christian?' The holy Speratus said: 'I am a Christian.' Likewise also said all the other holy ones. The proconsul said: 'Will ye not have a space for reflection?' The holy Speratus said: 'In a matter so approved[1] there is no deliberation and no reflection.' The proconsul said: 'What books have you in your satchel?'[2] The holy Speratus said: 'Our holy writings and the letters also of the holy man Paul.' The proconsul said: 'Ye shall have a space of thirty days, if so be ye may perchance come to reason.' The holy Speratus answered thereto: 'I am unchangeably[3] a Christian.' The others also with one voice affirmed the same thing. Then the proconsul Saturninus pronounced judgment over them in the following way: 'Inasmuch as Speratus, Martzallus, Cittinus,

---

[1] ἐγκρίτῳ.

[2] ποῖαι πραγματεῖαι ἐν τοῖς ὑμετέροις ἀπόκεινται σκεύεσιν; No doubt the question points to a suspicion of magic.

[3] ἀμετάθετος.

Donata, Hestia and Secunda, as well as the others who have not appeared before us, have professed that they live according to the Christian mode of life, and inasmuch as they remain obstinate in their resolution, notwithstanding that a space was allowed them in which to return to the Roman worship, we give orders that they be executed with the sword.'[1]

There is no sign in this account of any departure from the principles of Trajan's rescript. If M. Aurelius inaugurated a severer course, Saturninus at any rate did not carry it out. He clearly had not hunted out the Christians who were brought before him; he not only offers pardon on condition of recantation, even pressing on them a delay of thirty days, but he goes so far as to dispense with the test of actual sacrifice to the emperor, if the accused would only swear by his genius. On the other hand the Christians are punished for the name, in consequence of their obstinate profession of it (ἀκλινεῖς τὴν γνώμην), their disobedient refusal to return to the Roman cult, and their refusal to recognise the authority of the kingdom of this world in religious concerns.[2] There is no question of *maiestas*; no mention of any charge of immorality; if any suspicion of magic is implied,[3] no stress is laid on any such charge, and the whole trial is evidently summary and informal, the number of questions asked being solely due to the anxiety of the proconsul to avoid, if possible, extreme measures.

The other document, if anything a still more interesting one, is an account—probably the original ' Acta '—of the trial of Apollonius in Rome. This martyrdom is, as is

---

[1] Τοῦ Σπερατοῦ κ. τ. λ. ὅσοι τῷ Χριστιανικῷ θεσμῷ ἑαυτοὺς κατεπηγγείλαντο πολιτεύεσθαι ἐπεὶ καὶ χαρισθείσης αὐτοῖς προθεσμίας τοῦ πρὸς τὴν τῶν Ῥωμαίων ἐπανελθεῖν παράδοσιν ἀκλινεῖς τὴν γνώμην διέμειναν, ξίφει τούτους ἀναιρεθῆναι δεδίκακα.

[2] ἐγὼ τὴν βασιλείαν τοῦ νῦν αἰῶνος οὐ γινώσκω.

[3] See p. 200, note 2.

well known, mentioned by Eusebius,[1] who states that an accuser, stirred up by the devil, caused Apollonius to be brought before Perennis; that Perennis, after ordering the informer to be executed, requested Apollonius to give an account of himself before the senate,[2] and that the martyr, after giving a reasonable account of his faith before that body, was beheaded, ὡσὰν ἀπὸ δόγματος συγκλήτου, since an old precedent had been established that Christians who were once brought to trial could be released in no other way than by giving up their profession.[3] Eusebius adds that anyone who wishes to know what the martyr said and what he answered to the questions of Perennis, and his whole apology before the senate, can learn it ἐκ τῶν ἀρχαίων μαρτυρίων συναχθείσης ἡμῖν ἀναγραφῆς. The document thus referred to has almost certainly been discovered in an Armenian version, belonging to the fifth century, of a Greek original, by Mr. F. C. Conybeare, 'in a repertory of Martyrdoms published by the Mechitarists of Venice in 1874.' Mr. Conybeare has published in the *Guardian* for June 21, 1893, an English translation of the 'Acta,' while Professor Harnack has since published a German translation by Herr Burchardi, with a commentary of his own in the 'Sitzungsbericht der königlich Preussischen Akademie der Wissenschaften zu Berlin,' xxxvii. 1893.

After a brief introduction, probably by Eusebius, the 'Acta' begin abruptly, the first portion being lost. Perennis, the prefect, commanded that he should be brought before the senate, and said to him : 'O Apollonius, wherefore dost

---

[1] Euseb. *H. E.* v. 21.

[2] ὁ δέ γε θεοφιλέστατος μάρτυς, πολλὰ λιπαρῶς ἱκετεύσαντος τοῦ δικαστοῦ καὶ λόγον αὐτὸν ἐπὶ τῆς συγκλήτου βουλῆς αἰτήσαντος, λογιωτάτην ὑπὲρ ἧς ἐμαρτύρει πίστεως ἐπὶ πάντων παρασχὼν ἀπολογίαν κεφαλικῇ κολάσει ὡσὰν ἀπὸ δόγματος συγκλήτου τελειοῦται.

[3] μηδ' ἄλλως ἀφεῖσθαι τοὺς ἅπαξ εἰς δικαστήριον παριόντας καὶ μηδαμῶς τῆς προθέσεως μεταβαλλομένους ἀρχαίου παρ' αὐτοῖς νόμου κεκρατηκότυς..

thou resist the invincible law and decree of the emperors,[1] and dost refuse to sacrifice to the gods?' Apollonius said: 'Because I am a Christian;[2] therefore I fear God, who made heaven and earth, and sacrifice not to empty idols.' The prefect said: 'But thou oughtest to repent of this mind of thine, because of the edicts of the emperors,[3] and take oath by the good fortune of the autocrat Commodus.' Apollonius replied: '.... it is best to swear not at all, but in all things to live in peace and truth; for a great oath is the truth, and for this reason is it a bad and an ill thing to swear by Christ, but because of falsehood is there disbelief, and because of disbelief there is swearing. I am willing to swear in truth by the true God that we, too, love the emperor and offer up prayers for his majesty.' The prefect said: 'Come then and sacrifice to Apollo[4] and to the other gods and to the emperor's image.' Apollonius said: 'As to my change of mind and as to the oath, I have given their answer; but as to sacrifices, I and all Christians offer a bloodless sacrifice to God .... Wherefore according to the command of the God-given precept, we make our prayers to him who dwells in heaven, who is the only God, that men may be justly ruled upon this earth, knowing for certain that he, your emperor, also is established, not through anyone else, but only through the one King, God, who holds everyone in his hand.' The prefect said: 'Surely thou wast not summoned hither to talk philosophy. I will give thee one day's respite that thou

---

[1] This need imply no more than the *de facto* procedure which we have seen was pursued in such cases, and which no doubt rested on rescripts from different emperors.

[2] Cf. Plin. *ad Trai.* 96, 5: 'Quorum nihil posse cogi dicuntur qui sunt re vera Christiani.'

[3] Cf. Trajan's words: 'Qui negaverit se Christianum esse idque re ipsa manifestum fecerit, id est supplicando deis nostris.'

[4] Probably, as Harnack suggests, the senate was held in the temple of Apollo on the Palatine.

mayest consider thine interest and advise thyself concerning thy life.' And he ordered him to be taken to prison. After three days he ordered him to be brought forward and said to him: 'What counsel hast thou found for thyself?' Apollonius answered: 'To remain firm in my religion as I told thee before.' The prefect said: 'Because of the edict of the senate [1] I advise thee to repent and to sacrifice to the gods to whom all the earth gives homage and sacrifices for it is far better for thee to live among us than to die a miserable death. Methinks thou art not unacquainted with the edict of the senate.' Apollonius said: 'I know the command of the Omnipotent God, and I remain firm in my religion,[2] and I do no homage to idols made with hands. . . . .' The prefect answered: 'You have philosophised enough and filled us with admiration; but dost thou not know this, O Apollonius, that it is the command of the senate that no one shall anywhere be named a Christian?'[3] Apollonius answered: 'Ay, but it is not possible for a human statute of the senate to prevail over the command of God. . . . .' The prefect said: 'Art thou bent upon death? . . . . I would fain let thee go, but I cannot, because of the command of the senate,[4] and yet with benevolence I pronounce sentence on thee.' And he ordered him to be beheaded with a sword. Apollonius said: 'I thank my God for thy sentence.' And the executioners straightway led him away and beheaded him.

[1] The edict of the senate was probably a resolution that Apollonius should be treated in the same way as other Christians were.

[2] Apollonius manifests the same *obstinatio* as that displayed by the Bithynian Christians, which Pliny considered to be deserving of death.

[3] *i.e.* the senate sanctioned, in this particular case of a member of their own body, the course usually pursued, that the *nomen* or profession of Christianity was punishable with death.

[4] The motive of Perennis in putting the matter in this light is obvious.

There are several points which are unusual about this trial. In the first place the accused is brought before the court, not of the *praefectus urbi*, as Ptolemaeus and his companions were under Pius, and as Justin was under M. Aurelius, but of the *praefectus praetorio*. This, however, is sufficiently explained by the exceptional position of Perennis, who occupied under Commodus a position similar to that of Sejanus under Tiberius. There was at no time a very distinct line separating the judicial sphere of the *praefectus urbi* and the *praefecti praetorio*, and as the latter became more and more civil rather than military functionaries, their court, even in ordinary circumstances, came to encroach upon and to overshadow that of the senatorial *praefectus*.

A more difficult problem is the part taken in the trial by the senate. Apollonius was clearly first brought before Perennis, evidently because the crime of Christianity was one for the police administration to deal with. Perennis, however, insists that the accused should give an account of himself before the senate. But this by no means meant that the senate was to try the case. This is conclusively proved against Neumann in two ways: (1) by the fact that even in the senate it is Perennis—though not a senator, and strictly having no right to be present in the senate at all, except as an escort to the emperor—who puts the questions and conducts the examination; (2) after the reprieve of three days, Apollonius was brought, as Harnack very clearly shows,[1] not before the senate again, but before Perennis, who passes sentence upon him. We

[1] (1) Whereas on the first day, the prefect based his action on the edicts of the emperors, he on the second hearing mentions only the resolution of the senate. (2) The way in which Perennis refers to the senate makes it impossible that the proceedings were still in the presence of that body. (3) A philosopher interposes a remark: which might happen in the prefect's court, but was hardly possible in the senate, where non-senators were not admitted.

therefore have no instance here, as Neumann thinks, of a Christian trial before the senate. The expressions of Eusebius, ὡσὰν ἀπὸ δόγματος συγκλήτου and ἐπὶ τοῦ δικαστοῦ, were in themselves against this view, and the 'Acta' clearly show it to be wrong. What then was the part which the senate took? and what was the cause of its exceptional interference? The answer, it seems to me, can only be that Apollonius was a senator. Eusebius does not say so: but he tells us that about this time several persons in Rome conspicuous by wealth and birth became Christians.[1] There had clearly been Christian senators when Tertullian wrote the 'Apology,'[2] and he had been in Rome under Commodus; and Hieronymus[3] describes Apollonius as 'Romanae urbis senator'—a statement which, whether due to evidence independent of Eusebius, or to an inference from his account, as Harnack thinks, is not without its weight. Professor Harnack is inclined to give up the view that Apollonius was a senator, apparently on three grounds: (1) neither Eusebius nor the 'Acta' speak of him as one; (2) he was not tried by the senate, but by Perennis; (3) his appearance before the senate is quite well explained by the following passage from Mommsen's 'Staatsrecht:'[4] 'Wenn in der Stadt die capitale Coercition in Fällen von politischer Wichtigkeit zur Anwendung kam, ist dabei wohl regelmässig der Senat hinzugezogen worden. Dasselbe geschieht bei ausserordentlicher Gefährdung der öffentlichen Sicherheit, namentlich bei weit und insbesondere über die Bürgerschaft hinaus sich verzweigenden Verbrechen, also bei religiösen Associationen mit criminellen Tendenzen, bei den Gruppenverbrechen der Giftmischerei, der Brandstiftung u. s. w. Das für diese Judication erforderliche Imperium kann der Senat nicht verleihen, wohl aber die ihm zustehende Einwirkung auf

[1] Euseb. *H. E.* v. 21, 1.
[2] *Apol.* 37.
[3] *De Vir. illust.* c. 42
[4] *Staatsr.* iii. 1066.

die effective Competenz der Imperienträger in der Weise ausüben, dass er einen Consul oder einen Prätor mit der Handhabung dieser Criminaljustiz beauftragt. In Folge eines derartigen Auftrags richtet der betreffende Magistrat, je nach Umständen mit Zuziehung eines Consilium: der Senat selber fungirt auch in diesem Fall niemals als Gerichtshof.'

Of these reasons the first alone seems to me to have any force, and, as Professor Harnack himself allows, it is not conclusive, even apart from the possibility that Apollonius is described as a senator in the lost beginning of the 'Acta.' The second reason proves nothing. Senators were by no means invariably tried by the senate, except perhaps in the reign of Tiberius. Apollonius, if a senator, would much more naturally have been tried, as no doubt Flavius Clemens and Acilius Glabrio were, by the emperor himself. But Commodus, as we learn expressly from Dio Cassius, neglected all the duties of his position, and Perennis was compelled to administer, not only military affairs, but all other matters as well, and, in fact, to act as vice-emperor.[1] This by itself seems a sufficient explanation why a senator, accused of being a Christian, should come before Perennis rather than the *praefectus urbi*. With regard to the passage quoted from Mommsen, it is enough to say that it has reference solely to republican times, and is quite inappropriate even to the first century of the empire, and still more to the second.

On the other hand, the hypothesis that Apollonius was a senator enables us to suggest a consistent account of what really happened. Apollonius, a senator, was accused by an informer—perhaps, as Hieronymus states, by one of his own slaves—of being a Christian. An ordinary Chris-

---

[1] Dio Cass. lxxii. 9: τοῦ Κομμόδου ... τῶν τῇ ἀρχῇ προσηκόντων οὐδὲν ὡς εἰπεῖν πράττοντος ὁ Περέννιος ἠναγκάζετο οὐχ ὅτι τὰ στρατιωτικὰ ἀλλὰ καὶ τἄλλα διὰ χειρὸς ἔχειν καὶ τοῦ κοινοῦ προστάττειν.

tian would have been tried by the *praefectus urbi*, a senator naturally by the emperor. Commodus, however, delegated all such duties to Perennis, and accordingly before Perennis the accused was brought. The prefect, in these somewhat exceptional circumstances, may naturally have desired to relieve himself of some of the responsibility of putting a senator to death, especially as at the beginning of his reign the emperor, perhaps with a rather bad grace, made some show of deference to the senate's authority,[1] and he accordingly not only allowed but ordered Apollonius to make a statement to him in the presence of the senate, and induced the senate to pass a resolution that the ordinary course of procedure was to be observed in this case, viz. that pardon could only be secured by retractation.[2] Armed with this semi-official authority,[3] Perennis resumed the trial in his own court, and as Apollonius persisted in his profession of Christianity and refused to worship the emperor, he was condemned to death, the only concession made to his senatorial rank being that he was beheaded instead of being exposed to wild beasts.[4]

---

[1] Schiller, *Gesch. der röm. Kaiserz.* i. 663.

[2] This seems the best explanation of the words μηδ' ἀφεῖσθαι ἄλλως τοὺς ἅπαξ εἰς δικαστήριον παριόντας καὶ μηδαμῶς τῆς προθέσεως μεταβαλλομένους ἀρχαίου παρ' αὐτοῖς νόμου κεκρατηκότος ; cf. Hieronym. *ad loc. cit.* : 'veteri apud eos obtinente lege absque negatione non dimitti Christianos.'

[3] This seems to give exactly the force required by ὡσὰν ἀπὸ δόγματος συγκλήτου.

[4] Professor Harnack gives a different explanation. He supposes that the favourable attitude of Commodus towards the Christians under the influence of Marcia had already commenced; that it was with reluctance that the information of the slave was received; that Perennis was expected by the emperor to bring the matter to a favourable termination; that he sought to do this by inducing the senate to pass a resolution exempting Apollonius from the consequences of his obstinacy, and that it was only because he failed in this that he passed sentence on the accused, to whom he showed his

For the rest it is sufficient to point out (1) that Apollonius was not sought out, but accused; (2) that it was the mere profession of Christianity apart from any more specific charge which was laid against him, (3) that the worship of the emperor was, as in other cases, used as a test and sign of retractation; (4) that Perennis, no less than the provincial governors, is anxious to induce this recantation, and so to avoid the necessity of capital punishment.

favourable attitude by a lighter sentence. This account leaves quite unexplained the position of the senate in the matter, and probably antedates by several years the more indulgent attitude of Commodus.

A Selection of Works
IN
THEOLOGICAL LITERATURE
PUBLISHED BY
Messrs. LONGMANS, GREEN, & CO.
39 Paternoster Row, London, E.C.

Abbey and Overton.—THE ENGLISH CHURCH IN THE EIGHTEENTH CENTURY. By CHARLES J. ABBEY, M.A., Rector of Checkendon, Reading, and JOHN H. OVERTON, M.A., Rector of Epworth; Rural Dean of Isle of Axholme. *Crown 8vo.* 7s. 6d.

Adams.—SACRED ALLEGORIES. The Shadow of the Cross—The Distant Hills—The Old Man's Home—The King's Messengers. By the Rev. WILLIAM ADAMS, M.A. *Crown 8vo.* 3s. 6d.
    The four Allegories may be had separately, with Illustrations. 16mo. 1s. each.

Aids to the Inner Life.
  Edited by the Rev. W. H. HUTCHINGS, M.A., Rector of Kirkby Misperton, Yorkshire. *Five Vols.* 32mo, *cloth limp*, 6d. each; *or cloth extra*, 1s. each.
    With red borders, 2s. each. *Sold separately.*
    OF THE IMITATION OF CHRIST. By THOMAS À KEMPIS.
    THE CHRISTIAN YEAR.
    THE DEVOUT LIFE. By ST. FRANCIS DE SALES.
    THE HIDDEN LIFE OF THE SOUL.
    THE SPIRITUAL COMBAT. By LAURENCE SCUPOLI.

Allen.—THE CHURCH CATECHISM: its History and Contents. A Manual for Teachers and Students. By the Rev. A. J. C. ALLEN, M.A., formerly Principal of the Chester Diocesan Training College. *Crown 8vo.* 3s. 6d.

Barnes.—CANONICAL AND UNCANONICAL GOSPELS. With a Translation of the recently discovered Fragment of the 'Gospel of St. Peter,' and a Selection from the Sayings of our Lord not recorded in the Four Gospels. By W. E. BARNES, B.D., Theological Lecturer at Clare College, Cambridge. *Crown 8vo.* 3s. 6d.

Barry.—SOME LIGHTS OF SCIENCE ON THE FAITH. Being the Bampton Lectures for 1892. By the Right Rev. ALFRED BARRY, D.D., Canon of Windsor, formerly Bishop of Sydney, Metropolitan of New South Wales, and Primate of Australia. *8vo.* 12s. 6d.

Bathe.—Works by the Rev. ANTHONY BATHE, M.A.
 A LENT WITH JESUS. A Plain Guide for Churchmen. Containing Readings for Lent and Easter Week, and on the Holy Eucharist. 32mo, 1s.; *or in paper cover*, 6d.
 AN ADVENT WITH JESUS. 32mo, 1s.; *or in paper cover*, 6d.
 WHAT I SHOULD BELIEVE. A Simple Manual of Self-Instruction for Church People. *Crown 8vo.* 3s. 6d.

Benson.—THE FINAL PASSOVER: A Series of Meditations upon the Passion of our Lord Jesus Christ. By the Rev. R. M. BENSON, M.A., Student of Christ Church, Oxford. *Small 8vo.*
 Vol. I.—THE REJECTION. 5s.
 Vol. II.—THE UPPER CHAMBER. [*In preparation.*
 Vol. III.—THE DIVINE EXODUS. Parts I. and II. 5s. each.
 Vol. IV.—THE LIFE BEYOND THE GRAVE. 5s.

Bickersteth.—YESTERDAY, TO-DAY, AND FOR EVER: a Poem in Twelve Books. By EDWARD HENRY BICKERSTETH, D.D., Bishop of Exeter. *One Shilling Edition*, 18mo. *With red borders*, 16mo, 2s. 6d.
 The Crown 8vo Edition (5s.) may still be had.

Blunt.—Works by the Rev. JOHN HENRY BLUNT, D.D.
 THE ANNOTATED BOOK OF COMMON PRAYER: Being an Historical, Ritual, and Theological Commentary on the Devotional System of the Church of England. *4to.* 21s.
 THE COMPENDIOUS EDITION OF THE ANNOTATED BOOK OF COMMON PRAYER: Forming a concise Commentary on the Devotional System of the Church of England. *Crown 8vo.* 10s. 6d.
 DICTIONARY OF DOCTRINAL AND HISTORICAL THEOLOGY. By various Writers. *Imperial 8vo.* 21s.
 DICTIONARY OF SECTS, HERESIES, ECCLESIASTICAL PARTIES AND SCHOOLS OF RELIGIOUS THOUGHT. By various Writers. *Imperial 8vo.* 21s.
 THE BOOK OF CHURCH LAW. Being an Exposition of the Legal Rights and Duties of the Parochial Clergy and the Laity of the Church of England. Revised by Sir WALTER G. F. PHILLIMORE, Bart., D.C.L. *Crown 8vo.* 7s. 6d.
 A COMPANION TO THE BIBLE: Being a Plain Commentary on Scripture History, to the end of the Apostolic Age. *Two Vols. small 8vo. Sold separately.*
 THE OLD TESTAMENT. 3s. 6d. THE NEW TESTAMENT. 3s. 6d.
 HOUSEHOLD THEOLOGY: a Handbook of Religious Information respecting the Holy Bible, the Prayer Book, the Church, etc., etc. *Paper cover*, 16mo. 1s. *Also the Larger Edition*, 3s. 6d.

Body.—Works by the Rev. GEORGE BODY, D.D., Canon of Durham.
 THE LIFE OF LOVE. A Course of Lent Lectures. *Crown 8vo.* 4s. 6d.
 THE SCHOOL OF CALVARY; or, Laws of Christian Life revealed from the Cross. 16mo. 2s. 6d.
 THE LIFE OF JUSTIFICATION. 16mo. 2s. 6d.
 THE LIFE OF TEMPTATION. 16mo. 2s. 6d.

Bonney.—CHRISTIAN DOCTRINES AND MODERN THOUGHT: being the Boyle Lectures for 1891. By the Rev. T. G. BONNEY, D.Sc., Hon. Canon of Manchester. *Crown 8vo.* 5s.

Boultbee.—A COMMENTARY ON THE THIRTY-NINE ARTICLES OF THE CHURCH OF ENGLAND. By the Rev. T. P. BOULTBEE, formerly Principal of the London College of Divinity, St. John's Hall, Highbury. *Crown 8vo.* 6s.

Bright.—Works by WILLIAM BRIGHT, D.D., Canon of Christ Church, Oxford.
WAYMARKS IN CHURCH HISTORY. *Crown 8vo.*
MORALITY IN DOCTRINE. *Crown 8vo.* 7s. 6d.
LESSONS FROM THE LIVES OF THREE GREAT FATHERS: St. Athanasius, St. Chrysostom, and St. Augustine. *Crown 8vo.* 6s.
THE INCARNATION AS A MOTIVE POWER. *Crown 8vo.* 6s.

Bright and Medd.—LIBER PRECUM PUBLICARUM ECCLESIÆ ANGLICANÆ. A GULIELMO BRIGHT, S.T.P., et PETRO GOLDSMITH MEDD, A.M., Latine redditus. *Small 8vo.* 7s. 6d.

Browne.—AN EXPOSITION OF THE THIRTY-NINE ARTICLES, Historical and Doctrinal. By E. H. BROWNE, D.D., formerly Bishop of Winchester. *8vo.* 16s.

Campion and Beamont.—THE PRAYER BOOK INTERLEAVED. With Historical Illustrations and Explanatory Notes arranged parallel to the Text. By W. M. CAMPION, D.D., and W. J. BEAMONT, M.A. *Small 8vo.* 7s. 6d.

Carter.—Works edited by the Rev. T. T. CARTER, M.A., Hon. Canon of Christ Church, Oxford.
THE TREASURY OF DEVOTION: a Manual of Prayer for General and Daily Use. Compiled by a Priest. 18mo. 2s. 6d.; *cloth limp,* 2s.; *or bound with the Book of Common Prayer,* 3s. 6d. *Large-Type Edition. Crown 8vo.* 3s. 6d.
THE WAY OF LIFE: A Book of Prayers and Instruction for the Young at School, with a Preparation for Confirmation. Compiled by a Priest, 18mo. 1s. 6d.
THE PATH OF HOLINESS: a First Book of Prayers, with the Service of the Holy Communion, for the Young. Compiled by a Priest. With Illustrations. 16mo. 1s. 6d.; *cloth limp,* 1s.
THE GUIDE TO HEAVEN: a Book of Prayers for every Want. (For the Working Classes.) Compiled by a Priest. 18mo. 1s. 6d.; *cloth limp,* 1s. *Large-Type Edition. Crown 8vo.* 1s. 6d.; *cloth limp,* 1s.

[continued.

Carter.—Works edited by the Rev. T. T. CARTER, M.A., Hon. Canon of Christ Church, Oxford—*continued.*
SELF-RENUNCIATION. 16mo. 2s. 6d.
THE STAR OF CHILDHOOD: a First Book of Prayers and Instruction for Children. Compiled by a Priest. With Illustrations. 16mo. 2s. 6d.
NICHOLAS FERRAR: his Household and his Friends. With Portrait engraved after a Picture by CORNELIUS JANSSEN at Magdalene College, Cambridge. *Crown 8vo.* 6s.

Carter.—MAXIMS AND GLEANINGS FROM THE WRITINGS OF T. T. CARTER, M.A. Selected and arranged for Daily Use. *Crown 16mo.* 1s.

Conybeare and Howson.—THE LIFE AND EPISTLES OF ST. PAUL. By the Rev. W. J. CONYBEARE, M.A., and the Very Rev. J. S. HOWSON, D.D. With numerous Maps and Illustrations.
LIBRARY EDITION. *Two Vols.* 8vo. 21s.
STUDENTS' EDITION. *One Vol. Crown 8vo.* 6s.
POPULAR EDITION. *One Vol. Crown 8vo.* 3s. 6d.

Copleston.—BUDDHISM—PRIMITIVE AND PRESENT IN MAGADHA AND IN CEYLON. By REGINALD STEPHEN COPLESTON, D.D., Bishop of Colombo. *8vo.* 16s.

Devotional Series, 16mo, Red Borders. *Each* 2s. 6d.
BICKERSTETH'S YESTERDAY, TO-DAY, AND FOR EVER.
CHILCOT'S TREATISE ON EVIL THOUGHTS.
THE CHRISTIAN YEAR.
FRANCIS DE SALES' (ST.) THE DEVOUT LIFE.
HERBERT'S POEMS AND PROVERBS.
KEMPIS' (À) OF THE IMITATION OF CHRIST.
WILSON'S THE LORD'S SUPPER. *Large type.*
*TAYLOR'S (JEREMY) HOLY LIVING.
*——— ——— HOLY DYING.
　　　　* These two in one Volume. 5s.

Devotional Series, 18mo, without Red Borders. *Each* 1s.
BICKERSTETH'S YESTERDAY, TO-DAY, AND FOR EVER.
THE CHRISTIAN YEAR.
FRANCIS DE SALES' (ST.) THE DEVOUT LIFE.
HERBERT'S POEMS AND PROVERBS.
KEMPIS (À) OF THE IMITATION OF CHRIST.
WILSON'S THE LORD'S SUPPER. *Large type.*
*TAYLOR'S (JEREMY) HOLY LIVING.
*——— ——— HOLY DYING.
　　　　* These two in one Volume. 2s. 6d.

IN THEOLOGICAL LITERATURE.   5

Edersheim.—Works by ALFRED EDERSHEIM, M.A., D.D., Ph.D., sometime Grinfield Lecturer on the Septuagint, Oxford.

THE LIFE AND TIMES OF JESUS THE MESSIAH. *Two Vols.* 8vo. 24s.

JESUS THE MESSIAH : being an Abridged Edition of 'The Life and Times of Jesus the Messiah.' *Crown 8vo.* 7s. 6d.

PROPHECY AND HISTORY IN RELATION TO THE MESSIAH : The Warburton Lectures, 1880-1884. 8vo. 12s.

Ellicott.—Works by C. J. ELLICOTT, D.D., Bishop of Gloucester and Bristol.

A CRITICAL AND GRAMMATICAL COMMENTARY ON ST. PAUL'S EPISTLES. Greek Text, with a Critical and Grammatical Commentary, and a Revised English Translation. 8vo.

1 CORINTHIANS. 16s.	PHILIPPIANS, COLOSSIANS, AND
GALATIANS. 8s. 6d.	PHILEMON. 10s. 6d.
EPHESIANS. 8s. 6d.	THESSALONIANS. 7s. 6d.

PASTORAL EPISTLES. 10s. 6d.

HISTORICAL LECTURES ON THE LIFE OF OUR LORD JESUS CHRIST. 8vo. 12s.

Epochs of Church History.—Edited by MANDELL CREIGHTON, D.D., LL.D., Bishop of Peterborough. *Fcap. 8vo.* 2s. 6d. each.

THE ENGLISH CHURCH IN OTHER LANDS. By the Rev. H. W. TUCKER, M.A.

THE HISTORY OF THE REFORMATION IN ENGLAND. By the Rev. GEO. G. PERRY, M.A.

THE CHURCH OF THE EARLY FATHERS. By the Rev. ALFRED PLUMMER, D.D.

THE EVANGELICAL REVIVAL IN THE EIGHTEENTH CENTURY. By the Rev. J. H. OVERTON, M.A.

THE UNIVERSITY OF OXFORD. By the Hon. G. C. BRODRICK, D.C.L.

THE UNIVERSITY OF CAMBRIDGE. By J. BASS MULLINGER, M.A.

THE ENGLISH CHURCH IN THE MIDDLE AGES. By the Rev. W. HUNT, M.A.

THE CHURCH AND THE EASTERN EMPIRE. By the Rev. H. F. TOZER, M.A.

THE CHURCH AND THE ROMAN EMPIRE. By the Rev. A. CARR.

THE CHURCH AND THE PURITANS, 1570-1660. By HENRY OFFLEY WAKEMAN, M.A.

HILDEBRAND AND HIS TIMES. By the Rev. W. R. W. STEPHENS, M.A.

THE POPES AND THE HOHENSTAUFEN. By UGO BALZANI.

THE COUNTER REFORMATION. By ADOLPHUS WILLIAM WARD, Litt.D.

WYCLIFFE AND MOVEMENTS FOR REFORM. By REGINALD L. POOLE, M.A.

THE ARIAN CONTROVERSY. By H. M. GWATKIN, M.A.

Fosbery.—Works edited by the Rev. THOMAS VINCENT FOSBERY, M.A., sometime Vicar of St. Giles's, Reading.

VOICES OF COMFORT. *Cheap Edition. Small 8vo.* 3s. 6d.
The Larger Edition (7s. 6d.) may still be had.

HYMNS AND POEMS FOR THE SICK AND SUFFERING. In connection with the Service for the Visitation of the Sick. Selected from Various Authors. *Small 8vo.* 3s. 6d.

Gore.—Works by the Rev. CHARLES GORE, M.A., Principal of the Pusey House; Fellow of Trinity College, Oxford.

THE MINISTRY OF THE CHRISTIAN CHURCH. 8vo. 10s. 6d.
ROMAN CATHOLIC CLAIMS. *Crown 8vo.* 3s. 6d.

Goulburn.—Works by EDWARD MEYRICK GOULBURN, D.D., D.C.L., sometime Dean of Norwich.

THOUGHTS ON PERSONAL RELIGION. *Small 8vo.* 6s. 6d. *Cheap Edition*, 3s. 6d. ; *Presentation Edition*, 2 vols. small 8vo, 10s. 6d.

THE PURSUIT OF HOLINESS : a Sequel to 'Thoughts on Personal Religion.' *Small 8vo.* 5s. *Cheap Edition.* 3s. 6d.

THE GOSPEL OF THE CHILDHOOD : a Practical and Devotional Commentary on the Single Incident of our Blessed Lord's Childhood (St. Luke ii. 41 to the end). *Crown 8vo.* 2s. 6d.

THE COLLECTS OF THE DAY : an Exposition, Critical and Devotional, of the Collects appointed at the Communion. With Preliminary Essays on their Structure, Sources, etc. 2 vols. *Crown 8vo.* 8s. *each.*

THOUGHTS UPON THE LITURGICAL GOSPELS for the Sundays, one for each day in the year. With an Introduction on their Origin, History, the modifications made in them by the Reformers and by the Revisers of the Prayer Book. 2 vols. *Crown 8vo.* 16s.

MEDITATIONS UPON THE LITURGICAL GOSPELS for the Minor Festivals of Christ, the two first Week-days of the Easter and Whitsun Festivals, and the Red-letter Saints' Days. *Crown 8vo.* 8s. 6d.

FAMILY PRAYERS, compiled from various sources (chiefly from Bishop Hamilton's Manual), and arranged on the Liturgical Principle. *Crown 8vo.* 3s. 6d. *Cheap Edition.* 16mo. 1s.

Harrison.—Works by the Rev. ALEXANDER J. HARRISON, B.D., Lecturer of the Christian Evidence Society.

PROBLEMS OF CHRISTIANITY AND SCEPTICISM ; Lessons from Twenty Years' Experience in the Field of Christian Evidence. *Crown 8vo.* 7s. 6d.

THE CHURCH IN RELATION TO SCEPTICS : a Conversational Guide to Evidential Work. *Crown 8vo.* 7s. 6d.

Holland.—Works by the Rev. HENRY SCOTT HOLLAND, M.A., Canon and Precentor of St. Paul's.

THE CITY OF GOD AND THE COMING OF THE KINGDOM: Four Addresses delivered at St. Asaph on the Spiritual and Ethical Value of Belief in the Church. To which are added Sermons on kindred subjects. *Crown 8vo. 7s. 6d.*

PLEAS AND CLAIMS FOR CHRIST. *Crown 8vo. 7s. 6d.*

CREED AND CHARACTER: Sermons. *Crown 8vo. 3s. 6d.*

ON BEHALF OF BELIEF. Sermons preached in St. Paul's Cathedral. *Crown 8vo. 3s. 6d.*

CHRIST OR ECCLESIASTES. Sermons preached in St. Paul's Cathedral. *Crown 8vo. 2s. 6d.*

LOGIC AND LIFE, with other Sermons. *Crown 8vo. 3s. 6d.*

Hopkins.—CHRIST THE CONSOLER. A Book of Comfort for the Sick. By ELLICE HOPKINS. *Small 8vo. 2s. 6d.*

Ingram.—HAPPINESS IN THE SPIRITUAL LIFE; or, 'The Secret of the Lord.' A Series of Practical Considerations. By W. CLAVELL INGRAM, D.D., Dean of Peterborough. *Crown 8vo. 7s. 6d.*

INHERITANCE OF THE SAINTS; or, Thoughts on the Communion of Saints and the Life of the World to come. Collected chiefly from English Writers by L. P. With a Preface by the Rev. HENRY SCOTT HOLLAND, M.A. *Crown 8vo. 7s. 6d.*

Jameson.—Works by Mrs. JAMESON.

SACRED AND LEGENDARY ART, containing Legends of the Angels and Archangels, the Evangelists, the Apostles. With 19 Etchings and 187 Woodcuts. *Two vols. Cloth, gilt top, 20s. net.*

LEGENDS OF THE MONASTIC ORDERS, as represented in the Fine Arts. With 11 Etchings and 88 Woodcuts. *One Vol. Cloth, gilt top, 10s. net.*

LEGENDS OF THE MADONNA, OR BLESSED VIRGIN MARY. With 27 Etchings and 165 Woodcuts. *One Vol. Cloth, gilt top, 10s. net.*

THE HISTORY OF OUR LORD, as exemplified in Works of Art. Commenced by the late Mrs. JAMESON; continued and completed by LADY EASTLAKE. With 31 Etchings and 281 Woodcuts. *Two Vols. 8vo. 20s. net.*

Jennings.—ECCLESIA ANGLICANA. A History of the Church of Christ in England from the Earliest to the Present Times. By the Rev. ARTHUR CHARLES JENNINGS, M.A. *Crown 8vo. 7s. 6d.*

Jukes.—Works by ANDREW JUKES.

> THE NEW MAN AND THE ETERNAL LIFE. Notes on the Reiterated Amens of the Son of God. *Crown 8vo.* 6s.
>
> THE NAMES OF GOD IN HOLY SCRIPTURE: a Revelation of His Nature and Relationships. *Crown 8vo.* 4s. 6d.
>
> THE TYPES OF GENESIS. *Crown 8vo.* 7s. 6d.
>
> THE SECOND DEATH AND THE RESTITUTION OF ALL THINGS. *Crown 8vo.* 3s. 6d.
>
> THE MYSTERY OF THE KINGDOM. *Crown 8vo.* 2s. 6d.
>
> THE ORDER AND CONNEXION OF THE CHURCH'S TEACHING, as set forth in the arrangement of the Epistles and Gospels throughout the Year. *Crown 8vo.* 2s. 6d.

King.—DR. LIDDON'S TOUR IN EGYPT AND PALESTINE IN 1886. Being Letters descriptive of the Tour, written by his Sister, Mrs. KING. *Crown 8vo.* 5s.

Knox Little.—Works by W. J. KNOX LITTLE, M.A., Canon Residentiary of Worcester, and Vicar of Hoar Cross.

> SACERDOTALISM, WHEN RIGHTLY UNDERSTOOD, THE TEACHING OF THE CHURCH OF ENGLAND: being a Letter addressed in Four Parts to the Very Rev. WILLIAM J. BUTLER, D.D., Dean of Lincoln, etc., etc. *Crown 8vo.* 6s.; *or in Four Parts, price* 1s. *each net.*
>
>> Part I. CONFESSION AND ABSOLUTION.
>> Part II. FASTING COMMUNION AND EUCHARISTIC WORSHIP.
>> Part III. THE REAL PRESENCE AND THE EUCHARISTIC SACRIFICE.
>> Part IV. THE APOSTOLIC MINISTRY.
>
> SKETCHES IN SUNSHINE AND STORM: a Collection of Miscellaneous Essays and Notes of Travel. *Crown 8vo.* 7s. 6d.
>
> THE CHRISTIAN HOME. *Crown 8vo.* 6s. 6d.
>
> THE HOPES AND DECISIONS OF THE PASSION OF OUR MOST HOLY REDEEMER. *Crown 8vo.* 2s. 6d.
>
> CHARACTERISTICS AND MOTIVES OF THE CHRISTIAN LIFE. Ten Sermons preached in Manchester Cathedral, in Lent and Advent. *Crown 8vo.* 2s. 6d.
>
> SERMONS PREACHED FOR THE MOST PART IN MANCHESTER. *Crown 8vo.* 3s. 6d.
>
> THE MYSTERY OF THE PASSION OF OUR MOST HOLY REDEEMER. *Crown 8vo.* 2s. 6d.

[continued.

Knox Little.—Works by W. J. KNOX LITTLE, M.A., Canon Residentiary of Worcester, and Vicar of Hoar Cross.—*continued.*
THE WITNESS OF THE PASSION OF OUR MOST HOLY REDEEMER. *Crown 8vo.* 2s. 6d.
THE LIGHT OF LIFE. Sermons preached on Various Occasions. *Crown 8vo.* 3s. 6d.
SUNLIGHT AND SHADOW IN THE CHRISTIAN LIFE. Sermons preached for the most part in America. *Crown 8vo.* 3s. 6d.

Lear.—Works by, and Edited by, H. L. SIDNEY LEAR.
FOR DAYS AND YEARS. A book containing a Text, Short Reading, and Hymn for Every Day in the Church's Year. 16mo. 2s. 6d. *Also a Cheap Edition,* 32mo. 1s.; *or cloth gilt,* 1s. 6d.
FIVE MINUTES. Daily Readings of Poetry. 16mo. 3s. 6d. *Also a Cheap Edition,* 32mo. 1s.; *or cloth gilt,* 1s. 6d.
WEARINESS. A Book for the Languid and Lonely. *Large Type. Small 8vo.* 5s.
THE LIGHT OF THE CONSCIENCE. 16mo. 2s. 6d. 32mo. 1s.; *cloth limp,* 6d.
CHRISTIAN BIOGRAPHIES. *Nine Vols. Crown 8vo.* 3s. 6d. *each.*

MADAME LOUISE DE FRANCE, Daughter of Louis XV., known also as the Mother Térèse de St. Augustin.

A DOMINICAN ARTIST: a Sketch of the Life of the Rev. Père Besson, of the Order of St. Dominic.

HENRI PERREYVE. By A. GRATRY.

ST. FRANCIS DE SALES, Bishop and Prince of Geneva.

THE REVIVAL OF PRIESTLY LIFE IN THE SEVENTEENTH CENTURY IN FRANCE.

A CHRISTIAN PAINTER OF THE NINETEENTH CENTURY.

BOSSUET AND HIS CONTEMPORARIES.

FÉNELON, ARCHBISHOP OF CAMBRAI.

HENRI DOMINIQUE LACORDAIRE.

DEVOTIONAL WORKS. Edited by H. L. SIDNEY LEAR. *New and Uniform Editions. Nine Vols.* 16mo. 2s. 6d. *each.*

FÉNELON'S SPIRITUAL LETTERS TO MEN.

FÉNELON'S SPIRITUAL LETTERS TO WOMEN.

A SELECTION FROM THE SPIRITUAL LETTERS OF ST. FRANCIS DE SALES.

THE SPIRIT OF ST. FRANCIS DE SALES.

THE HIDDEN LIFE OF THE SOUL.

THE LIGHT OF THE CONSCIENCE.

SELF-RENUNCIATION. From the French.

ST. FRANCIS DE SALES' OF THE LOVE OF GOD.

SELECTIONS FROM PASCAL'S 'THOUGHTS.'

Liddon.—Works by HENRY PARRY LIDDON, D.D., D.C.L., LL.D., late Canon Residentiary and Chancellor of St. Paul's.

LIFE OF EDWARD BOUVERIE PUSEY, D.D. By HENRY PARRY LIDDON, D.D., D.C.L., LL.D. Edited and prepared for publication by the Rev. J. O. JOHNSTON, M.A., Vicar of All Saints', Oxford; and the Rev. ROBERT J. WILSON, M.A., Warden of Keble College. *Four Vols.* 8vo. *Vols. I. and II., with 2 Portraits and 7 Illustrations.* 36s.

ESSAYS AND ADDRESSES: Lectures on Buddhism—Lectures on the Life of St. Paul—Papers on Dante. *Crown 8vo.* 5s.

EXPLANATORY ANALYSIS OF PAUL'S EPISTLE TO THE ROMANS. 8vo. 14s.

SERMONS ON OLD TESTAMENT SUBJECTS. *Crown 8vo.* 5s.

SERMONS ON SOME WORDS OF CHRIST. *Crown 8vo.* 5s.

THE DIVINITY OF OUR LORD AND SAVIOUR JESUS CHRIST. Being the Bampton Lectures for 1866. *Crown 8vo.* 5s.

ADVENT IN ST. PAUL'S. Sermons bearing chiefly on the Two Comings of our Lord. *Two Vols. Crown 8vo. 3s. 6d. each. Cheap Edition in one Volume. Crown 8vo.* 5s.

CHRISTMASTIDE IN ST. PAUL'S. Sermons bearing chiefly on the Birth of our Lord and the End of the Year. *Crown 8vo.* 5s.

PASSIONTIDE SERMONS. *Crown 8vo.* 5s.

EASTER IN ST. PAUL'S. Sermons bearing chiefly on the Resurrection of our Lord. *Two Vols. Crown 8vo. 3s. 6d. each. Cheap Edition in one Volume. Crown 8vo.* 5s.

SERMONS PREACHED BEFORE THE UNIVERSITY OF OXFORD. *Two Vols. Crown 8vo. 3s. 6d. each. Cheap Edition in one Volume. Crown 8vo.* 5s.

THE MAGNIFICAT. Sermons in St. Paul's. *Crown 8vo.* 2s. 6d.

SOME ELEMENTS OF RELIGION. Lent Lectures. *Small 8vo.* 2s. 6d.; or in paper cover, 1s. 6d.
  The Crown 8vo Edition (5s.) may still be had.

SELECTIONS FROM THE WRITINGS OF H. P. LIDDON, D.D. *Crown 8vo.* 3s. 6d.

MAXIMS AND GLEANINGS FROM THE WRITINGS OF H. P. LIDDON, D.D. Selected and arranged by C. M. S. *Crown 16mo.* 1s.

DR. LIDDON'S TOUR IN EGYPT AND PALESTINE IN 1886. Being Letters descriptive of the Tour, written by his Sister, Mrs. KING. *Crown 8vo.* 5s.

Luckock.—Works by HERBERT MORTIMER LUCKOCK, D.D., Dean of Lichfield.

> AFTER DEATH. An Examination of the Testimony of Primitive Times respecting the State of the Faithful Dead, and their Relationship to the Living. *Crown 8vo.* 6s.
>
> THE INTERMEDIATE STATE BETWEEN DEATH AND JUDGMENT. Being a Sequel to *After death*. *Crown 8vo.* 6s.
>
> FOOTPRINTS OF THE SON OF MAN, as traced by St. Mark. Being Eighty Portions for Private Study, Family Reading, and Instructions in Church. *Two Vols. Crown 8vo.* 12s. *Cheap Edition in one Vol. Crown 8vo.* 5s.
>
> THE DIVINE LITURGY. Being the Order for Holy Communion, Historically, Doctrinally, and devotionally set forth, in Fifty Portions. *Crown 8vo.* 6s.
>
> STUDIES IN THE HISTORY OF THE BOOK OF COMMON PRAYER. The Anglican Reform—The Puritan Innovations—The Elizabethan Reaction—The Caroline Settlement. With Appendices. *Crown 8vo.* 6s.
>
> THE BISHOPS IN THE TOWER. A Record of Stirring Events affecting the Church and Nonconformists from the Restoration to the Revolution. *Crown 8vo.* 6s.

LYRA GERMANICA. Hymns translated from the German by CATHERINE WINKWORTH. *Small 8vo.* 5s.

MacColl.—CHRISTIANITY IN RELATION TO SCIENCE AND MORALS. By the Rev. MALCOLM MACCOLL, M.A., Canon Residentiary of Ripon. *Crown 8vo.* 6s.

Mason.—Works by A. J. MASON, D.D., Hon. Canon of Canterbury and Examining Chaplain to the Archbishop of Canterbury.

> THE FAITH OF THE GOSPEL. A Manual of Christian Doctrine. *Crown 8vo.* 3s. 6d.
>
> THE RELATION OF CONFIRMATION TO BAPTISM. As taught in Holy Scripture and the Fathers. *Crown 8vo.* 7s. 6d.

Mercier.—OUR MOTHER CHURCH: Being Simple Talk on High Topics. By Mrs. JEROME MERCIER. *Small 8vo.* 3s. 6d.

Molesworth.—STORIES OF THE SAINTS FOR CHILDREN: The Black Letter Saints. By Mrs. MOLESWORTH, Author of 'The Palace in the Garden,' etc., etc. *With Illustrations. Royal 16mo.* 5s.

Mozley.—Works by J. B. MOZLEY, D.D., late Canon of Christ Church, and Regius Professor of Divinity at Oxford.

ESSAYS, HISTORICAL AND THEOLOGICAL. *Two Vols.* 8vo. 24s.

EIGHT LECTURES ON MIRACLES. Being the Bampton Lectures for 1865. *Crown 8vo.* 7s. 6d.

RULING IDEAS IN EARLY AGES AND THEIR RELATION TO OLD TESTAMENT FAITH. Lectures delivered to Graduates of the University of Oxford. 8vo. 10s. 6d.

SERMONS PREACHED BEFORE THE UNIVERSITY OF OXFORD, and on Various Occasions. *Crown 8vo.* 7s. 6d.

SERMONS, PAROCHIAL AND OCCASIONAL. *Crown 8vo.* 7s. 6d.

Newbolt.—Works by the Rev. W. C. E. NEWBOLT, M.A., Canon and Chancellor of St. Paul's Cathedral, Select Preacher at Oxford, and Examining Chaplain to the Lord Bishop of Ely.

SPECULUM SACERDOTUM; or, the Divine Model of the Priestly Life. *Crown 8vo.* 7s. 6d.

THE FRUIT OF THE SPIRIT. Being Ten Addresses bearing on the Spiritual Life. *Crown 8vo.* 2s. 6d.

THE MAN OF GOD. Being Six Addresses delivered during Lent at the Primary Ordination of the Right Rev. the Lord Alwyne Compton, D.D., Bishop of Ely. *Small 8vo.* 1s. 6d.

THE PRAYER BOOK: Its Voice and Teaching. Being Spiritual Addresses bearing on the Book of Common Prayer. *Crown 8vo.* 2s. 6d.

Newnham.—THE ALL-FATHER: Sermons preached in a Village Church. By the Rev. H. P. NEWNHAM. With Preface by EDNA LYALL. *Crown 8vo.* 4s. 6d.

Newman.—Works by JOHN HENRY NEWMAN, B.D., sometime Vicar of St. Mary's, Oxford.
  PAROCHIAL AND PLAIN SERMONS. *Eight Vols. Cabinet Edition. Crown 8vo. 5s. each. Cheaper Edition. 3s. 6d. each.*
  SELECTION, ADAPTED TO THE SEASONS OF THE ECCLESIASTICAL YEAR, from the 'Parochial and Plain Sermons,' *Cabinet Edition. Crown 8vo. 5s. Cheaper Edition. 3s. 6d.*
  FIFTEEN SERMONS PREACHED BEFORE THE UNIVERSITY OF OXFORD *Cabinet Edition. Crown 8vo. 5s. Cheaper Edition. 3s. 6d.*
  SERMONS BEARING UPON SUBJECTS OF THE DAY. *Cabinet Edition. Crown 8vo. 5s. Cheaper Edition. Crown 8vo. 3s. 6d.*
  LECTURES ON THE DOCTRINE OF JUSTIFICATION. *Cabinet Edition Crown 8vo. 5s. Cheaper Edition. 3s. 6d.*

*** *A Complete List of Cardinal Newman's Works can be had on Application.*

Osborne.—Works by EDWARD OSBORNE, Mission Priest of the Society of St. John the Evangelist, Cowley, Oxford.
  THE CHILDREN'S SAVIOUR. Instructions to Children on the Life of Our Lord and Saviour Jesus Christ. *Illustrated. 16mo. 2s. 6d.*
  THE SAVIOUR KING. Instructions to Children on Old Testament Types and Illustrations of the Life of Christ. *Illustrated. 16mo. 2s. 6d.*
  THE CHILDREN'S FAITH. Instructions to Children on the Apostles' Creed. *Illustrated. 16mo. 2s. 6d.*

Overton.—THE ENGLISH CHURCH IN THE NINETEENTH CENTURY. By the Rev. JOHN H. OVERTON, M.A., Canon of Lincoln, Rector of Epworth, Doncaster, and Rural Dean of the Isle of Axholme. *8vo. 14s.*

Oxenden.—Works by the Right Rev. ASHTON OXENDEN, formerly Bishop of Montreal.
  PLAIN SERMONS, to which is prefixed a Memorial Portrait. *Crown 8vo. 5s.*
  THE HISTORY OF MY LIFE: An Autobiography. *Crown 8vo. 5s.*
  PEACE AND ITS HINDRANCES. *Crown 8vo. 1s. sewed, 2s. cloth.*
  THE PATHWAY OF SAFETY; or, Counsel to the Awakened. *Fcap. 8vo, large type. 2s. 6d. Cheap Edition. Small type, limp, 1s.*
  THE EARNEST COMMUNICANT. *New Red Rubric Edition. 32mo, cloth. 2s. Common Edition.* 32mo. 1s.*
  OUR CHURCH AND HER SERVICES. *Fcap. 8vo. 2s. 6d.*

[continued.

Oxenden.—Works by the Right Rev. ASHTON OXENDEN formerly Bishop of Montreal—*continued.*
>FAMILY PRAYERS FOR FOUR WEEKS. First Series. *Fcap.* 8*vo.* 2*s.* 6*d.* Second Series. *Fcap.* 8*vo.* 2*s.* 6*d.*
>>LARGE TYPE EDITION. Two Series in one Volume. *Crown* 8*vo.* 6*s.*
>
>COTTAGE SERMONS; or, Plain Words to the Poor. *Fcap.* 8*vo.* 2*s.* 6*d.*
>THOUGHTS FOR HOLY WEEK. 16*mo, cloth.* 1*s.* 6*d.*
>DECISION. 18*mo.* 1*s.* 6*d.*
>THE HOME BEYOND; or, A Happy Old Age. *Fcap.* 8*vo.* 1*s.* 6*d.*
>THE LABOURING MAN'S BOOK. 18*mo, large type, cloth.* 1*s.* 6*d.*

Paget.—Works by FRANCIS PAGET, D.D., Dean of Christ Church, Oxford.
>THE SPIRIT OF DISCIPLINE: Sermons. *Crown* 8*vo.* 6*s.* 6*d.*
>FACULTIES AND DIFFICULTIES FOR BELIEF AND DISBELIEF. *Crown* 8*vo.* 6*s.* 6*d.*
>THE HALLOWING OF WORK. Addresses given at Eton, January, 16-18, 1888. *Small* 8*vo.* 2*s.*

PRACTICAL REFLECTIONS. By a CLERGYMAN. With Prefaces by H. P. LIDDON, D.D., D.C.L., and the BISHOP OF LINCOLN. *Crown* 8*vo.*
>THE HOLY GOSPELS. 4*s.* 6*d.*
>ACTS TO REVELATIONS. 6*s.*
>THE PSALMS. 5*s.*
>THE BOOK OF GENESIS. 4*s.* 6*d.*

PRIEST (THE) TO THE ALTAR; or, Aids to the Devout Celebration of Holy Communion, chiefly after the Ancient English Use of Sarum. *Royal* 8*vo.* 12*s.*

Puller.—THE PRIMITIVE SAINTS AND THE SEE OF ROME. By F. W. PULLER, M.A., Mission Priest of the Society of St. John Evangelist, Cowley, Oxford. *Crown* 8*vo.* 7*s.* 6*d.*

Pusey.—LIFE OF EDWARD BOUVERIE PUSEY, D.D. By HENRY PARRY LIDDON, D.D., D.C.L., LL.D. Edited and prepared for publication by the Rev. J. O. JOHNSTON, M.A., Vicar of All Saints', Oxford, and the Rev. ROBERT J. WILSON, M.A., Warden of Keble College. *Four Vols.* 8*vo.* Vols. *I. and II., with* 2 *Portraits and* 7 *Illustrations.* 36*s.*

Pusey.—Works by the Rev. E. B. PUSEY, D.D.
>PRIVATE PRAYERS. With Preface by H. P. LIDDON, D.D. 32*mo.* 1*s.*
>PRAYERS FOR A YOUNG SCHOOLBOY. With a Preface by H. P. LIDDON, D.D. 24*mo.* 1*s.*

Sanday.—Works by W. SANDAY, D.D., Dean Ireland's Professor of Exegesis and Fellow of Exeter College, Oxford.
> INSPIRATION: Eight Lectures on the Early History and Origin of the Doctrine of Biblical Inspiration. Being the Bampton Lectures for 1893. 8vo. 16s.
> THE ORACLES OF GOD: Nine Lectures on the Nature and Extent of Biblical Inspiration and the Special Significance of the Old Testament Scriptures at the Present Time. *Crown 8vo.* 4s.
> TWO PRESENT-DAY QUESTIONS. I. Biblical Criticism. II. The Social Movement. Sermons preached before the University of Cambridge. *Crown 8vo.* 2s. 6d.

Seebohm.—THE OXFORD REFORMERS—JOHN COLET, ERASMUS, AND THOMAS MORE: A History of their Fellow-Work. By FREDERICK SEEBOHM. 8vo. 14s.

Stanton.—THE PLACE OF AUTHORITY IN MATTERS OF RELIGIOUS BELIEF. By VINCENT HENRY STANTON, D.D., Fellow of Trinity Coll., Ely Prof. of Divinity, Cambridge. *Cr. 8vo.* 6s.

Swayne.—THE BLESSED DEAD IN PARADISE. Four All Saints' Day Sermons, preached in Salisbury Cathedral. By R. G. SWAYNE, M.A. *Crown 8vo.* 3s. 6d.

Twells.—COLLOQUIES ON PREACHING. By HENRY TWELLS, M.A., Honorary Canon of Peterborough. *Crown 8vo.* 2s. 6d.

Welldon.—THE FUTURE AND THE PAST. Sermons preached to Harrow Boys. By the Rev. J. E. C. WELLDON, M.A., Head Master of Harrow School. *Crown 8vo.* 7s. 6d.

Williams.—Works by the Rev. ISAAC WILLIAMS, B.D.
> A DEVOTIONAL COMMENTARY ON THE GOSPEL NARRATIVE, *Eight Vols. Crown 8vo.* 5s. *each. Sold Separately.*

THOUGHTS ON THE STUDY OF THE HOLY GOSPELS.
A HARMONY OF THE FOUR GOSPELS.
OUR LORD'S NATIVITY.
OUR LORD'S MINISTRY (Second Year).
OUR LORD'S MINISTRY (Third Year).
THE HOLY WEEK.
OUR LORD'S PASSION.
OUR LORD'S RESURRECTION.

> FEMALE CHARACTERS OF HOLY SCRIPTURE. A Series of Sermons, *Crown 8vo.* 5s.
> THE CHARACTERS OF THE OLD TESTAMENT. *Crown 8vo.* 5s.
> THE APOCALYPSE. With Notes and Reflections. *Crown 8vo.* 5s.
> SERMONS ON THE EPISTLES AND GOSPELS FOR THE SUNDAYS AND HOLY DAYS. *Two Vols. Crown 8vo.* 5s. *each.*

[continued.

16 A SELECTION OF THEOLOGICAL WORKS.

Williams.—Works by the Rev. ISAAC WILLIAMS, B.D.—*continued.*
PLAIN SERMONS ON CATECHISM. *Two Vols. Cr. 8vo. 5s. each.*
SELECTIONS FROM ISAAC WILLIAMS' WRITINGS. *Cr. 8vo. 3s. 6d.*
THE AUTOBIOGRAPHY OF ISAAC WILLIAMS, B.D., Author of several of the 'Tracts for the Times.' Edited by the Venerable Sir GEORGE PREVOST, as throwing further light on the history of the Oxford Movement. *Crown 8vo. 5s.*

Woodford.—Works by J. R. WOODFORD, D.D., Bishop of Ely.
THE GREAT COMMISSION. Addresses on the Ordinal. Edited, with an Introduction, by H. M. LUCKOCK, D.D. *Crown 8vo. 5s.*
SERMONS ON OLD AND NEW TESTAMENT SUBJECTS. Edited by H. M. LUCKOCK, D.D. *Two Vols. Crown 8vo. 5s. each.*

Wordsworth.
For List of Works by the late Christopher Wordsworth, D.D., Bishop of Lincoln, see Messrs. Longmans & Co.'s Catalogue of Theological Works, 32 pp. Sent post free on application.

Wordsworth.—Works by ELIZABETH WORDSWORTH, Principal of Lady Margaret Hall, Oxford.
ILLUSTRATIONS OF THE CREED. *Crown 8vo. 5s.*
THE DECALOGUE. *Crown 8vo. 4s. 6d.*
ST. CHRISTOPHER AND OTHER POEMS. *Crown 8vo. 6s.*

Wordsworth.—Works by CHARLES WORDSWORTH, D.D., D.C.L., Lord Bishop of St. Andrews, and Fellow of Winchester College.
ANNALS OF MY EARLY LIFE, 1806-1846. *8vo. 15s.*
ANNALS OF MY LIFE, 1847-1856. *8vo. 10s. 6d.*
PRIMARY WITNESS TO THE TRUTH OF THE GOSPEL, to which is added a Charge on Modern Teaching on the Canon of the Old Testament. *Crown 8vo. 7s. 6d.*

Younghusband.—Works by FRANCES YOUNGHUSBAND.
THE STORY OF OUR LORD, told in Simple Language for Children. With 25 Illustrations from Pictures by the Old Masters. *Crown 8vo. 2s. 6d.*
THE STORY OF THE EXODUS, told in Simple Language for Children. With Map and 29 Illustrations. *Crown 8vo. 2s. 6d.*

Printed by T. and A. CONSTABLE, Printers to Her Majesty,
at the Edinburgh University Press.

www.ingramcontent.com/pod-product-compliance
Lightning Source LLC
Chambersburg PA
CBHW021807230426
43669CB00008B/664